LOUD MEDICINE

LOUD MEDICINE

DISPATCHES FROM THE MUSICAL UNDERWORLD

JAMES KENNEDY

Calon

2025

www.uwp.co.uk

British Library Cataloguing-in-Publication Data
A catalogue record for this book is available from the British Library.

ISBN: 978-1-83760-007-6

For GPSR enquiries please contact: Easy Access System Europe Oü, 16879218. Mustamäe tee 50, 10621, Tallinn, Estonia. gpsr.requests@easproject.com

Cover design by Andy Ward
Typeset by Agnes Graves
Printed by in Great Britain by Bell & Bain Ltd, Glasgow

To all the dreamers, artists, freethinkers, rebels and fighters of the good fight.

Don't ever stop.

CONTENTS

Readers may want to note that the start of Chapter 14 references suicide and take this into consideration when reading this chapter.

INTRODUCTION

Writing about music is like dancing about architecture, as the late, great Frank Zappa once said – and when Frank says something, you shut up and nod (although, he also wrote songs about dildos and dental floss – just saying). But he had a point. How *do* you describe with mere words the mystical, life-defining, soul-rattling maelstrom of pure intangible awesomeness that is music? And what would be the point? Well, here's my problem. I love music. But it frustrates me that so many books on the subject are either a needlessly academic, self-indulgent trudge through fifty shades of brain ache, OR another multimillionaire bragging about the drugs they've taken, the hotels they've trashed, their questionable sexual conquests and the grossly unfair quota of good luck they've had (although, I think those books are pretty damn exciting too, but don't tell anyone). Neither of them are a true reflection of *most* people's relationship with music, and both mislead the honest reality of how most musicians actually live in the real world. And that's a shame because there's a much bigger story to be told – and the truth, as they say, is way sexier.

So I'm not here to lie to you. And I'm not here to try to impress you either. But I (along with countless others) have lived for many years inside a secret society that is so exciting, so challenging, painful, rewarding, awe-inspiring, frustrating and so addictively exhilarating, it just begs to be shared! No garnish needed. Sans bullshit. Real magic in the raw. We're called the underdogs and I want to invite *you* into our crazy underworld, show you around and teach you some moves. Why? Well, because it's great fucking fun down here, that's why! And our vibrantly bustling ecosystem has been hidden in plain sight for far too long. No longer should we remain in the shadows cast down by 'the real guys', the guys you've heard of, the mere 1 per cent of our sprawling, noisy metropolis. Because the music industry is not the charts, the radio hits, Spotify, pop stars, Coachella, platinum albums, award shows and heroin overdoses – no, the music industry is down here with all of us. We, the invisible musical masses, are the engine that keeps this whole lopsided industry afloat. Us and you. So where's our book?! And that's my problem. Until now you've been mostly misinformed, so I want to break down the many misconceptions, the misleading mythologies, the myriad misunderstandings – and other things beginning with 'm'.

We also need to get better acquainted because it's important. It's important if my kind are going to survive (let alone thrive). You see, we're under threat. Our enemies are many and they get stronger by the day and only you – you reading this right now – can save us. If you want us to keep the good stuff coming, there're some things you should know – and the rock stars are definitely *not* going to be the ones to tell you. In fact, it wasn't all that long ago that we had a real-life practice run of what life without a music scene is like. And I know we never want to think about those brutal lockdowns ever again, but if we can quickly rewind our minds back a little, the Covid-19 pandemic did shine a white-hot stage light on some stark truths about the love affair we all have with music and the people who make it. Joni told us a long time ago that we wouldn't know what we'd got till it was gone, and for that year or so, music (specifically, live music) was *gone* gone. Like shutters-down, empty-streets, tumbleweed-in-the-desert gone. And we all felt it big time, as if a dull, grey, lifeless void now occupied the space where floor-shaking bass, bright lights and screaming your heart out used to be.

Yet within days of the lockdowns, like weeds squeezing through the Tarmac to smell the sun, the underdogs found a way. New ways to provide solace with everyone's favourite moonshine. New ways to smuggle just a little taste of that former euphoria, to share the healing powers of a good tune, even if only through our screens. Musical speakeasies popped up in every home, with live streaming, interactive chats, games and competitions all seeking to lift the collective mood and help us through the claustrophobia. And who *were* these legends who came to our rescue when we were bored, alone, depressed and frustrated? Who lit up our nights with home-made Glastonburys in bedrooms and kitchens? Who was it who, despite having their industry and livelihoods thoroughly ravaged by the restrictions, continued to play on regardless – nourishing all our primal needs – for free? It sure wasn't the owners of Wetherspoons or Topshop. We know that much now. Neither was it the major labels trying to cash in on our captivity by charging us to see artists perform in their attics. Nope, you know *exactly* who it was. It was us – your friendly neighbourhood noise doctors. And even though it wasn't quite the *same* as having it loud and live in a packed, sweaty venue with mates beside us and a beer in hand... it helped. It helped some people a lot.

So what's become of those legends since then? Caught up as we are in the back-to-normal chaos of congestion, deadlines, pubs and a thousand other distractions. Where did they all go? Probably back to their cocaine, yachts and groupies, right? Not exactly. They went back to the shadows from whence they came. Back to the unknown. Back to the underground secret society that I would love to lure you into on the pages that follow.

Many things were learned during the times of the ole 'rona virus – about ourselves, our society, our governments and just *how* mental conspiracy theorists really can be – but one realisation I'm confident almost all of us shared was how much music means to us. Not only in how much we missed the live shows, but how much it gave us strength in moments of weakness, consoled us in times of sorrow and made our familiar four walls all the more colourful to be stuck inside. Life without music is like food without flavour – joyless, routine, functional. We've had a taste of that meal now, and everyone thought it sucked. But it doesn't take a pandemic to kill a music scene; it takes negligence. As in politics, as in music. We get what we deserve – and Judgement Day is watching us all like a hawk.

So let's not simply coexist any more. I want to invite you into our world. The world us musicians actually live in – not the one on Instagram or ghostwritten memoirs from a golden age long past. Who *are* the people that make the music you know and love? What goes on in their mysterious, hidden world? What are the issues endangering their existence? How can you help? Why do they do what they do, and what the hell *is* music anyway? This book is a tribute to all the underdogs, the unsigned, the unsung, the unheard and the unknown. And it's a love letter to everyone's favourite medicine.

But what's it got to do with me anyway? What do I care? Well, I'm one of them. I'm *in* the secret club and have been for a very long time. So don't worry; you're in safe hands. As a veteran of the music world with over twenty years' service behind me, I've done the dirty work so you don't have to. I've gigged, toured, busked, taught, won, lost, been to the parties and been screwed hard (by the industry). I run a label, I've released many albums, performed thousands of shows and I'm very well acquainted with that fascinatingly unique species known as *Homo musicus*. It'd be my honour to be your guide. There will be rants, truth-bombs, F-bombs, big ideas, scam-busting shockers, the likely crucifixion of a beloved music icon or two – and yes, of course, there will be road stories.

I'm stoked to have your company. So whack on your favourite albums, crank 'em up and let's hit the road.

Enjoy the show.

1.

THE CRUSADE

The heat has got me on the ropes. I'm starting to hallucinate from the torturous cocktail of sleepless nights, relentless travel and sadistic service station sandwiches. We've been on the road for weeks now and we're sunburnt, running on empty and massacred by mosquitos. Being stuck (like, literally stuck) shoulder to shoulder in the front of a sweltering hot transit van all day – our sweaty, naked arms mushing and chafing together hour after hour as the merciless heatwave batters us from above and the never-ending road to Milan hammers us from the front – is... let's say... taking its toll on our humanity. But we have a quest to fulfil. A brave and noble mission that has lain waste to many before us – and we *will not* surrender. So we soldier on. But truth be told, we're exhausted. Broken, bruised and beaten down.

Except him. God, I wish he'd shut up. Rory is being Rory. Still. Does he ever fucking stop? The ever-excitable drummer has been bellowing a hundred-decibel mock-opera mash-up and doing flamboyant Italian impressions at us ever since we crossed the border into Italy – complete with wild gesticulations and dashboard drumming. It was funny at first. Except that he's behind the wheel now, and every time he does it, he throws the van towards the cliff edge that he's hurtling us along at 100 miles an hour. Vespas attack from all directions, wild blind bends jump out of nowhere and I'm so delirious I can't tell if that's a tunnel he's flying us towards or a giant, grinning devil emoji. Whizzing past on our left, the rock face. Mere inches to our right… a sharp and sudden plunge into the Mediterranean sea, hundreds of feet below. And this fucking maniac thinks it's funny, his eyes dilated maniacally with his size-tens firmly forcing the pedal to the metal as we warp-speed our way across narrow, rickety old Italian bridges in a jumbo-size transit van with the wheel on the wrong side. I won't lie – I'm shitting myself.

This is the downside to having The Clown type in your band (see Chapter 2). They're bloody brilliant most of the time, but then they also might just send the entire band plummeting to a gory, mangled-up death down the side of a mountain. I guess it's the price you pay for the good times. But we're all going to die today. That much is clear. I reach for the sick bag. I don't know if it's the heat, the exhaustion, the hunger or this wanker's driving, but I can feel it coming. Fast. The saliva, the sweats, the dizziness. Yep, it's coming.

'Dude, fucking slow *down*, man!' barks bassman Ace, unable to hold it together any more.

'You're going to kill us, you crazy bastard!'

'YEEEEHAAAAW! Squeal, piggy! SQUEEEEEEEAL!' is his response, frantically thrusting his dick and slapping the wheel – a mime that he's… I don't know… screwing a wild pig?

This motherfucker fears no death. Ignoring our pleas for sanity, he powers on even faster while rummaging under his seat for a CD with one hand and guzzling a Coke with the other, steering with his knees and nearly driving us face-first into the side of a tunnel in the process. If Ace hadn't panic-grabbed the wheel at the last second, you'd have read about us in the news. Here it comes.

'Shit, man, pull us over! I'm gonna speeeeew!'

× × ×

Like you, I've read the books and watched the documentaries, and rock folklore has always led me to believe that touring is basically about jamming on the tour bus, drinking whisky and shagging groupies. Oh, and maybe performing a few shows along the way. But what those assholes never mention is that 'that' type of touring is exclusive only to a select subgroup of musicians known as 'Major Label Lucky Bastards' – and, my friend, that's not most bands. In fact, that's hardly *any* bands. Most bands don't have a tour bus. They have a van. Or even a car (yes, four bodies and an entire band backline *can* fit in a car; you're just not doing it right). And when I say 'they have a van', I mean that is *all* they have. Sleeping? That happens in the van. Eating? Van (usually while in motion). Changing clothes, doing hair and brushing teeth? Well, what else do you think the wing mirrors are for?! Got lucky after a gig? Well, your poor, gullible victim had better be happy doing it on top of the drum cases... in the van (to no doubt be interrupted by a bass player arriving halfway through to fumble around for his 'fucking beers'). These things stink. In the true sense. They're where we sleep, fart, eat, wash and sit all day, each day getting sweatier, fartier and stickier. After a few weeks, a band van looks like a Hong Kong coffin cubicle invaded by beasts.

And of course, there is always the infamous 'Evian Shower'. For those of you who don't yet know, the regal-sounding Evian Shower is where you strip down to your pants in a public car park or on a dusty roadside and throw bottled water over yourself with one hand while 'lathering up' erratically with the other. Depending on the circumstances, the water will either be the barely warm sloppy seconds of someone's – *anyone's* – drinking water, or it'll be fresh from the shop fridge, Siberian-grade cold. Choose your weapon. This is called 'showering', band style. And where do all those dirty clothes live once you've peeled them off? You guessed it! The van. Bags of stinky socks and pants all sitting there for weeks on end, festering in the airless heat. Are you getting the picture? Is the violent stench wafting up from the pages yet?

So bear this in mind, people. That awesome out-of-town band playing your local venue tonight are not smashing up the Hilton afterwards; they're living in mobile squalor – sleeping together in a van, eating cheese sandwiches and fantasising about brutally murdering one another. Like I told you, I'm not here to lie to you, and neither am I going to feed you any of the clichéd, mythological bollocks peddled in far too many other books. I'm bringing you along for a ride into the real world of most musicians. And trust me – it's way more fun than heroin and hotel-trashing. But if you're coming with us, you'd better get used to the smell – and the food.

Now... the reason we put ourselves through all this godforsaken hell in the first place is because we're addicted. Addicts, all of us. It *loses* us money to go through this hurt! Along with our time, our relationships, our health and our sanity. But at the end of the day... we get our fix. We get another quick, fleeting shot of the good stuff before departing again in search of more, more, more! There's a theory that us musicians do what we do because we secretly crave attention or love, or that we yearn for connection, respect or appreciation. Bullshit. If I wanted love and attention, I'd buy a puppy. I certainly wouldn't haul my broke ass around half the world's toilet circuit like a mangy hobo in dirty denim and leather. Nope, we're on today's pitiless pilgrimage in search of one thing and one thing only. That holy grail of musicians everywhere. That cathartic purge, that electric surge, that glorious hypnotic trip to the heavens that cleanses the body, mind and spirit of its toxins. For tonight... we get to play a show – and that makes *all* of the other shit worthwhile. No question about it. As far as drugs go, all fall impotent to the euphoric religious rapture of a thousand watts running through your veins on a sticky stage with your mates (and I've tried). It's an addiction that grips your soul by the throat and never lets go. There is nothing better, and the addicted will endure unspeakable horrors to get another hit.

Which is why we're in Milan. After surviving near-death, hours of gridlocked traffic and the guitarist's insistence that we all listen to this 'awesome new German industrial band' on the stereo for the past two hours, we make it to soundcheck on time and intact. And thank God. Trust me, after six hours stuck in a van with Rory, you'd welcome a kick in the balls if it meant just two minutes' fucking silence. But now we're here and *this* is when the fun begins. The excitement kicks in and we transform instantly from witless wanderers to Professional Rock Band Who Didn't Come Here To Fuck Around. I want that stage, dammit! This is when you get your first peek at tonight's battleground (or 'venue' as some people prefer to call them). A battle is how we think of it. Us against the airwaves. When we head out on tour, it's more like we're going off to war. A band of Spartans en route to the battlefields in a rickety old van, fully loaded with musical weapons of mass destruction. Drugs and booze? Forget it. That's for *rock bands* – WE are here for war, and you can't fight a war when you're high.

More than ready for our fix after that harrowing journey, we promptly assess the terrain, weigh up the opposition (which is everyone – the other bands, the audience, innocent bystanders), plot our battle tactics and mark out our trenches. Last night's venue was of the vast, open-hall variety. Tonight it's a pokey underground dungeon with anaemic-looking mic stands held together with Sellotape – my favourite. That means no barrier between the band and our prey... I mean, audience. That means sweat, heat, chaos and not enough room to thrash around without bashing each other in the face. It means lock-ins and after-parties and an owner who doesn't give a shit if you play over time. I smell fresh blood.

But before one can play, one must unpack their toys. And fast, because you're soundchecking everything you own in half an hour. Tons of guitar cases, amps, drums and bass cabs are manhandled down winding, narrow staircases by – correct – the band themselves, and thus begins the frenzied 'set everything you own in the world up in ten minutes please' routine. Still delirious from travel, lack of food and sleep deprivation, you do as you are bid and you make it happen. After fifteen minutes of mumbling 'one two' and the drummer making a racket, you gotta get the hell outta the way so the next band can get up and do the same. Side note: soundchecks go in reverse order, so if you're headlining, you soundcheck first (and usually for the longest), and if you're opening the show, you soundcheck last (usually for five minutes and in front of the audience). Yep, us humans even managed to make hierarchies out of fucking soundchecks.

Once we're done, in unspoken formation, we each disappear into our own individual Zen-like pre-battle ritual. The next hour or two will be the last bit of calm you get until you pass out in a service station car park in the early hours of tomorrow morning – so use them wisely. For Ace, that involves the physical – focused stretching, lunging, lifting and working up a sweat before limbering up on his instrument and selecting the appropriate thrash band T-shirt for the night. For me, I go into my silent place. Don't try to strike up a convo with me before a show; I'm not listening. If I'm not warming up my vocals, I'm pacing, brooding, checking stuff, tweaking stuff and working myself up like a fight dog on a leash (a dog that wears guyliner). And in contrast to mine and Ace's eagle-eyed centredness, Rory (of course) continues down the hyper route: bashing things, singing, roaming, clowning around, bouncing off the walls, taking a thousand pictures, making a hundred new best mates, and keeping us all fully stocked with the excitable, optimistic faith one must have before one goes into battle. So long as he doesn't kill you on the way there.

We don't have trinkets, a special drink, a group hug, or a god that we pray to – and we save the rocking and rolling for the stage and the after-party. We don't need good luck, because we've got the unspoken conviction that we are a well-prepared, well-oiled juggernaut that has conquered many miles with one simple purpose – to blast as many skulls as possible and take no fucking prisoners. We wait. And we wait some more. Adrenaline fizzing through every vein. Has that damn support band finished yet or what?! I haven't eaten since that plastic croissant and crisps when we stopped for fuel in France, and although I need it, I simply can't stomach another stale cheese and ham buffet laid on by the club. So instead, I'm just gonna ride this adrenaline rush all the way to breakfast, baby.

And then... it happens. Cattle Smasher, or whatever they're called, have finished and now... it's our turn. Our turn to satiate our bloodlust, to gorge ourselves silly on the best dope in the world, to be absolved of our sins and ignite some new ones. Our turn to fool our repressed yearning for connection, to get another faint whiff of the dream we've clutched on to since forever, to float formless in intense oneness with fellow addicts and to scratch the itch that gnaws away at us every dull second we're not doing it. It's our turn.

'*Buona sera*, Milano!'

X X X

'Am I turning right here, dude?' Ace mutters for the third time in fifteen minutes.

'Urgh, hang on,' I groan, reaching across a snoring Rory to get a closer look at the satnav.

'No, dude, you're turning right in 210 kilometres. That's ages away yet.'

'Are you *sure*?'

'Yes, dude, it says it right there!'

Christ, I'm tired. I've hit the post-gig crash. Hard. That point around 3 a.m. when the last dregs of adrenaline have sputtered out and the aggregate of exhaustion, hunger and lack of sleep finally kicks you in the guts. And it's not Ace's fault. He's as wrecked as I am. Tonight, it was me that got the first lucky stint of the night drive, still riding high on post-gig euphoria. Ace has drawn tonight's short straw, and I know how much that hurts around now. But still, if he asks if we're turning right one more fucking time, I swear to God, I'm gonna grab the wheel and throw us all into the black. I *need* sleep. Why won't he let me sleep?! I've *done* my share of the driving. Please just let me sleep. I swear I'm losing my grip. Edgy, irritable and impatient, I'm jumping at the passing road signs like a scatty meth head. I'm hallucinating again. We're ploughing on for as many miles as we can, trying to make tracks towards tomorrow's gig in Germany while the roads are dead – but now it's hit us. Thus far and no further.

'Dude, are you *sure* we're not turning right here?'

'Aaaaaaaaargh!' I rip the satnav from the windscreen and shove it right up to Ace's face.

'In 200 kilometres, dude! It says it right there, man!' I cry desperately, hoping that proximity and volume are what's causing his confusion.

'But it's *showing* that we turn right.'

'Yes! But not for 200 fucking kilometres , man!'

He pauses for a moment's careful consideration. And then...

'Are you *sure*?'

'Yeeeeeeeeeeeeeeeeeees!!'

'Well, all right. But if we get lost, we'll miss soundcheck tomorrow,' he reasons.

'Dude, I've gotta sleep, man. I've *got* to. Can we call it a night at the next service station?' I beg.

'Yeah, cool, man. I'm dropping off at the wheel here.'

Although sandwiched snuggly between us, Rory is blissfully unaware of our anguish as he nods back and forth in a deep, beautiful slumber. We banned the bastard from driving after the episode in Italy, meaning Ace and I have to pull double shifts if we're to make it out of the tour alive. And, boy, are we feeling it. It wasn't just the 'nearly killing us in a tunnel' incident – or even the 'nearly throwing us off a cliff' thing. That would have all been fine if it weren't also for the 'pulling out in front of a high-speed artic lorry' debacle, which we survived by a mere inch, the force of the lorry's momentum alone nearly toppling our van over. Or the time he got distracted on the motorway and nearly steered us into a ravine, still looking the other way as we crashed over the kerb and into the greenery at ninety miles an hour. We can't relax when that psycho is driving anyway – every time he drives, my heart is in my throat. If I'm going to die in a van, I want to be the one gripping the wheel when it happens. So we've banned him from driving, and although we're paying for it, at least we're still alive. Kind of.

'Awww, look at him. The poor little lamb has worn himself out,' Ace says with genuine affection.

A contemplative silence falls over us both like a soft quilt, as we each begin to imagine how awesome *our* sleep is going to be when it finally happens. And then... as if on cue, as if by divine decree, a blessing from the gods! A star appears in the heavens, gently guiding these three daft men towards it, coaxing us lovingly into its car park. There she is... that thing of beauty, lit up in a sparkly fluorescent halo... the '*Autohof*'. We're home. Ace has been banging on about turning right ever since we left Cardiff and now he gets to do it. Finally! My bed awaits me. You really learn to love these soulless, overpriced purveyors of junk food and creepy souvenirs when you're a desperate band of homeless road dogs. We wake Rory.

'Huh?! What? Is it my turn to drive?!' he rambles, bouncing straight back into action.

'We're there, dude. Get out of my bed,' I reply.

That's right. That farty, crisp-covered front cabin seat... is mine, baby! All mine! The other two get the full length of the van to stretch out in the back of together, but me being a short-arse, I can stretch out just fine across the passenger and driver seats of this bad boy – and it means I get my own space for a mere few hours of suffocating semi-sleep. But first I need to put my curtains up. By curtains, I mean the dirty towels and T-shirts that I stick to the windows with gaffer tape. Aaaah, bliss! Today was a good day. We kicked absolute ass in Milan (and they knew it too). What a show, what a ride, what a rush! With the warm embrace of victory caressing me to sleep, I'm happy, content and secure in the front of this rusty old workman's van on the side of a motorway just off the border of Switzerland. In a few hours' time it'll be another cheap morning coffee, another plastic croissant and another Evian Shower.

But for now, we sleep. And tomorrow, we do it all again.

2.

MONO/STEREO TYPES

Musician. The dictionary simply says they're 'a person who plays a musical instrument, especially as a profession'. But let's be honest. The image that shudders through *some* people's minds when they hear that word is often one of the following:

The Hippie. Long, scraggly hair in face. Smelly. Stoned. Late. Broke-ass job dodger. Almost always associated with the guitar. Or worse... the bongo.

The Metalhead. Tattoos. Leather. Piercings. Tough guy. Scary. A danger to your child, a menace to society and probably a satanist.

And it makes me so angry to see the community that I know and love denigrated to such narrow and derogatory stereotypes when there isn't merely one sweeping, negative generalisation one can make about us – but many! For a start, *no one* considers hippies to be real musicians! Not even hippies! As with all stereotypes, they exist because, as much as we don't like to admit it, there is a whiff of truth in them. The problem with the above examples is that they're woefully incomplete. There are a hundred other bitchy stereotypes that us musicians have about *each other*, so allow me to introduce some of the lesser-known subgroups before we break it down further in an attempt to clear up exactly *who* and *what* musicians are. What do they eat? Where do they burrow? And are they friendly towards humans? There are lots to choose from, but here are some of the classics:

The Jazzer. Often confused with geography teachers. Smug. Friendless. Poor and proud of it. Not into music half as much as they're into being clever (and smug).

The DJ. Permanently whizzing their tits off. Unfathomably popular and grotesquely well paid, despite dressing like they've mugged the Primark pyjama department. Most musicians have no clue what these guys actually do and openly dispute their place in the 'real musician club' (and it's not because they're jealous, honestly).

The Orchestra Darling. Do *not* be fooled. Ozzy Osbourne is cute compared to these animals. If you want sex, drugs and rock 'n' roll; if you want excess, debauchery and filth – forget the guitar; go learn the flugelhorn.

The Session Musician. Only in it for the money. Literally. Otherwise they'd be working in finance. Lovely guys when you're paying them. Cash would be great, pal.

The Singer-Songwriter. See The Hippie. A close relative of the Folk Family. Plays acoustic guitar (or ukulele) and is usually found singing about their girlfriend, their boyfriend or… no, that's it.

The Prog Rocker. Basically Jazzers who think they're from space. There will be keyboards, lots of keyboards. There will be solos, loooong solos. Nerds assemble.

Now, I can sense some eyes rolling already. 'Pfff, what's next? Drummer jokes?!' But banter aside, let's be honest… there *is* some truth here. We've all met these guys at some point and if you're offended, it's probably because you're a Jazzer. There are many more, of course – punks, hip-hoppers, Britpoppers, goths and dudes with the blues – but you get the point. However, within these *totally* accurate groupings, we find a further plethora of sub-personalities, but my belief is that these too can be shortlisted into the following camps:

The Leader. Every band has one. That one member who is indispensable. That hard-working pain in the arse who everyone else leans on way too much and then blames when things go tits up. These can vary in style from flat-out military dictator to martyred band babysitter. You will see them setting up the PA, updating the socials, selling merch, packing the van and wiping the drummer's arse. Often found among the guitarist community.

The Wingman (or woman). These absolute angels are a rare find, but if you catch one, hold on to them with loving hands! The lukewarm, diplomatic glue between the frazzled Leader and the useless but iconic singer. Happy to not be in the driving seat, but forever supporting the Leader from the rear, the Wingman (or woman) plays a vital role in holding the whole operation together. These can often come in the form of bass players. They like beer.

The Diva (also known as The Arsehole). Shockingly populous despite their belief that they stand without equal. They believe that their unspeakable musical genius voids the usual necessity to carry equipment, drive, chip in, cooperate or help in any way. A complete dependency whose relentless, pretentious bullshit is usually the cause of the whole group's downfall. Unfairly attributed to singers, diva status can often be found among the drummer community. Weed them out as fast as you can.

The Clown. Another drummer affliction, but of the good kind. Laughter in times of tension, positivity in times of struggle – these morale-boosting fun machines can be vital when things get tough but can also grate everyone's balls when they're still doing it at 4 a.m. You will find them banging things, playing pranks, causing trouble and being permanently hilarious – even if you're laughing *at* them.

The Contrarian. Will challenge and belittle every idea proposed by another member of the unit but will never have a single idea of their own. Keyboard players, we're looking at you. They'll brag that they've played in 'every band in town', but we know that means they've been kicked *out* of every band in town. Closely connected to the Silent But Violent type – i.e. that member of the band who hardly speaks, seems to hate every second of it but shows up anyway. Don't cross them. In a few years' time you'll discover that they buried your gran under their floorboards because you said their solo was a 'little off' one night back in 2007.

The Show Stealer. Singers beware – they want your job. In fact, they want Freddie Mercury's job, but for some reason opted to learn the guitar. You will find them trampling on the singer's feet, barging in on the singer's mic, crowd-surfing and gyrating topless around the stage like it's their own personal playground. And that's just the soundcheck. Usually seen once in 'every band in town'.

The Rock Star. Another widespread irritant. These guys aren't usually *that* rock 'n' roll by nature, but they've bought into the popular mythology that in order to be a musician, one must also be an arrogant, pretentious throwback to the gory days of the eighties, when it was all about tantrums and Jack Daniels. It's usually an act put on by guys who aren't very musical – or a cover for nerves. Those of you familiar with the fifth law of thermodynamics ('the bigger the prick, the lesser the talent') will know who I'm talking about. Small local bands and cover bands have these in surprising numbers and, nope, nobody thinks they're cool.

The Team Player. Another rare find, but if you do get lucky, hold them tight. These beauties cause no fuss, they muck in, they stay in their lane and they 'get it'. They 'get' that it takes more than being able to shred fast or being popular on Instagram, and that being able to play well with others, not letting the side down and not being a needy, irritating wanker are far greater assets to everyone's long-term success. A close relative of the Wingman (or woman).

So what categories do our favourite chart-topping musical icons fall into? Well, I'm focusing here on the 99 per cent of musicians that actually exist in nature, not those 1 per cent of special cases who levitate above the rest of us with airbrushed auras and personal assistants. Nope, 'Major Label Lucky Bastard' is where you'll find them, but they don't mingle in the wild with the rest of us, and we've all heard way more than we need to about them already – so for the purposes of this particular field study, we'll be ignoring them (for now), and you can only imagine how much that hurts them.

So, us musical types are a broad, dysfunctional family, pervading all areas of society. A sprawling ragtag web of clashing personalities and tribal distinctions all loosely united by a common affliction called 'music'. There's at least one of us in every family, office, gym, factory and prison cell. We're everywhere. And although each camp has its own generally identifiable uniform (anything black for the goths, Gran's cardigan for the grungers), there are a myriad exceptions to the rule. Don't be deceived by the goofy Ned Flanders-looking guy in the accounts department; he might just be the death growler in a church-blazing doomcore band called Foetus Burner. You can't get lazy. We're everywhere. Stay vigilant. Hell, you might even be one yourself!

And that doesn't mean that we all get along either. Far from it. I'd love to say that beneath our superficial differences, we're all on the same side, but we're not. The Metalheads hate the DJs, the Prog Rockers hate the keyboard-less Singer-Songwriters, the Hippies love everyone and we all hate the Jazzers. Objects of my personal vitriol include *any* band that wear stupid raincoats done all the way up under steaming hot stage lights, walk like their knees have been confiscated and sing glorified Oasis covers in a fake Manc accent when they're from Bournemouth. I don't need to hear their music; I already know that I hate them with a passion bordering on violence.

So I guess what I'm trying to say is that it's tricky. In fact, it's damn near impossible to generalise about musicians, even though I've spent the last few paragraphs doing exactly that. Sure, some of us conform keenly to the clichés of our chosen gang, but most do not. We've got day jobs, families, diets. We stroke kittens and we like football. All the normal stuff – just cooler. The caricature of the workshy, unreliable musician simply isn't true. Neither is the popularised fantasy that we spend all of our time 'off our faces' and sleeping with anything that moves – and I'm still bitter about it. So here are some other things that likely don't spring to mind at the mention of a musician:

We can bench. Yep, even the weedy ones. I've seen an eight-stone skeleton carry a two-tonne bass cab down a flight of stairs... in skinny jeans. You see, we're well practised at lugging. In fact, we spend more time hurling heavy equipment around than most builders. 'So you think you're 'ard, mate? Then let me see you run with a case of drum hardware (known as a "body bag") through the crowded streets of Camden on a Saturday night... without dropping the Fender Deluxe in the *other* hand. Yes, I'm challenging you – come at me, bro!'

We've seen some stuff. To the weekend revellers reading this: after a long week of following orders, pushing through traffic, paying your bills, stressing your stresses and carrying your woes, what do you do? You cut fucking loose, right? And who's there for you when you're doing it? Who's egging you on with a bone-rattling beat and a call to reckless abandon? Why it's us, isn't it? While you're crawling topless and bloodied through a pool of your own fluids and shouting 'one more for the road, lads', who gives you one fucking more? Your friendly local band of amigos have got your back. I've seen blood, I've seen vomit, I've seen affairs, drugs, violence, crime and the most unspeakably mental behaviour from my hard-working, otherwise upstanding countryfolk on a weekend, and I'm pretty sure that neither our politicians, our police nor our marketeers (or indeed many bosses or partners) have seen such an unrestrained and uncensored insight into the full nature of our society as us musicians have. My life as a musician has led me to meet people from all walks of life – rich and poor from every conceivable corner of beyond to the other – and these experiences have given me a depth of social insight that is a rare treasure. We've seen it all. But don't worry; your secrets are safe with us.

We work hard. If anyone still thinks that us musicians don't live in the 'real world' and wouldn't know a 'real day's work' if it bit us on the arse, then we need to take a walk. In an average week we'll juggle several bill-paying jobs by day, followed by practising, gig booking, promoting and performing by night (when others are rightfully relaxing in front of the TV). Come the weekend, while most people are out busting shapes and livers, we're driving across the country, dragging tonnes of equipment with us to entertain those crazy, drunken bastards until the early (really early!) hours before having to drive home and do it all again the next day. We put in some serious hours for the cause here, people. And we don't get any of the perks of that 'real job' either, with the real monthly wage, the real pension, paid leave and free evenings and weekends (but we do get to play live and that's way better). We survive in a world with zero job security, in an industry that's essentially died and an ever-dwindling live circuit on which to earn an honest shekel – and we don't do it by sitting on our arse. These days, it's not enough to simply be good at your instrument; you've also got to be a graphic designer, photographer, social media influencer, web designer, brand marketer, producer, video maker and secretary. Us musicians have adapted to the challenges of our changing times and we're still fucking here doing our thing. We're handy, resilient dudes to know.

And we provide a noble social service. Whether you're a music lover or couldn't tell your Johns from your Pauls, whether you're a musician yourself and whether you know it or not, *we* are the soundtrack to your life. Whether it's on the radio, a playlist, the town streets or in the bars, we're there for you. That's us. Giving you a little line of noise candy to help you through your day. We're a million different faces with a million different stories to tell. We played your wedding, those banging nights at the local boozer, those tear-drenched stadium memories. We're your escape, your confidant, your devil, your voice. We wrote your special song. We got the party started and gave a send-off to your deceased. We made you question. We made you dream. We made you laugh, cry, dance, fight and fuck. We're hard-wired into who you are and what you're about. We touched your heart; we left our mark. That's us.

So, who exactly is making *your* music? I guess it's a case of how long is a guitar string, but I'm pretty sure that, armed with the above info, you'll be far better equipped now to spot them out in the wild. You may even be able to tell if what you see is a Wingman, a Leader, a Clown or an Arsehole – and next time you hear about a bunch of musicians trashing the local wine bar, at least you'll know it wasn't that burly, leather-clad metal band, but the polite, rosy-cheeked orchestra that was in town for the night. So good luck out there and be careful; as I said, they're everywhere. But next time you see a musician, try this: send them over a firm, respectful nod that says 'I know; I get it', thank them for their service – and then sleep with them proudly.

3.

NOISE CANDY

After food, sex and violence, what's the one thing you're guaranteed to find in every tribe, commune, urban metropolis, gutter, palace, desert and backwater shanty town throughout the ages? What is the one thing that unites people of every nationality, race, social class, age, gender, religion or political persuasion? And no, I'm not talking about the universal confusion at the staggering success of Coldplay... but close. I'm talking about bongos, rain dances, dodgy thrash-metal dungeons, backalley jazz clubs, opera, hip-hop, bone flutes, songs around the campfire, illegal raves, ragas, twinkling bells, that crazy throat-singing stuff, hymns at church, samba, symphony orchestras and... you get the point. Rhythms and noises that have spoken to every soul that's ever existed. Hell, they've even got it in space, man!

Yet nobody even knows what it is. What *is* music? We can't touch it. We can't see it, smell it or taste it. What *is* it? *Where* is it? Along with earth, water, fire, air and space, it's our sixth element for living (isn't it?), except we know what fire, air and water are.

But music? What *is* that formless, ethereal elixir that has kept us all dancing, romancing, raving and wallowing since the *sapiens* first boogied? Maybe let's start with what it's not.

It's not sound. It *has* sound, but it's not sound. Let me explain with a jam session...

Me blasting radio static at you (noise) is unlikely to make you hit the dance floor and fall in love (unless you're into Japanese noisecore music). Similarly, you stamping on a lone kick drum (rhythm) or twanging a solitary note on a guitar (pitch) over and over again isn't going to provoke any mosh pits any time soon. So sound – even *musical* sound with pitch – is not musical by itself; it's just bloody irritating. But if I took that same radio static and yanked the volume up and down on it in a consistent rhythm, and if you then added your kick drum and guitar – still playing the same one note, but in *alternate* rhythms to my crazy radio thing... well now... now we've got ourselves a party! Now we've got ourselves some music, baby! So what's changed? Not the ingredient parts (noise, pitch and rhythm) but the *interplay* between them. The rub and flow of how those different sounds push and pull against each other to make that undeniably sexy groove (nice job by the way; let's form a noisecore band). So it's the sum of the parts together – and each part has to be *relative* to the other or it just doesn't make any sense. Like a pizza without the tomato and cheese, just the base – it ain't a pizza.

So is 'music' merely the interaction of different sounds? Hell no. If we were all standing in a room, randomly slamming the crap out of our instruments at the same time, would that be music? Experimental Jazzers would, of course, say yes but literally everyone else on the planet would thankfully say no. So the simultaneous playing of sounds isn't *only* what it takes to make music – there's a little bit of craft involved too. The sounds need to engage with each other in certain ways before heads start a-bobbing, each part getting its purpose in life from what it does in relation to the other sounds playing. There are no lone heroes in music land. That shredelicious guitar solo only sounds awesome in context with the kick-ass beat and backing riff it's playing over. If anyone's in any doubt about that, try staying in a musical instrument shop for more than an hour and tell me you didn't ponder genocide. A kick drum only starts to sound funky when it's played in relation to a hi-hat and a snare – otherwise it's just some dude stamping on something. So it's all relative, man, and all of those crashes, bangs and twangs need to come together as one big hippie commune in the airwaves before they turn into... music.

Interaction doesn't always have to mean 'nice' interaction, however. It can mean aggression. It can mean discord and shock. And this is where I draw my flag. Because the thing is, I like heavy and experimental music. I like noisy, clashy, weird, difficult music. The idea that music *has* to have a melody, a toe-tappable rhythm and 'right'-sounding chords is an idea that I actively enjoy smashing. I genuinely enjoy listening to music that has none of the above. Dissonant, brash, unrhythmic anarchy with no structure, lyrics or familiar sounds – that's my Sunday! I *like* that shit. To me, it's still music, glorious music. And I'm not alone. But as we're talking technicalities here, I stand my ground that one lone sound in and of itself is not music – even in such experimental music. It's just a sound. And a sound doesn't become *music* until it gels (or clashes) with other sounds or other notes on the same instrument.

So what are some of the main elements of such musical witchcraft? What are some of the trade secrets we can use to turn a humble tabletop into a dance-off, to conjure a collection of lifeless noises into the irresistible magic of music? On my worryingly bizarre and practically unlistenable album *9.i.P*, I experimented with making music that was devoid of any melody, discernible rhythm, conventional pitch or recognisable sounds. Needless to say, it didn't get much radio play on Smash Hits Radio, but the purpose of this musical masochism was to test whether emotional responses could still be sparked in the listener, without using any of the tried and tested gizmos like rhythm, melody, harmony and structure.

And the answer was... well... kind of, but not really. I mean, if dark, discombobulating, unsettling weirdness is your happy place then I've made you a gift. But the entire record was essentially limited to that one narrow shade of horror, and if I wanted to do anything else with the poor listeners' emotions, like make them happy, sad or get down and boogie, I would have to lean on some reliable old pals. Let's introduce the gang.

Melody: The tune. The bit we sing along to. The thread that stitches the other bits together.

Rhythm: How often the sound happens. The bit that makes us nod and twerk.

Harmony: The backing. The context giver. Is a tomato a pizza or a salad?

Structure: The boundaries. The journey. Establishing home, leaving home and returning victorious.

Some other notable and wildly important mentions are:

Silence: That's right. The spaces between stuff are crucial. The stars at night without any sky between them would just be a migraine. Silence is the difference between randomly hitting something and playing a 'beat'. It's the air; it's the breath; it's vital.

Expression: Like *how* is the piece played? The feel. Are we swelling the notes in dramatically or just smashing them all out at full volume? Expression turns an A minor chord into an A minor chord that has you sobbing into your sleeve.

Timbre: The type of sounds used. I can play the same melody on a piano, a synth or a distorted Les Paul, but which one 'fits' best for the vibe we're creating? Timbre is super important. It's the difference between cute and cuddly – and torturous and terrifying. Same tune, different timbre.

Let's also give a little shout-out here to 'tension'. On their own, clashy, dissonant earloads of pure sonic evil are just that – and they quickly lose their edge (like my *9.i.P* hell broth). But when used tactfully, tension is the very thing that makes the nice bits sound so damn good. Too much, however, will ruin the dish. Too much sugar and we've got another sickly-sweet, forgettable pop hit soon to be on the scrapheap once we're all bored of it in two weeks. Too much salt and we're back to me pissing about with that radio again. It's about working that pan like an evil alchemist – a little sugar here, a little spice there, a little tension, a little more, is it coming, please tell me it's coming, oh shit it's getting really tense now... and then BOOM, there's the fucking chorus I've been waiting for! Heaven. Pass me the smokes, hun.

It's a metaphor for life. Those moments of friction, joy, suspense and release are all equal parts of what makes for an exciting mortal ride. Similarly, a song where all the parts play perfectly in unison, all the time, nice and orderly with no moments of unrest or tension, would be a grooveless, predictable, artificially sweetened march towards madness and tyranny. Kind of like the North Korea of music. Or the Phil Collins of life.

This is, of course, an offensively skimmed-over tour of the brilliant and beautiful musical devices that we could delve into further, but hey, both you and I have got monkey videos vying for our attention, so let's just keep it snappy. However, if anyone is looking for the keys to the musical gun locker, they can find them above.

So that's a super-speedy sneak peek into the arsenal that musos use to fool people into thinking that a thick, flappy string is funky. Are we getting closer now? Have we answered that seemingly simple question: what is music? Could we say perhaps that music is 'the creative arrangement of sounds'? I guess if we're being stone-cold boring about it then yeah, perhaps that's it – but it's so much *more* than that, isn't it? Come on, us humans *love* the stuff! We *need* it! What is it about those bundles of jostling noises that just hits us all right in the feels? Take a look around: wherever there are people, there is music. The stuff *means* something to us! It's not only evident in the tunes blasting out of every phone, car stereo, drinking hole, food stop, movie soundtrack, shop, stadium and theatre, providing a soothing balm or an energy power-up to get us all through the day; it's in the immortal folklore of our musical icons; it's in the fashion and lifestyle identity that comes with our chosen juice (are we a punk, a mod, hip hop or Orchestra darling?); it's where we lose ourselves and find ourselves; it's in the memories that are triggered when we hear that special song; it's in the goosebumps on our arms, the tears on our cheeks and the big dopey grin on our face. So no, music is not just the creative arrangement of sounds. Far fucking from it.

It's a force. Music is a force. And not just a force that draws us all to the dance floor but an immense force for personal and social change too. It wasn't my teachers who taught me about the world, my place in it and what really matters – it wasn't my leaders either. It was my musical heroes. Swaggering, sunglasses-wearing, instrument-wielding, cool-looking badasses who agreed with me that school sucks, war sucks, love sucks and fitting in is for suckers. I'd found my home, my natural habitat. It was rock stars who taught me to challenge authority, question conformity, be a decent dude and celebrate who I am with a firm middle finger for anyone who didn't like it. It's thanks to music that I had an identity during my teens, a safe place of escape in a sometimes ugly world, a friend who was always there for me, a mentor, a big brother and a role model. Music gave me confidence, focus and drive, and it stopped me from stealing the neighbours' car. It wasn't just about the music with the bands I obsessed over; it was a lifestyle. It was a gang, a purpose and a belief system. It was everything. It still is.

And it's not just me. Recent history is filled with examples of music being a force for social unity, change and progress – from the blues to reggae to hip hop. Why? Because a good beat and a good chorus is physically irresistible whoever you are, wherever you're from. It's a universal language that speaks louder than any propaganda or racist bullshit. It pulls us all together like a magnet, and before you know it, former enemies are meeting in the club and making babies. Just as it made it harder to be racist as a young white guitar player if your hero was Chuck Berry, it makes it hard today for toxic parents to pass on their ignorance to their kids who are upstairs bingeing on hip hop. I'm not saying that it's the whole story, but it's certainly a factor. It's a diluting agent, gradually eroding the prejudices and accepted norms of the unsuspecting listener from inside the safety of their own homes and ears. The generation who voted for the first black president in American history was the generation who grew up listening to hip hop. That's significant.

With a different style, mood and vibe available for every conceivable personality, purpose, setting and need, music is an unstoppable, all-pervasive little virus that we just cannot escape. And despite us still not knowing what it even *is* – it's proving to have a pretty impressive résumé. But there's more. Before I became a full-time soldier for the rock 'n' roll cause, I had to juggle a variety of day jobs alongside playing in pubs and sleeping on gear sticks. One such day job was as a music teacher in schools around south Wales. I'd drive between several different schools each day – some primaries, some high schools, some rich, some poor – and bestow upon my many willing victims the life-changing miracle of… the 'power chord'. Two fingers, two strings and a thousand classic songs just fell into my pupils' hands. I'm sure there was probably, like, a syllabus or something, more than likely involving dusty old dead dudes in wigs – but I've never much cared for syllabuses or Bach, so my guys all got Green Day, Metallica, Guns N' Roses and Nirvana. And you won't *believe* what happened…

Within a few weeks I'd see the kids transform, right in front of my eyes! The shy, always-getting-bullied kid started strutting around with head held high. The troublesome, always-getting-suspended kid started to excel in their studies. Why? Because instead of music class being just another place where they *couldn't* do something, where they were forced to regurgitate stuff that had no relevance to surviving the harsh world outside the school gates, suddenly *they* were a dude who could play fucking 'Raining Blood' on the electric guitar! This simple injection of self-esteem and a newfound passion to focus on was all it took for them to realise that they didn't want to screw their life up. That life could be better, that *they* could be better.

I saw grades improve, I saw bad attitudes improve, and soon I couldn't accommodate any more students in my eager line of punctual young metal converts, hungry for more. The divisions between the bullies and the bullied evaporated as all were desperate to jam with each other, and I witnessed a stark social development in even the most introverted kids. Teary thank-yous, letters and gifts were sent from parents, astonished at the rapid transformation of their previously challenging child. Because of a power chord! It really was something to behold. Out of everything I've done, those times still stand alone as the most rewarding. The moral? If you want the best for your kids, for God's sake support the arts. It was yet another priceless benefit the world gets as a result of this elusive music stuff. But don't thank me, thank Slayer.

And have you heard of the mysterious effects that music and the playing of an instrument can have on the brain? The way it fires up like a Christmas tree when it hears the stuff – both the left and right sides together. Like how when we play an instrument, we're flexing many different parts of our brain at the same time – physical coordination, memory, creativity, vision, language and others. Learning a musical instrument at an early age has been proven to supercharge the brain, leaving lifelong benefits in the areas of memory recall, creative problem solving and mental dexterity (I'm assuming drummers weren't included in the study). It has been suggested that learning an instrument (or even just listening to music) is one of the best things we can do to keep our brains fit and nimble. And because music seeps its way into every part of the brain, it has been proven to have some staggering results in the care of those suffering with dementia and other cognitive disorders. There's just something about music that ignites the brain in a truly unique and puzzling way. Science knows it to be true, but it doesn't yet know why it happens.

Music is also used as a form of therapy for a whole range of conditions, from depression to schizophrenia and speech disorders. Many years back, I was loosely connected with the cancer research charity Tenovus in Wales, who used music – specifically the running of choirs composed of cancer patients – to study what effects music and singing might have on those involved. What they found was so exciting that Channel 4 did a documentary on it. Across the board, well-being was lifted, a sense of hope was instilled, feelings of isolation disappeared and a measurable positive impact was found in the body chemistry of all involved. From singing! Music truly is remarkable, powerful, important stuff, and I'm proud to be a disciple of its cause – but one doesn't have to be a *musician* to be a music-ist.

So what is it, then? I don't know if I've brought us any closer to answering that question or pushed us further away, but you can rest assured that the experts haven't got a damn clue either. There are countless scientific theories about music and why we have it. Does it have an evolutionary purpose? Is it because of its socialising factor? Is it linked to certain resonances of frequency found in the laws of nature? Is it connected to the orbits of the stars? For more than a thousand years, studies have been done, long, dry academic books have been written and outlandish theories have been tested, but still, the song remains the same. We don't really know what it is. It's an anomaly. A beautiful, magical, otherworldly anomaly – and I hope it stays that way. I would hate it if the enigma code of music was one day cracked and demoted to such a drab and clinical description as the one found in dictionaries:

'Music is the art of arranging sounds in time so as to produce a continuous, unified and evocative composition, as through melody, harmony, rhythm and timbre.'

Urgh! No, it's not! It's the wine of the gods, the poetry of the Devil, the Big Bang, the reason, the answer and the cure. It's a comfort, a friend, a saviour and the best drug in the world. What music is depends on who you ask. It means so many different things to all of us, so perhaps there's no 'right' answer after all. But the one thing I'm certain we can we all agree on is that music... is fucking awesome. Do not trust anyone who says otherwise.

Ok, class dismissed.

4.

SAVE OUR VENUES

The suspense has reached bursting point. You can feel the collective heart rates galloping like speedballing stallions as we wait... and wait. This room is essentially a bomb. A bomb that is soon to explode like a motherfucker on the count of one, two, three and four. You can feel it coming. It's hot, it's dark and it's getting tense. A mass of bodies sway as one organism in fidgety anticipation as the pent-up turmoil inside each and every soul that's been squeezed inside this monastic dungeon is about to be exorcised in a high-volume transcendental cleanse. Bring on the band already!

As always, I've got the best seat in the house – as does everyone, because there *are* no seats in this house and there are certainly no special seats. Nope, in *this* church, we stand. And we stand as one – as equals. And if you want to commune with the clergy during service, you just push your way through the crowd and high-five them right there and then, because not only are there no seats here but no barriers either – literal or otherwise. That's right, folks, tonight I'll be standing mere inches away from your next favourite band as they thrash out the bangers that will soon be exclusive to the far-away stages of arenas and festivals. It's a view that the most expensive concert ticket in the world couldn't buy you – and it only cost me fifteen bucks (for THREE bands). Tonight, both band and audience will be bound together in intimate, sweaty communion, the dividing lines between us removed as they should be – eye to eye, heart to heart, soul to soul. None of that squinting-at-what-you-think-*might*-be-the-singer-on-a-giant-TV-screen-ten-miles-away-from-the-stage nonsense. Fuck that. Not in this house, dude. Here, everyone gets an all-access pass as standard.

The punishingly never-ending wait is in fact only fifteen minutes, as that is the standard (and humanly impossible) amount of time allocated to each band to 1) get all their shit offstage or 2) get all their shit *on*stage and prepare to rock. As the support band does the former – breathlessly hurling tons of amps and drums off the tiny stage where they just spent every last ounce of blood, sweat and tears pleasuring us blessed bastards – the headliner quickly does the latter and hastily assembles their ten-tonne wall of sonic destruction, each band weaving seamlessly in and around each other in a kind of builders' ballet. I know their pain. I've done that dance a thousand times and, man, let me tell you, when your final chord chokes out and you stand there victoriously drenched in sweat with your heart punching its way out of your chest, having to immediately weightlift ten tonnes of heavy metal off the stage within mere minutes before drink, rest or reflection is a killer. But hey, tonight, that's their problem. The support band will now be standing next to you downing beers and enjoying the rest of the night, their noble work of kicking in eardrums dutifully and beautifully delivered. Their work here is done. Now, it's the headliner's turn to step it up one higher and give us what we've all been waiting for... a delicious hit of that loud, loud medicine. And here it comes.

'One, two, three, four!'

BOOM! The room erupts in a mass frenzy of euphoric, demented contortions. Primal release. Violence without the violence. Happy faces everywhere. Is it dancing? Therapy? Or a connection to a higher power? We may never know but it feels... good. A cardinal cure for the relentless drudgery and shackles of daily life. For that moment, we're human again, dancing around the fire, wailing at the wilderness and wondering at the stars. Except we're in Tony's Rock Bar on a Wednesday night in Newport. And it's loud. Gloriously loud. Every kick of the kick drum is a thundering kick to the eardrum, heart and chest. The sound doesn't politely *arrive* at your ears after being gently spring-cleaned by the open air; it physically assaults you, gripping you by the spine and shaking all of the bad stuff out. The bass wraps itself around you in a warm, sexy bass bath. The instruments howl in perfect clarity because, well... you're standing in front of the actual fucking amps rather than being five acres away. You hear the band as the band sounds when they play in a room together – which is exactly what they're doing. And there's nothing like it on Earth.

The band blitzkriegs its way through a perfect set as we bob, bounce and bump around for what feels like bare minutes before the 'final song' is introduced. Hugs and fist bumps are exchanged between band and fan, and in twenty minutes, we'll all be sharing drinks together like lifelong friends. You see, there's no backstage bar here – there's just *the* bar – so if the band want to hang out and sink a few brewskis after the show, they'll be doing it with you. And they saved the best for last too – the song we've all been waiting for. As that loving sonic tsunami floods the room, washing the body and soul of everyone in it, we are once more under its black magic in a variety of supernatural spasms and seizures – literally exorcising our demons. When it's all over, both band and audience stand spent, reeling from the trip to nirvana and back. Soaked to the bone and fully purged of our collective poisons. Humanity restored. If only it didn't have to end. If only life could just be one big concert. The whole room bellows, heckles and begs for 'more, more, more', but the band look unsure – there are rules for this sort of thing now, aren't there? Noise laws and stuff. But then, from behind the bar, the main man from whom this holy sanctum derives its name, Tony, gives the signal we've all been praying for – a big, fat thumbs up for the more.

Thanks to Tony being such a consummate fucking legend, we're all once more aboard the high-speed bliss train. With the official sanction of the mythical dude who runs the joint, the band eagerly embrace the chance to be freed from the chains of an immorally short set and give us an exclusive premiere of some new songs, never before heard – and they're stunning. It feels like a real moment. Everyone knows this band is gonna be the next big deal, and yet here we are, standing three feet away from them as they grace us with an intimate first airing of next year's mega-banger. We've witnessed something special tonight and we know it. You can feel it. Not only did my favourite band in the world just feed me the goods in dirty, decadent helpings half an hour away from my front door, but I discovered a new band too – that tasty little opener from out of town who I'd never even heard of before coming here tonight but who (almost literally) blew the top of my fucking head off. You just can't put a price on nights like these. Except you can – as I said, it was fifteen bucks.

And now for the aftershow party! I was so busy busting shapes and fighting invisible monsters that I completely forgot that other essential component of the evening's proceedings – beer – and boy, do I need one about now. The gift that keeps on giving that is Tony and his hard-working crew are busting the frothy-topped jugs of salvation out with more speed than a Motörhead blood test – and unlike at those arena shows where you have to queue for hours to get fleeced for lager, Coke or... did I mention lager... here, you've got a fully stocked bar of all sorts of trouble-inducing elixirs for a price you can actually afford. Because, despite the perception of this being a music venue, this, my friends, is a fucking bar – like, a proper bar – and I intend to fully explore its magical bounty. Hit me up, Tony, my good man.

The aftershow DJ starts cranking out the classics while I chat with the singer from the headline band at their merch stand. Even though this dude has been sleeping in a wet van and showering in a car park for the past three weeks, he still takes the time to hang with me, take a selfie and share a beer. I'm actually hanging out with my favourite band! Now I'm sure you don't need me to tell you this, but the rule at these type of shows is that you *always* buy at least *something* from the merch stand – whatever you can afford – so I bag myself one of those killer tees and a physical copy of the new album, content with the knowledge that every penny will be going straight to the band's survival fund and keeping the show on the road. Pretty soon, there's a whole gang of us laughing and hammering shots with the band, listening to their road stories and adventures before some absolute hero informs us all that they live a few doors down and we're all welcome to take the *after*-after-party back to theirs and sleep where we may fall.

There have been times in my life when I myself have been such a hero and there have been other times when I have been a hanger-on or an invited band member. Folks who do this have no idea of the level of heavenly luxury enjoyed by a member of a travelling band in getting to sleep on a sofa for a night instead of guitar cases and dirty laundry, so if you are ever able to be such a legend sometime, please do it. Anyway, before long we're back at some random dude's flat getting royally trolleyed with my new best mates who happen to be in my favourite band. The guitars are out, the tunes are playing, the beers are flowing and we're all having a pretty awesome Wednesday – now Thursday! Falling where we fall after 4 a.m. 'deep talk', tonight is a night we will never forget. And yet, somewhere out there, there is a long, loooong line of pissed-off drivers sitting in a motionless, 10-mile gridlock after leaving whatever gig they just '*kind of saw*' at the big arena in town and paying the entire ticket price of our gig on one pint of watered-down piss. Because, let's be honest, arenas suck – and stadiums suck even harder. The whole process is a piss-take. From the cost of the ticket (if you can get one) to the queueing, parking, more queueing, being herded in like cattle, being rinsed at the bar for shite beer, seeing nothing of the band, with dire sound, and then being herded out again and sitting in a traffic jam for hours. Fuck that. I'd rather be at Tony's Rock Bar any night of the week, wouldn't you? So it's a shame that it's closing down next month to be turned into 'luxury' flats.

X X X

Up and down the country, grass-roots music venues are being culled at a truly disturbing rate. Many of the venues where I honed my craft in my early days were considered iconic cultural landmarks, vital players in this country's proud musical history and a coveted rite of passage for any band hoping to get on the scene. Almost all of them are now gone. Imagine being a starry-eyed young band, about to play your first gig in London, and walking down the mysterious staircase into the black mouth of the underground Borderline club, passing photos on the wall of Jeff Buckley, Muse, PJ Harvey, Frank Turner, Rage Against the Machine, Pearl Jam and loads of others, all playing intimate sets on the very same stage where you'll be playing tonight. A younger me made that exact walk, and I can still feel the intoxicating wave of awe, inspiration and wonder at seeing those pictures of many of my heroes gracing that small stage at the same entry point of their fabled musical journey. The Borderline is gone. As is TJ's in Newport, The Haçienda, Moles, The Moon, all of the Barflys, The Roadhouse, The Arches, The Square and The 12 Bar Club where I personally witnessed the sit-in protests at the rampant gentrification of the area on the day that police dragged people out of the building. All of these are now gone, along with too many others to list. And by the time you read this, many more will have befallen a similar fate. Travesty isn't the word. Scandalous national disgrace would be more like it.

Why is this happening? Well, in a nutshell, it seems as though it's because music, art, culture, fun and history no longer have a place in this country unless they're making grotesque amounts of money for a tiny cartel of super-rich, soulless drones. We can dress it up however we want, but that's the gist. Choose your villain. First there are the landlords. These guys couldn't give two turds about iconic cultural heritage or maintaining the fertile breeding ground that produces the musical genius that this country is known and respected for worldwide. Nope, all these guys want is M.O.N.E.Y. As much as they can get their hands on. Actually, forget hands; they want truckloads of the stuff, they want tubs full of it to rub over their heartless bodies, to invest it in more properties so they can make even more of that dirty, sweet M.O.N.E.Y! Fuck your band, fuck music and fuck you. That gritty haven of loud sounds, good times, bad mistakes and memories for life means nothing to the dude who owns the joint. To them it's just bricks and mortar, and whoever stumps up the most filthy lucre for access to those bricks will get the keys. And so it turns out that there's not enough money in happiness – but *loads* to be made from an endless supply of laughably small, rip-off city-centre apartments deceivingly listed as 'luxury flats'. I have no idea who's renting these flats or why there seems to be such a wildly insatiable demand for them, but up and down the country, buildings that were once a thriving hub of each city's cultural identity and history are being converted en masse into generic, super-expensive cubicles for God knows who.

It's a result of the lean towards the yuppification of city centres generally, known as gentrification. Our cultural centres are now increasingly catering to high-salaried professionals working in the city – who else is buying the luxury flats? And the accompanying explosion of glitzy, expensive high-end chain stores that are making every town in the land look identical is matched only by the even sadder explosion of desperate poverty, extreme homelessness and scores of boarded-up shops we see on too many of our city streets. It's the yuppie effect, and it destroys everything good. The money brigade want to make all of our city centres the exclusive playgrounds of the rich. I guess it's what happens when we elect the Tories over and over again – but don't get me started. As the yuppification level increases, so do things like rents and peripheral costs, so that even when venues are not having the premises tugged out from under them, it's ever more impossible for them to scratch out a sustainable existence.

It also transpires that these new settlers don't much like noise either – unless it's at a pricey sports bar with a cover band 'bashing out noughties bangers'. Ah, noise pollution, oh how I miss you. I mean, one shouldn't have to tolerate the sound of the city's communal beating heart when they're paying over the odds for a prime-location glorified bathroom, should they? How is one supposed to give one's full attention to the *Financial Times* when some grubby band of peasants is bashing a bastard drum kit three doors down?! Apparently it's perfectly acceptable to move into a city-centre apartment and expect the rest of the city that was there long before you to shut the fuck up immediately. And the law agrees – because of course it does. I personally know of several venues that have been embroiled in such draining, time-consuming and costly legal tussles, with a complaint from a *single* resident, to the point that they have had to move location several times before eventually closing down for good. If anyone reading this *is* one such resident, close the book now; you're not welcome here. If these people don't want noise, they should go and buy a place in the countryside, the entitled, fun-murdering asshats. Otherwise, they need to get their ass downstairs, buy a beer and remember how good it feels to be on the highway to fucking hell.

So that's one reason for the heartbreaking horror show we see taped across the closed doors of our favourite venues – landlords, yuppies and Tories. They don't care about rock 'n' roll, they care not for joy; they care only for filthy lucre and a quiet place to plot their evil. Against this changing tide, and despite the truly heroic efforts of club owners and promoters everywhere whose doors *are* still open to keep the good times rolling, it's just become impossible for many. But why? Surely there's still demand for live music, right? People still like beer, don't they? Well, I hate to say it, but *that one*... that one's on us.

If we don't show up and support our venues, they simply can't survive. Not so long ago, going to a local show was just what we *did* on the weekend, but these days there are so many more contenders for our attention and our pounds that our vital grass-roots venues often get neglected. And I get it, I really do; times have been hard for all of us. But there is so much at stake here that we all have a moral duty to treat gig-going as an act of cultural defiance – to stand not as an audience but as a resistance movement defending our sacred breeding grounds of sonic awesomeness. That one's on us. All of us. It's time for us to reclaim our music scene from the cold, undead hands of the money men and bring it roaring back to the streets – our streets.

But then again, I'm a romantic. I've spent much of my life in places like Tony's Rock Bar – both onstage and off – and I have an unashamed love for their sticky floors and stickered walls. And being an active musician, of course, I have a horse in the race. But does it *really* matter? Is it *that* big of a deal? Things change don't they? Get over it. Well, here's why it matters. This little island upon which we graze may suck at many things – cuisine, weather, an embarrassingly archaic class system and a frustrating lack of revolutionary fervour – but one thing we are top of the global league table in, one thing we are the undisputed world champions in and one thing we are recognised and respected for worldwide is our music. No contest. If anyone needs a reminder, here are some of the biggies:

Pink Floyd, The Beatles, Queen, Adele, David Bowie, Ed Sheeran, Led Zeppelin, The Rolling Stones, The Clash, Radiohead, Motörhead, Black Sabbath and Kate Bush.

Yeah, read it and fucking weep, Germany. Now that is one fat CV for a country that's smaller than the state of Oregon – and I've not even scratched the surface. Here in the UK, music is *what we do*. We're knocking out more bangers per capita than anywhere else on earth, and we should all revel in the sickly jealousy of those lands with better food, better weather but tragically disastrous music. They know it; everyone knows it. Don't try to get cute with the UK when it comes to music. You'll come back with your arse bagged up in a Union Jack and a safety pin. And here's the stinger: every single one of those iconic guys and gals honed their wizardry on hundreds of rickety stages up and down this great, grey land. It's where they got good. It's where they got exceptional. It's where they learned to mesmerise a crowd, how to craft ever-better songs and how to steal our hearts. Nobody gets exceptional in the bedroom except porn stars. Us Brits used to have a global empire powered by horrific brutality and exploitation, but now we make the world sing, and that's a form of soft power that should not be understated.

And what about the jaw-dropping amount of money that this industry makes for the country? Billions upon billions of pounds every year. Not to mention the enormous tax boost made from all of our multi-platinum, stadium-hopping legends – that is, of course, the ones who don't identify as a vague business entry in the Cayman Islands. These tax-paying titans wouldn't exist were it not for the grass-roots furnaces that spawned them, and hundreds of millions would be lost to us if they'd had to keep their jobs at KFC. Back at the grass-roots level, the substantial boost to the local economy stimulated by the presence of live music venues should not be downplayed either – and I'm sure we'd all rather see that money going into the tills of our local bars, takeaways and strip clubs than to some giant arena's dubious parent company based overseas.

In any other industry, these venues would be classed as R & D departments. Research and development for the 'products' that will ultimately create a shitload of money for the broader economy and the taxman. And just as the R & D departments of many other (and much less savoury) industries such as arms and big tech are subsidised heavily by the government, our grass-roots venues should also be subsidised as part of a national cultural development programme. It really is quite simple: no local venues, no Adele, no Oasis, no Ed Sheeran, no Queen – and none of the tax revenue and industrial stimulus that comes with them. The relatively tiny cost of subsidising our local venues would be dwarfed by the gargantuan gains, both economic and cultural, that would be reaped by the nurturing of tomorrow's megastars, teachers and techies. Because, after all, it's not just artists who are cooked up in these grass-roots cauldrons – it's entire industries.

Muse's lighting engineer didn't figure out how to work all those lasers on their first night at Wembley. Hell no – they'd done a thousand club nights first. Adele's sound tech didn't go to uni and then, hey presto, here's a stadium to play with. It doesn't work like that. And that's not to mention the drivers, riggers, backstage techs and crew – whole industries of people without whom there would be no Glastonbury or Wembley Stadium. Grass-roots music venues are the literal engine of this country's proud cultural standing. Lose them and it's all over. I'm being dead serious. As things get rapidly and terminally worse for our glorious local factories of rock, I strongly believe we need a nationwide emergency programme of assistance from the government just as we do with public libraries and community centres. Yet in recent years, government support for cultural industries across the board has been pissed on from a great height – or 'streamlined', to use their vernacular. So it's highly unlikely we'll receive any help from our grinning emperors any time soon – and what a surprise that is.

What, then, can be done? What will *have* to be done in order to stave off the pandemic of yuppification before it swallows up everything good and every town becomes an indistinguishable bore of hipster bars, sports bars and piss-takingly exorbitant arenas and stadiums hosting the same rotating menu of mega artists? Many brilliant ideas already exist, such as putting a levy on all ticket sales at arenas and stadiums and investing that money back into the industry's R & D departments: the grass-roots venues. But as important and necessary as that is, we don't want to be held at the mercy of our overlords. It's better we do the heavy lifting ourselves, and while it's going to take a committed effort to reclaim what was rightfully ours, luckily we already have everything we need to make a swift and punishing retaliation: each other. Because what is the counter-attack to the social warfare of the Thatcherite creep towards banality? Community. The exact opposite of the weapon of yuppification that they've used to divide and downgrade us all this time. Community. Whether it's in politics, labour disputes, climate change or saving our venues, the solution is in all of us standing together as one immovable army – like the mosh pit at the start of this chapter. And nothing brings the people together like music. Our local grass-roots venues are our resistance bunkers in a world becoming worryingly sterile and uniform, and it is paramount that we fight to save our communal heart.

One easy thing we can all start doing immediately is start showing up. It's hardly a raw deal, is it? Pay a few quid to watch some bands on a Thursday night who might turn out to be the best fucking thing we've ever heard. Or we could stay at home and watch *The Apprentice* – it's our call. But when our grandkids ask, 'What were *you* doing during the great collapse, Granddad, before the world became a digital dust-bowl dystopia?' that's what we'll have to tell them. So show up and keep showing up – as an act of resistance, if nothing else. Spread the gospel and bring your converts. Once the place starts making decent dough again, they'll have the weapon they need to keep the slumlord from the door. And the second our venues have enough active local support, they'll be impenetrable to the encroaching tentacles of yuppification. This is not only about supporting the scene; it's a matter of what kind of society we stand for and whether we're going to be passive accomplices in our own cultural eradication. The battleground is right outside our door. So show up and buy a beer. Buy two.

Another thing we can do is own the buildings. That's right. This absolutely genius idea has been successfully pulled off by those heroes at the Music Venue Trust where you can become a micro-investor in the building and, along with others, enable it to be run as a cooperative – either for profit or not. What cooler thing is there to say on a night out after someone says, 'Where to next, guys?' than... 'Let's go to *my* place.' Not only has my place got the best up-and-coming original live music in the whole goddamn town, not only has my place got a better range of booze than all the rest, not only can I get us in for free because... well, it's my fucking place, but once inside, you'll be part of a bustling, thriving community that's responsible for advancing this country's enviable cultural melting pot. Once you're in, you'll never want to leave. And what cooler way to fend off the various evil shit stains of capitalism than to collectively buy the fucking building out from under them. I love that. WE make the music, WE support the music and now WE can own the very room where it happens. Whether it's through collective ownership of the buildings or collective support of the venues within them, the point here is that it is the unconquerable power of community spirit – *us* – that is our most effective death blow against the well-manicured talons of doom. So come together, my comrades in rock, and let's do this!

It's time to reclaim what's ours. To light a fire under the arses of all those who've been stealing our culture and selling it back to us. To take it back to the streets from where it came and the communities that build it. Music isn't some elite spectator sport to be worshipped from a distance; it is forged in the fertile kitchens of our streets, our struggles, our stories and our sounds. New styles of music are a collaboration between creator and listener that grows and mutates synergistically within the laboratory walls of our local music scene before exploding outwards as the next giant leap in our shared musical evolution. It's time we all got back in the lab. Let us once again rejoice in our proud local musical history and keep it safe for the next generation of noise-makers, soul shakers and game-changers. Because this isn't just about supporting venues; it's about supporting the very bedrock of our immense music heritage, and each and every one of us must be a militant protector of that coveted grail. Rip it back from the limp clutches of those who seek to sterilise, clownify and monetise our essential life force. Our enemies are nothing against us. So I'll see you down the front at next week's triple bill with Cattle Smasher – and you'd better buy some merch. *Viva la revolucìon*!

But wait, what if I'm wrong? What if the lure of 'Mr Brightside', small-batch pale and luxury flats is simply too alluring for us to defeat? What if every last Tony's Rock Bar shrivels away under the shiny boot of yuppification and all that's left is a sprawling, identical chain of "Slippery Joe' sports bars in every town? What will become of our noble cause and our once beautiful scene then? Will we be doomed to a life sentence of being eternally violated by the same safe, syrupy songs from the same industry-approved elite of out-of-touch multimillionaires? Will *that* be the day the music died? Will we have suffered the final defeat? And where will all the musicians go? The real ones. The artists, the dreamers, the icons, the visionaries? I'll tell you where. They'll go underground. Like a secret rebel group of guerilla fighters, they'll continue to operate – but under the radar. I guarantee you that if the small local venue circuit ever got completely decimated, it wouldn't be long before we saw an explosion of living-room concerts, illegal gigs, shows in derelict buildings, on rooftops, industrial estates and street corners. Why? Because music isn't going anywhere – we can be assured of that. Music is an essential, non-negotiable element of life and us musicians and music lovers alike will always need our fix. And we're a creative bunch... try us. Even if we lose the battle, we'll be back. We'll be back like a phoenix from the ashes, roaring as lions and scaring the living vacuum out of the yuppies who put us there. New scenes will sprout everywhere like weeds, necessitating new venues, and before long we'll be making speedy advances into enemy territory and they won't know what hit them. So keep the faith, my follow rebels, for we are the deliverers of truth in an era of lies – and the truth always prevails. So let's get out there and save our venues, save our music and save our souls. The fight is on. Godspeed.

5.

QUIET MEDICINE

I was nine years old when I fell head over heels in love with music. I was ten when the doctor said I would soon be deaf. Both events are seared into my memory like the tattoo of a dead lover. The baby-sized, second-hand Spanish guitar for my birthday, the simple two-finger blues riff my dad taught me that had me transfixed and hell-bent on torturing my family with it for evermore. It was immediate. Love at first strum. The light had been flicked on inside me. A Pandora's box had burst open, spewing a whirlwind of multicoloured adventures, dreams and wonder into my innocent nine-year-old world. From that moment on, the first thing I did in the morning, the last thing I did before bed and pretty much the only thing I did... well, ever... was play that sweet 'Boogie in G' over and over with a wide, maniacal grin on my face. Footballs, skateboards and He-Man became instantly redundant next to the hypnotic grip of this mystical, magical music machine. I dashed around obsessively soaking up riffs from everywhere. The local stoner guitar guy in my village, grainy VHS tapes, the neighbours' vinyl and home-made mixtapes that I would rewind, study, rewind and study, painstakingly teaching myself to play, one note at a time. To this day, I can still feel the intoxicating rush and thrill of it all – my nimble nine-year-old brain blazing like a furnace with my new six-stringed lightsabre.

And then it was over. I'd been having this sticky discharge coming out of my ears, along with constant pain, balance problems and a significant loss of hearing. 'It's what happens to little boys,' the doctor said. 'They're kind of grubby, aren't they?' seemed to be his general vibe on it. 'It'll pass,' he guessed. My poor mum did the best she could to clean and comfort me through it – and so it went on. By sheer chance, we moved house later that year – and with it came a change of doctor. Unlike the previous douche, this new guy actually did some doctoring and promptly referred me to a specialist, who wasted no time in writing (in block capital letters) that I needed urgent surgery on both ears and that there could be no guarantee that I would survive with any of my hearing intact. It turns out that it wasn't general little-boy grubbiness that was causing the problem, but the two giant tumours that had been chewing their way through both of my middle ears while I'd been blissfully practising the blues for the past year. Cholesteatoma (as the horrible bastard is called) is rare. Having one in both ears at the same time? Man, that's some cruel shit.

At the time, my starry-eyed, floppy-haired, ten-year-old self couldn't really grasp the concept of 'no more music, no more hearing, ever again' and I just wanted to get the whole boring ordeal over and done with so I could get back to learning 'Whole Lotta Love'. So it's probably a good thing I had no idea said ordeal would end up dragging on for over three years. A life of toys, mates and carefree kid stuff had deformed into a life of cold steel implements, masked strangers, fluorescent lighting, relentless prodding, drugging, drilling, poking, nil-by-mouthing and the horror of nineties general anaesthetic. Looking back, my heart breaks for that shy, well-behaved, mop-topped, music-loving little dude who was still wearing his pants on the outside of his jeans in solidarity with Superman.

I ended up having three major operations because the dreaded cholestea-bastard came back. It dragged on and on. And these were heavy-duty surgeries, which meant slicing my ears half off my head (I've still got the scars), removing the bad guys from inside my skull and rebuilding my ear canals (which is why you can now park a tour bus in my right ear – a fact very much enjoyed by bullies when I finally got back to school). Time off the meat slab meant weeks of recovery time wrapped in a ginormous head bandage filled with antiseptic packing, which wasn't very conducive to listening to Hendrix. It wasn't very conducive to listening to bugger all, actually – the sympathetic words of upset loved ones included. Soon I had to start relying on lip-reading. Life without sound had begun.

But it was in my blood. I just *had* to play my guitar, man! I needed my six-stringed buddy now more than ever. Life had fast become silent, isolated, confusing, sad and bitterly unfair, but as soon as I'd feel the strings under my little fingers, I'd be instantly teleported back to my happy place. This was beyond hobby – this was food-water-and-shelter stuff. But I couldn't hear the damn thing. No matter how hard I tried, I just couldn't hear it. After weeks of trying, it was futile.

It is impossible to convey with words, the crushing, paralysing terror of seeing the strings dance before my eyes and not hearing a single, delicious decibel of it. Nothing. Zero. Cold, dead, silence. Think on that for a minute, while the ice tightens around your spine. This was no gradually-losing-it-over-the-years type of deal; this was complete and instant disconnection from the outside world. The speaker cord had been yanked out. No more banter with mates, no 'I love yous', no TV, no hearing that car coming at you, no jokes, no school, no work, no play, no music – just the maddening, disorientating, endless nothingness of the soundless abyss. Every day.

I wasn't frustrated. I wanted to bite my own arm off and beat my stupid, useless ears to death with it. I wanted to torture the doctor who let my condition get this far. I harboured a boiling hatred for every ungrateful son of a bitch who took for granted the daily miracle of working ears. There were tears, there were 'why mes', there was seething rage and awful breakdowns. But hope is a foolish romantic – and happy accidents rule. For one afternoon, leaning my neck towards the strings in yet another desperate attempt to hear something, anything, I sulkily rested my chin on the body of the guitar in despair… and there it was. For the first time since my previous life, there it was. I heard it. The impossible.

What the? *How* the? I did it again. I pushed my chin hard into the top of that Spanish bad boy, twanged a string and, yep, like a head massage from God, that glorious E string resonated around my skull in clear, bell-like clarity – at full volume! Archimedes said 'eureka'; I said, 'Muuuuuuum!' Rather than going in through my ears, the sound was vibrating directly into my skull – something I now know to be called… 'conductive hearing'. I fell downstairs racing to show my parents how I could hear… like completely, truly hear… and hear *well*, so long as I gritted my teeth and forced my chin into the top of the guitar. The light had been flicked back on. In all of us – even my dad shed a sneaky tear – in one strum, a ten-year-old boy was alive again. The awestruck, maniacal grin was back, the frenzied, obsessive blues riffery was back, and even though I still couldn't hear anything else at all in the world, I could hear my guitar, and that was good enough for me.

As the months passed, I continued teaching myself the guitar with my newly discovered 'chin technique'. It was the first (but certainly not the last) time that music saved me. That guitar lived with me in hospital, and much to the torment of my ward, I caught up on a hell of a lot of playing (although my teeth and chin took a hell of a hammering). I'd got my swagger back, my mojo, my purpose, my friend. All of the fundamental stuff one learns on a musical instrument, I learned this way – I pulled off my first full barre chord hunched upon a sterile hospital bed with a dopey, lead-heavy bandage helmet on my head while digging my chin into the top of that faithful little Spanish guitar. Let's hear it for my ward buddies!

Fast-forward through a few more years of surgery, recovery, check-ups, rebuilding of ear canals, more bandages and school disruption, and guess what? It was over. Finally. Thanks to the indefatigable heroes and geniuses at the NHS, both of my ears survived this brutal attack with a staggering 60 per cent of my hearing still intact! From an original prognosis of *any* hearing being highly unlikely, this was more than a miracle. And although I was essentially half-deaf with a newly acquired balance problem and an infuriatingly loud jet engine noise in my left ear that hissed and roared away non-stop all day and night (and still does), I knew I was the luckiest kid in the world – and I threw myself head first into my musical obsession with a fanatical vigour.

Within two years, I was out gigging the local clubs with my first band. Five years later and I released my first album – which I self-produced. Fast-forward a few decades and I'm still here. I've released many more albums, played thousands of shows and lived my childhood dream – not bad for a half-deaf guy who taught himself to play guitar by grinding his teeth into the top of it, eh? I still struggle; I still miss things; I still stare at people's lips when they talk to me; that annoying bloody hissing noise still blasts away inside my head all day. But I know that what I've got can be stolen away from me in a drumbeat – and as someone who has lived the horror of deafness, the gravity of that is not lost on me.

Which is why I'm fucking furious. Furious with anyone who casually mumbles, 'Sorry, dude, can you speak up? I've wrecked my ears.' It brings out the Stalin in me. I hear it all the time (no pun intended), and in rock 'n' roll circles, it's usually offered with an air of proud normalcy – as if it's perfectly acceptable for our ears to be annihilated, for we are, after all, professional musicians. Contradiction much? This is a needless and self-inflicted sabotage of our vital hearing that many people don't have a choice in avoiding – like the one in six people in the UK who live every day with some degree of hearing loss. Or the one in eight in the US. Pick a country and the picture's the same. But sadly, we're not just talking about genetics, disease or Nan and Grandad here. We're also talking about young club-goers, bar staff, teachers, people who work in construction or the military, and douchebags who listen to their headphones way too loud when they're sat next to me on the Megabus. That is to say, all cases where this abuse of our hearing could be avoided.

And that's not to mention the tinnitus. Apparently, one in eight of my fellow countryfolk also suffer this lifelong nightmare – that godawful radio static that howls away at full blast inside my left ear all day, all night, every day, every night. It's there now. It's always there. It's louder than the TV; it's louder than the stereo; it's louder than all of the noise in the pub; it's louder than whoever's talking to me. It doesn't quit for a spilt second, and there is absolutely nothing I can do about it. There's no cure. Tinnitus never gets better; it only gets worse, and some people have been driven to take their own life to escape its sleep-stealing, silence-butchering, emotional-bullying misery. Trust me, you *don't* want this. Once you've got it, it's there for life. How do you get it? Well, it can start for many reasons, but one surefire way to get it is by recklessly abusing your awesome, delicate ears.

The problem is that it's taboo. Off-limits. Quite frankly rude to even bring it up. Offensive even! But people, we need to talk about hearing health. I SAID WE NEED TO TALK ABOUT HEARING HEALTH! The musicians I know who *aren't* suffering are in a minority – it's a shock when I meet one. And as crucial as it is, it's still a subject that no one seems to want to confront. We know it's happening, but we're all a bit ashamed to admit it – so we just turn the amp up a little louder. But living in denial sucks – and it's dangerous because it perpetuates the problem – so I'm going to put myself in the firing line here and bazooka the ugly elephant in the room once and for all: most musicians' ears are ruined, and that's a fact. Permanently, badly, irreversibly screwed.

We are 400 times more likely to have unusable lugs than anyone else. And it's not just rock musicians. Orchestral musicians, who sit for hours with a tuba blasting in their left lobe every night, have got it bad too. DJs who play sets of bone-splitting, bass-heavy music for hours at a time have got it *real* bad. And anyone even remotely in the vicinity of a drum kit has had the top range of their hearing chopped off with the devil's sickle – and boy, did it feel good. Everyone in this industry is affected by this scourge in some way – and that includes the fans. There, I said it.

What we've got ourselves here is a deeply rooted cultural problem. Stamping your ears to death with loud guitars is seen as a well-earned battle scar. And I get it. It feels sooooo good. It's meant to be LOUD! If my amp doesn't punch me in the guts when I hit that low C, it's just bad sex. And our heroes who trailblazed the road before us aren't sending back any words of warning either. Very few will openly admit to having ears that are well and truly shagged. But even if they did, the problem is that I'm not Ozzy Osbourne – and neither are you. He's got people to do shit for him – we don't. And when your music career is over and you're trying to hold down a bill-payer at the local McDoucheDunker's, life is going to be very difficult for you once you've vandalised your hearing.

I know because I've tried. I lasted six months in a 'real job' before I *had* to quit, purely because I could barely hear a word anyone said to me. It was embarrassing, awkward. I made mistakes. I was ridiculed and, although I desperately needed the money, I ran away in shame. Let's be brutally honest here – it's far more likely that you're going to end up in a shirt and tie once Grave Raider has broken up than as a pampered millionaire whose deafness is accepted as an entertaining and eccentric affectation. The only people I know who are still firm evangelists for blowing eardrums in the name of rock just haven't had their reality check yet – but they'll get it.

Now sure, many people with hearing impairment or deafness live perfectly rich and happy lives – but we're talking here about the *preventable* carpet-bombing of our otherwise healthy hearing. Something that is rampant in the music industry and others. So do you want to know what else is in store for you once you've trashed your hearing for good? For those of you yet to join the quiet club, let me tell you from more first hand experience. To start with, a lot of people will treat you like you're ignorant, arrogant and a bit thick. They won't consider that you've misheard them – or not heard them at all. Always getting the wrong end of the stick and walking away while you're being spoken to won't get you laid; it'll just label you as a rude weirdo. Soon, social interaction becomes too taxing, too cringeworthy and too humiliating – so you stop doing it. Exclusion and isolation are common backdrops to the world of the newly hearing-impaired – and what does that lead to? That's right – depression. The black dog will lay heavy in your lap a lot in your new, muffled, musicless, friendless world. Am I scaring the shit out of you yet? I hope so.

But wait, there's more. Every trivial daily interaction becomes exhausting. Why? Have you ever tried playing three games of *Scrabble* at the same time? Let me explain. Only half of what is said to me gets heard – and that includes the TV news, YouTube, conversation, everything. So I have to maintain a clear line of vision with whoever is doing the talking so I can lip-read as well. That's two guessing games already. Then I have to mentally decode, in real time on the spot, what I think *might* be being said based on the context of what was just said a second ago. I have to do this three-handed juggle of sound, sight and context processing for every word of every sentence of every conversation I ever have. And, my God, it's draining. It fast becomes another reason you start avoiding social encounters altogether. And that means more time alone with the dreaded hissing, pinging and ringing in your head – and that unbearable black dog. I mentioned the tinnitus, right?! My friend, please, you really can spare yourself all of this drama. It's all so avoidable that my heart weeps for the needless new arrivals in busted-ear land.

Which brings me to the good news. There has never been a better time to have bad ears. Whether your lugs are as mangled as a clubhouse drum kit, or you've got a brand-new pair, straight out of the box, some super-clever people have got your ass covered. Firstly, nobody *needs* to butcher their hearing any more. Earplugs cost pennies, are available everywhere and even the cheapo versions now come tailored for hi-fi musical enjoyment. They range from the affordable, squidgy foam jobbies that you just mash into your earlobe, right up to custom-moulded gizmos that make the Terminator look like something from *Toy Story*.

You can still have it loud, you can still have it *fucking* loud – but stick something in your ear, for Lemmy's sake. There are no excuses any more. And I'm not just ranting at my musical comrades here; *anyone* who enjoys loud music, whether it's at the club, the rock dungeon or the orchestra – get some damn protection in your pocket, man! If you truly love music, prove it to me, show me your plugs. I didn't have a choice with my hearing hell – you do. With music, like sex, use protection – cos with deafness, like herpes, there is no cure.

And if you're already struggling to hear what the line manager is yelling at you, and the ringing sound is already keeping you awake at night, fear not – help is at hand for you too. For the past few years, I've had the honour of working with some insanely talented tech companies and hard-working hearing charities, and my mind has been both bent and blown by what I've seen. Walking into a modern-day hearing research lab is like walking into Iron Man's basement. But cooler. Floating rubber heads, lasers, robot arms and walls of flashing flat-screen futurism.

I was there to test some stuff and get the lowdown on where things are at these days, and my conclusion is thus: there is absolutely *no* reason for anyone to suffer in silence any more. None. Even if you're as deaf as a debt collector, there now exists, already on the high street, sci-fi wizardry that hides inside your ear canal, which you can discreetly control from an app on your phone, in real time, in order to turn down background noise in restaurants, automatically change your hearing settings depending on where you are (one setting for work, another for the pub) and give you a degree of directional accuracy that is indistinguishable from mere bone and gristle. Ears 2.0! When we hear the words 'hearing' and 'aid', we usually think of decrepit old dudes with cumbersome hunks of unworkable plastic hanging off their heads – and that image has *got* to go. The stuff that's out now... these aren't hearing aids – they're high-tech nuclear defence command centres that live inside your lobes! Prepare to be stunned, prepare to be born again.

Also easily available is a ton of help, support, guidance and advice from an array of tireless charities – super-knowledgeable folk who genuinely care. I've worked with many of them, and I deeply regret not knowing them when I was in my 'dark place'. If you're struggling, seek them out. It'll be the best thing you ever do for your mental, emotional and social well-being – not to mention your hearing. If nothing else, I hope that all this demonstrates that you are far, FAR from alone – and that help is more than available. These days, *no one* needs to struggle like I did.

My time with deafness and my subsequent life with hearing loss and tinnitus have given me a rather peculiar insight into this issue. Music is our life, our oxygen, our soul food – and as I know all too well, it can be ripped away in an instant. Don't take it for granted. Whether you're a musician or a music fan, we're all in the same club (literally), and without our ears, we're nothing. Please protect them. And if all else fails, remember this: as long as you've got a chin and a few teeth left, you can ram them into the top of a little Spanish guitar and still enjoy the beauty of a clumsily played blues riff. Funnily enough, after all these years, I still instinctively tune my guitar that way to this day – and it still works a charm!

PS, Wear earplugs.

6.

A WEEK IN THE LIFE

You thought it was all sleeping late, getting stoned all day and 'jamming, bro', huh? Or maybe you thought it was all hotel-trashing, groupies and private planes? Other music books would have you continuing to believe it, but I'm here to smash those miserable little fantasies with a sledgehammer. If you really want to know how most musicians spend their time offstage (not the pampered 1 per cent and their handlers), if you really want the nitty-gritty on what goes down in the day-to-day lives of 'the rest of us', then buckle up, broheim, and bring some beers – you'll be needing them. The following was a pretty regular week for me not so many years ago, and I think it's fairly typical of any artist who is really 'going for it' and juggling day jobs, band commitments, gigs, travel, admin, sleepless nights and binge drinking on the brink of madness. Don't be late – we're up at 5 a.m. sharp.

MONDAY

Wake-up call. 5 a.m. Urgh, I knew that 1 a.m. bedtime was going to hurt. Fucking Sunday night gigs! Still, I need the money – badly. That's another 100 bucks in the war fund (tour fund) and if it wasn't for that pisshead keeping me blathering on past closing time, I would have been home ages earlier. Still, the only pisshead keeping me up drinking until 1 a.m. on a Sunday night... was me. But a man needs *some* kind of a relief in this detached, one-dimensional, nomadic bubble world I exist in – and with everywhere else closed and everyone else asleep when I'm still reeling, wide awake from the frantic midnight packing of PA systems and lonely drives home down black, empty motorways, the only attainable treat for me at such a time is at the faithful twenty-four-hour petrol station that stocks more booze than most pubs. Every night is the same and it goes like this. Having scored my poison through the bulletproof window, I tiptoe upstairs in darkness so as not to wake my peacefully sleeping housemates and then, finally, at just gone midnight... it's 'me time'. A brief moment to sink some cold ones, pat myself on the back for another busy week and unwind down a YouTube wormhole. Or sink into a deep depression and question what the fuck I'm actually doing with my life as I sit silently getting hammered by myself in a small, square squat – the same four walls where I work, write, exercise, record, study, plan, dream, drink and occasionally... sleep. It looks like a landfill. A junkyard of electronics, instruments, cases, cables and only the devil knows what else fighting for space among clothes, deodorant cans, dirty plates and empty beer bottles – with a chair and a bed dumped in the middle. That's my bedroom, my office and my pub. It's called surviving on the bare minimum. It's called being in a band. By 1 a.m., I'm comatose in my chair.

But anyway, that was last night. Today is Monday, the start of a brand-new week, and I *need* to get my arse in gear! To me, exercise has always been thoroughly un-rock 'n' roll, but the lifestyle is rapidly annihilating my health, so my latest hack is to not think about it, just rise robotically out of bed *Manchurian Candidate* style and hit the pavement half-asleep. A swift half-hour jog around the block gives me time to rehearse today's sprawling to-do list; I leave for my *actual* job in two hours so every minute counts. One of last week's many projects had been to compile *another* Godzilla-sized spreadsheet of record labels and managers to contact – days and nights scouring the web for suitable companies and finding the right contact details somehow (something they don't make easy). Then repeat a few hundred times. It's time-guzzling and staggeringly boring work, but hopefully it'll pay off. So my first task this morning is to mail as many of these lucky reptilians as possible and attempt to lure them into giving the faintest of craps about my band. Slurping cereal with one hand and chain-draining coffees, on I crack. It's still dark outside.

My theory is that I set all of these bad boys sailing at the start of the week so that replies can trickle in while I'm racing around doing all the other crazy crap that you're joining me for this week. A hundred speed-mails later, my wrist has died and I've missed my window on the shower – so today will be double deodorant day! Throwing on my unironed and unsexy work attire, I'm sprinting out the door to begrudgingly embark on that dull necessity, that thief of time, that barrier to all things fun – the day job. The bill-payer. Every musician has their version of it and it's almost *always* dire pay. Why? Because for us, more important than a great salary, a pension and a company gym... is flexibility. Our employer *must* be cool with us randomly having a gig in Birmingham next Tuesday and needing yet another day off. *Our* dream job is one that pays us enough money to keep the van on the road and allows us the freedom to change our hours every two minutes – and sometimes be away for several weeks at a time. For some of us that means a music shop, for others a call centre or a driving job. For me, it's door-to-door surveys. That's right, traipsing around some of the scariest shitholes in the country in the pissing-down rain and doorstepping people who could easily murder me for fun. But hey, it's flexi-hours! We all hate them, but God bless the day job. After the standard two hours of mind-blowing rush-hour madness, *work* work begins.

Except the 'real' work begins when I get home afterwards. Eight soggy hours of low-paid, high-risk pavement-prowling only puts more fire in the belly – I *have* to make this music thing work out. I *have* to escape this shit. Now, I've perhaps wrongly always assumed that home time for 'normal people' meant a nice meal and feet up in front of the widescreen. But for me? Well, I've just lost a whole day's productivity to that damn day job and I've got to make up for it! Which means marching straight back to my room and hunching over the laptop, work clothes still on. Band practice is in T minus two hours, and I've got artwork to finish for our new album. A graphic designer I am not, but as we can't afford a real one, that'll just be another of the many roles I shall be blagging this week. I mindlessly gobble down any kind of food stuff while doing it, crumbs landing on the keyboard, the clock is ticking fast. After what seems like minutes, it's time to swap work trousers for skinny jeans, hurl a ton of heavy metal into my trusty, rusty old van and rush off to rehearsal. Oh, and I've had three replies to the 127 emails I sent this morning – all telling me to go pleasure myself.

Rehearsal requires further sweaty swinging of car-sized amps and drum kits down twisty hallways, followed by a quick few runs through the set. Man, I'm tired. But piss about one cannot, for you are paying by the hour, so on the fuck with it you must get. The said budgetary constraints also dictate where you are in the rehearsal-room hierarchy. Are you, for example, in the large, open, air-conditioned room with great acoustics and free drinks? Or are you attempting to polish your masterpieces while squashed into a tiny, plywood chicken coop – drum kit at your nose – in a volume war with the godawful death metal band next door? We're in the coop. Its extreme volume and lack of air can be nauseating, and whether anything of any use can ever be achieved here is debatable, but we're all completely convinced that we just rocked like no one has ever rocked before.

Load *out* equipment again by 9 p.m. (and not a minute later!), then a speedy, wet and breathless natter with the lads to confirm plans for tomorrow's gig and home by half past. Now... surely *this* is when we finally kick back and be all rock-star-ish and stuff, right?! Wrong. Although, this final segment of the working day can at least be done while under the influence, so that's something. After a long day of being band admin machine, art designer, roadie, kick-ass frontman and door-to-door irritant, this is when one must now become a marketing guru and update the socials, reply to comments, nag people about the show tomorrow and post the necessary selfies. I'm *way* behind on editing those bass tracks for the album, too, so I'd better blast a little bit of that before bed. Jesus, is it only Monday? By 1 a.m., I'm snoring in the chair again; it's bedtime. Even though this *is* my bedroom, technically it's more like my bed is in my office. I stand up, turn around and fall into it face-first. Zzzzzzzzzz...

TOTAL WORKING HOURS: 20

TUESDAY

Brrrrrring! Brrrrring! Round two. 5 a.m., same drill. Rise, jog, dribble breakfast in front of the computer. Today is gig day, so I've only got until midday to get everything done before we leave – a mere seven hours! Pressing priority: finish bass tracks for the album. But first, emails. Always more emails. And boom! Another reply from my mammoth mailout!

'Thank you for the information about your music, but we do not accept unsolicited material.'

Ah, that old chestnut. Just for the record, that whole 'not

accepting unsolicited material' thing is horse-shit. Don't believe it. If my name were Bono, they'd accept my mail pretty fucking sharpish – solicited or not – so here's my proud, unsolicited middle finger, Mr A & R man. Other classic music industry horse-shit excuses include:

We're only focusing on our existing roster right now ('unless your band is Metallica...')

You're way too early for our submissions (which is always followed by...)

You're too late for our submissions

You haven't got enough experience to work with the incredible likes of us yet (as they sign another teenage ukulele player who hasn't played a single gig yet)

I'm at a meeting (and will be for the next eleven years)

The music industry loves to present itself as an open, artistically driven meritocracy full of hip and groovy music lovers, but nothing is further from the truth. And I've learned the hard way that wasting hours, days and weeks sending polite emails to talent scouts, label guys, managers and agents is completely pointless. You might as well just punch yourself in the balls all day instead – it'd be less painful. In fact, *all* of the things the industry says we should do if we want to attract their heavenly gaze – write great songs, play lots of shows, build a buzz, get good press etc. – is bollocks. Bands that suck get signed. Artists without a single song or a gig get signed. Machine Gun Kelly got signed. And yet all of us have friends who make game-changing music, work their asses off and get slapped down and rejected every day, no matter *what* they do. It's a joke. At the creative level, the music industry hasn't got a fucking clue. But more on that later.

Do you wanna know what *does* work? Being friends with someone who's friends with someone. *That*, my friends, and that alone, is how the game works. Don't trust anyone who tells you otherwise. They say, 'It's all about the music, man.' It isn't – it's about who you know. Period. And this isn't bitterness talking either; it's the truth as I've seen it for over twenty years, and I've just saved you a whole lot of emails. So forget about making expensive music videos and start buying expensive drinks for rich dudes in city clubs. I have just given you *the secret*. You're welcome. But where was I… oh yes, editing. Urgh. Ok, so soundcheck in Sheffield is at 4 p.m., which means heading off at 12 p.m., so if I fucking GO FOR IT… I can do this (which will only leave mixing, mastering and… well, everything else to do, but whatever). So washing down the sour taste of this morning's routine rejection with another strong coffee, the next few hours will be spent moonlighting as an audio engineer – if the engineer was Del Boy.

Yet before I can say 'your phone is spying on you', it's here – gig o'clock. Yes! *This* is what it's all about! Brain fried and bleary-eyed from hours of click-click-clicking; I steal a quick shower, blast another round of promo posts online, drag all my shit back out to the van and scurry away. Now, bands always meet at the drummer's house (I think it's the law or something), so that's the first stop, whereupon the guys and all of *their* stuff squash into the van – and the road trip begins! The second stop is always petrol and supplies. Like, why bother making food in the house for free when you can spend six quid on a cardboard Chernobyl sandwich at a skanky-ass petrol station! Then again, if you've ever been stuck in a van with the violent stench of our bass player's home-made tuna pasta disaster, you'd welcome a Chernobyl of any kind.

Long story short, you know how the rest of Tuesday unfolds. I've told that story before. Hours of traffic, roadblocks and life in the slow lane. Junk food, offensive banter, bad smells and even badder music on the stereo. Parking tickets, cavorting of equipment into cold, sticky venues, waiting, Chernobyl buffet, getting a ten-minute soundcheck because the singer in the headline band spent two hours faffing with his monitor mix, and condensing a lorry load of equipment (plus ourselves) onto a glorified food pallet called a 'stage'. And we're right where we belong! Our natural habitat. In God's pocket. Ok, so there were only thirteen people there, almost all of them in the other bands. Ok, so the promoter may have lied about giving us 'fifty quid for petrol' and it being their 'biggest night of the month' – but what do we care! That half an hour on stage is why we do this. It's cost us each a day off work and more than a full day's pay on fuel and food – but that glorious, timeless moment of loud, sweaty endorphin overdose is *always* worth it. Victorious high fives and triumphant battle talk abound as we speed our way home, buzzing on post-gig adrenaline and energy drinks. The lights, the heat, the smells, the intense physical workout, the new city, the adventure – it keeps you buzzing for hours. That is, until the sudden and crushing comedown hits, just south of Birmingham. Despite leaving Sheffield at a sensible half ten, the inevitable road closures and typical UK motorway bullshit ensure that we don't make it back to the drummer's house until gone 3 a.m., hanging off the wheel like wet washing. Flaccid bro hugs and fist bumps do the rounds before going our separate ways with the additional half-hour drive home. Was it worth it? Do you kiss your priest with that mouth?!

I'm up in an hour and a half, but it's ritual to sink at least one beer...

TOTAL WORKING HOURS: 22.5

WEDNESDAY

5 a.m. Sleep was pointless. Barely worth bothering with. The jog can piss off too. The Megabus to London leaves in an hour and I'm already late. I knock back three strong coffees and hit the road. But then I see it. The staggering faux pas on my part – a van still full of gear from last night's gig! WTF! There is no way, NO WAY, that I'm parking *all of this* down some dodgy side street by the coach station, so before I can go *anywhere*... you got it: another high-speed, two-tonne equipment load-out into my hallway – at 5.30 a.m. You'll be amazed at how speed-lugging heavy amps on less than two hours' sleep can become normal when you're doing it every day. Amps, drums and guitars are breathlessly replaced with today's tools of the trade... my portable songwriting studio. For today is songwriting day at a posh hotel in London for a young singer who doesn't know how lucky she is.

Her manager thought he was being all cool and chill when he arranged for the session to start at a 'relaxed' 11 a.m. in Shoreditch, except that he made the fatal error that everyone in the music business makes in thinking that everyone on Planet Earth lives in fucking Shoreditch. To make it on time, I'm having to catch the 6.20 a.m. Megadouche out of Cardiff. Why not catch the train, you say? Because I could fly to Spain for less than the price of a train ticket to London and I'm a musician (read, poor). Drive? Not any more. I've learned that too many hours spent on the great British roads, tangled up in congestion, diversions and the subsequent panic driving are not conducive to one being 'on their A-game' when they arrive at the other end with the aura of a jangly meth head. And I drove to Sheffield and back last night so it's not gonna happen. At least on the Megaballs I can (in theory) work and maybe have a nap. And... it's cheap! Although it does come at a higher cost on the soul.

And so it is that I will spend the next four hours in cramped, toilet-out-of-use, the-wifi-is-off, the-heating-is-broken, existential turmoil. I arrive just as the bus is leaving, sprinting down the street with guitar case, suitcase and bags flopping around everywhere. And as such, I land the only seat left and it's next to 'that' guy. The guy who will spend the entire journey screaming into his phone at what sounds like family members in a country far away. What data plan is that dude on?! But sometimes being half-deaf has its perks – so in go the headphones and up goes Megadeth. Ah, Megadeth on the Megabus – my office for the morning is set. A claustrophobic, smelly pit of an office – much like my one back home. I spend the next few hours updating social media and dreaming of my forthcoming world domination amid the pungent waft of farts and crisps.

So why am I doing this? Well, let me tell you how hit songs get written…

It goes like this. You get a call from a label, manager or producer bigging up their latest artist and convincing you that writing songs for them would be an amazing opportunity for you (cos they're nice like that). You don't get paid, of course – but it's called 'taking a punt' on a winner.

'*This is the one, mate. I'm telling you! Major-label backing, a great team. Write 'em some songs and when this takes off, you'll be sorted, pal! Shall we say next Wednesday? A relaxed 11 a.m. start in Shoreditch?*'

All around the world, right now, there are thousands of super-talented songwriters writing incredible songs, for free, on the tiny off-chance that something may come of it. Because you just never know which one of these guys might be the next Ed Sheeran – and getting a piece of *that* royalty share means no more eating Pot Noodles in a squat and holding your guitar together with gaffer tape. In almost all cases, however, it just means that the label gets songs written for them without any financial risk of it not working out. Because that risk was paid for by a desperate, broke-ass musician – in this case, me. And I've been doing this for years – taking punts.

After dragging heavy and expensive equipment across London via several crammed tubes, walking the usual multi-mile, rain-soaked marathon and four hours aboard the Megahell, I arrive at the posh hotel. Finally! An excited, young singer who's just inked a deal with a major label is awaiting her songwriter for the day, and rather than collapsing in a foetal position on the fluffy cloud of expensive bedding right there, I must conjure from somewhere the illusion that I'm also super pumped and excited to write all day – when truthfully, I'm dying.

Fight or flight is a wonderful thing though (as are espressos), and somehow, the hours have passed and we've got three new killer songs in the bag. Great fun! Peripheral problems aside, *this* is what we're made for. That electric charge of creative energy as inspired ideas bounce between us, birthing new music in a previously musicless room. Something from nothing. The singer was a joy. Heartbreakingly talented, bursting with unscarred enthusiasm and high on the dream. I just pray to Strummer that she doesn't end up on the trash heap in a year's time along with all the other 'failed experiments' that the labels call their 'exciting new signing'. The probability, sadly, is that she most definitely will… along with the awesome songs we just wrote.

But my work here is done. Now I get to treat myself to a London-priced pasty and get royally mangled on cans from the off-licence – I'm gonna need it for the journey back. If all goes to plan, this will involve me sleeping through the entire thing in a drunken coma. Man, the amount of times I've stumbled around the bustling streets of London completely spannered of an eve, I dread to count – but it's a non-negotiable necessity for that long, torturous ride home on the Megashite. And it seems that my unhealthy wealth of experience in the fields of cheap transport and cheaper booze serves me well, for I manage a glorious half-sleep back to Cardiff, arriving at the station by 1 a.m. A brisk walk through the empty, orange-lit streets of a sleeping city, dragging recording equipment and instruments behind me to find my van – and, yes, no ticket! I'm fucking bossing this. Home by 2 a.m., a quick beer to de-frazzle and pass out in my clothes.

TOTAL WORKING HOURS: 21.5

THURSDAY

Brrrrrring! Brrrrring! Argh, that damn alarm clock! What a brutal, punishing, unrelenting bastard you are! I'm so tired I could cry. Is it really that time already? Despite only sleeping for two and a half hours, I feel guilty for not exercising yesterday – like I've 'let myself go' or something. So I heed the sweatshop mantra and I 'just do it'. And pounding the pavement gets the blood moving and puts some fresh air in my lungs, leaving me feeling surprisingly awake and revived – but I guess that's relative. The truth is that I've become adjusted, perhaps addicted to living in this highly adrenalised state of constant motion. Bereft of sleep, devoid of sustenance and stuck on 'on mode' as I charge face-forward without compass, anchor or good sense and a nervous system that's shot to bits. And I have to. The point of no return is far behind me now. I mean, what else am I gonna do?

'So do you have any experience in human resources, Mr Kennedy?'

'Does ten years of hard rocking count, sir?'

No. This *has* to work. It's my only option. I sold my soul to rock 'n' roll but I'm still chasing the invoice. And I've been living like this for years. This is normal. And it'll end in death or glory. But before all that... the day job. Remember that? A lot has happened since we last mentioned that old ball and chain – and it was only two days ago. Yep, I'm back at it today, making up for those hours I lost on Tuesday so I could play to the bar staff at The Bull's Arse in Sheffield, for free. It'll be the same routine as always: trudge around in the rain with soggy clipboard in hand, knocking the doors of people who may or may not bury me under their floorboards or wear me as a mask. Band debt, I hate you.

Before I set forth on that fateful journey, though... yep... emails! They've been mounting up as hoped over the last two days, and I've got about two hours to speed through all the lovely replies to my Monday morning mail blast, so let's be having ya! Save me, guys.

Please, someone save me from this grind. This life of poverty. This sleepless, desperate, never-ending 'trying'. I've got the goods, man! For once, someone *please* just get back to me and say:

'Dear Mr Kennedy, thank you for sending us your insanely godlike music. It is the soundtrack of a generation. Seriously. You are clearly the absolute megadon and I'd like to personally sign you to a million-pound global deal, take care of everything so you can just focus on being all awesome and stuff, and put you on a support tour with AC/DC. I hope you will consider my humble offer, oh talented one.'

You'd think that out of 1,283 meticulously researched and well-targeted emails, surely I'd hit *someone* with the remotest of shits for what we're doing? Well, after hours of brain-blasting, eye-trashing, wrist-wrecking mail-gunning, these are the stats:

Eight replies. All telling me to go jump. The rest? Generic robot responses about how busy they are and good luck... somewhere else. I've become immune to it now. My skin has calloused over from the years of daily rejection. But giving up is not possible. And anyway, there's always that list of 800 Spotify curators to get cracking on... oh, and the list of 2,543 radio stations I've been building up as well! I'll try them too. All is not lost! Woop woop! I begin immediately, with the forced faith of a man who literally has no other option. Remember when I said it's not all smoking weed and jamming? These days, an indie or unsigned artist has to perform *all* of the roles that would be done by entire teams at a major label. The digital department, marketing, distribution, PR, booking, merch, album production and bribing radio stations. Until you are signed, *you* must do all of these things and do them without a penny to your name. This leaves minus hours for actually enjoying your instrument like you used to, seeing friends or having any semblance of a normal life, and it quickly breeds a growing background anxiety to your life as your brain must bounce between all the myriad mindsets required just to exist as an artist each week. Frankly, the idea of a routine job with someone else in charge, paying your taxes, with sick pay, paid holiday, free weekends and a pension, seems pretty fucking tempting at times.

Back home after another eight hours of tempting death on the mean streets of Austerity Britain, I plunge once more into the fantasy of escaping it all by ploughing forth with more album editing, more emails and more unmemorable food scoffed down while not even looking at it. I stay here, in the same chair, in the same clothes, surrounded by the same mess, stooped over the same computer for the remaining six hours of Thursday, squeezing every last drop of productivity out of myself until I can physically take no more. Exhaustion plus a few beers has really hit me tonight, and at half past 11, I'm climbing into bed at what's a reasonably early hour for me. I'm praying that I sleep. What usually happens in my wired, overtired state is that I toss and turn all night trying to block out the din of clashing thoughts surging around my mind as my brain fails to disengage from the high-speed multitasking of its day. On nights like that, I get up and do more work – it's a better use of precious time. But I could really use some sleep tonight. And hey, I finished the album editing.

TOTAL WORKING HOURS: 18

FRIDAY

As suspected, sleep was shite. But at least I got some. And I'm not too hungover this morning, so the jog was only one battle, rather than two. Friday is technically a half day because we're gigging – not our own stuff, but what I call 'Wonderwalling'. I define it as:

'Any task undertaken exclusively for its financial gain, regardless of its detrimental effects on one's soul.'

It could be a bar job, a labouring job, working at Daddy's firm, or whatever. For us musicians it's playing godawful cover songs to obnoxiously drunk sports fans in deadly chicken-wire joints around the south Wales valleys. Wonderwalling, quite literally. In an industry where the vast majority of its workforce live at a loss, *this* is how we pay for shit. Our tours around Europe, our albums, videos, van, equipment, websites and the free money we give to PR companies for no services rendered – it's all paid for by the shameless whoring of ourselves on the local sports bar circuit. Whoever you are, Mr Brightside, thank you (and please die). Today, we've got two of them. Four hours of back-to-back satanic cheese and the prolonged risk of one of us being beaten to death by one of the patrons – but hey, it's another few hundred quid in the rock bank, and God knows we need it. We've got an album to feed.

And speaking of the album, those few hours of the day that won't be spent Wonderwalling will be spent mixing the album. We're on the final stretch! It's taken weeks to piece it together around our day jobs, gigs and neighbour-sensitive working hours. And we've done it all here in my tiny, cramped junk den – no fancy studios, no relocating to LA for a few months, no 'budget' – and now, NOW, we're this close to finally hearing the thing. After months of secluded passion, energy, toil and firefighting creating this bad boy, we'll soon be able to unleash it on a poor, unsuspecting public. But before that can happen, someone's got to mix it all. And that person (as always) is me, so I get to bashing out a few hours before the weekend carnage begins.

I used to hate – like, *really* hate – doing these cover gigs. I didn't devote all of my teens and twenties to practising my guitar (while everyone else was out getting shagged and spannered) so that I could strum the same four chords all night in the corner of The King's Cock. But sometimes, it can be a welcome respite from the intensity of the rest of my week. Having the power to drive a nightclub batshit crazy with the mere opening line of 'Summer of '69' has an innocent charm about it. And having half-dressed drunk women throw themselves at you, men lining up drinks for you and you getting *paid* for it may not be the stadium-strutting dream I still cling to, but it certainly beats doing more fucking emails or knocking on doors in the rain. It definitely beats sitting alone in a low-lit room for days on end, obsessively working on 'making it'. And it can be fun, in its own disturbing way. Like being dropped into a zombie apocalypse for a few hours and narrowly escaping with all of your flesh. For me, it's my only weekly holiday from the self-enforced gulag known as Monday to Friday. And I yearn for the day that I never have to do it again.

Tonight will involve the following:

The standard powerlifting of several tonnes of heavy equipment through drunken streets and crowded clubs, and squeezing it all into an area the size of a paddling pool.

Blasting our way through two hours of songs we loathe intensely while simultaneously defending our instrument-laden selves from repeated zombie attacks. This will include clutching at your mic, the pouring of cider on your equipment, falling into you and smashing the mic into your teeth, tripping over your cables, climbing up your speaker stands, throwing things at you, and the worst... talking to you while you're singing, always to ask for Gerry fucking Cinnamon.

Packing *down* said equipment and fighting your way out through the clambering hordes, before you refill van, eat Chernobyl sandwich and race to next gig.

Congratulations. You've just smashed the intermediate level. Now it goes to advanced – the end-of-the-night slot.

This is when shit gets serious. These late-night zombies have a few hours of drinking time under their belts already, they're excited and they *want* the fucking band. This excitement can oscillate wildly between a little *too much* love for you... and violent hatred. They want you set up, they want you started, they want it loud and you'd *better* play 'Wonderwall'.

You are now on the final level, and this is when the men get yanked from the boys. You will get started on, grabbed, pushed, kissed, licked, groped and argued with while playing 'Sweet Caroline'. Some twat will scream 'Phonics' in your face repeatedly.

Tracy, who's friends assure you can 'really sing' will join you for a spine-chilling butchering of 'Valerie'. Some bloke's wife will force your face into her breasts, resulting in him promising to kill you. There will be vomit, there will be blood and there will be stupidity of a horrific nature. This is the stuff of Nam flashbacks.

Two hours turn into three as you are physically refused exit from the 'stage', drinks are lined up as a bribe to 'keep fucking playing, lads', the paralytic bar manager tries to dazzle you into doing another set for 'an extra twenty quid', and as you finally put your foot down and walk off the stage, you go from being 'legends' to 'wankers' immediately.

Upon sinking a cheeky (and much needed) 'one for the road', you try to avoid getting locked into a painfully long, repetitive and unfathomably boring conversation with some drunk bloke, meaning that if you're lucky, you'll make it home in time to do some proper drinking.

Load out heavy equipment through a gauntlet of clasping hands, fights and beer-soaked floor, remove drunk women from back of van, refuse haggling with coke-heads into being their taxi service and, with God willing… you're out of there.

Getting home around 1 a.m., smelly, sticky and starving – you have just completed the advanced level. You win! You've put 500 big ones in the band kitty and now the victory drinks can commence. The festival of one – drinking alone in a sleepless, semi-traumatised state, wondering whether the bloke from Metallica has to put up with any of this shit. Unable to sleep from the sensory onslaught of the past few hours, a few 'wind-down' drinks turns into a 5 a.m. dribble-fest, accompanied by the increasingly common drunken existential meltdown about whether any of this is worth the life it's robbing me of. But we've been here before – remember Sunday? Me neither. And we'll be here again. Cue Saturday.

TOTAL WORKING HOURS: 19

SATURDAY

Aaah, Saturday. That beautiful bringer of lie-ins, brunches, afternoon pints and scenic days out. Unless you're a musician – in which case, Saturday is indistinguishable from any other. While everyone else is out shopping, drinking and hanging out, guess where I'll be? That's right, bent over my laptop, twiddling knobs and listening to the same sections of songs over and over (and over) again while fighting the hungover, sleep-deprived urge to spew violently all over the screen. This is what's called the 'mixing' part of the process, and it's the difference between a random collection of recorded noises and something that vaguely resembles a song you can listen to. Usually this pivotal work would be undertaken by a professional sound engineer but, ya know... money. So I'm doing it. And right now, in bedrooms the world over, there are musicians doing exactly the same. Hundreds of hours spent crafting and fine-tuning the masterpieces that other motherfuckers will get to enjoy for free. And if we're not doing that with our sexy Saturday, you'll find us melting inside a walk-in oven with the windows carpeted over – otherwise known as a rehearsal room – or editing videos, designing artwork, creating social media content, busking or travelling to a gig somewhere and spending half the day in a van. But please don't feel sorry for us; we bring it on ourselves because we're mental. Saturday also includes another savage round of Wonderwalling, and if I'm going to make any headway towards finishing the album (and therefore headway towards no longer having to *do* any more fucking Wonderwalling), I'd better get up and crack on. Stepping from the bed to the chair, this is where I will spend the rest of my day. It's sunny outside, I think.

You may have noticed by now that, so far, little mention has been made of 'girlfriends' or 'pints with the lads', but I'm sure you're getting a feel for why that might be. I mean, who in their right mind would want to be in any kind of relationship with with one of us lot anyway, given that we're fanatically committed to an excessively overbearing marriage already? The answer, of course, is everyone. But when people imagine being the oh-so-cool partner of an oh-so-cool musician, what they're imagining is endless parties, travel, excitement, sex, danger and rock 'n' roll. After three weeks, it hits them that they're just spending all of their time waiting around by themselves in dingy venues, sitting on a drum case, bored out of their fucking mind. Inevitably they do what all the others have done before them – they leave. For good. So my loyal girlfriend for the day goes by the name of 'New Song – Final FINAL Mix 13', but before you can say 'toxic relationship', it's that time again. Time to brave getting my teeth knocked out, my head kicked in and my soul shat upon – that's right, it's time to earn this girlfriend some money!

Starting, as all things do, with another Herculean van pack, the rest of the night follows the same format as last night to a tee. It's basically Groundhog Day – but with zombies. Except that, by the grace of God, tonight's courageous mission ends with that rare occurrence, that coveted prize, that centrepiece of rock folklore and myth – the groupie. Yes, they do exist. And even us lowly club-level musos occasionally get to indulge in those kind providers of guilt, trouble and STD tests. It began with the not-so-rare occurrence of a coked-up arsehole wanting to 'knock me out'. His essentially naked girlfriend had been enjoying the band too much, it seems, and... heaven forbid... dancing in full view of the other uber-males frequenting this fine establishment. She was happy. And it was my fault. It was I, not her, that was the root cause of his jealousy, so 'knocking me out' seemed a rational solution.

I foolishly stayed behind for a pint after the other boys had left, and met my retribution. His name was Kev. And Kev wanted justice. He informed me that if I didn't give him my drink, he was going to fucking kill me. I refused. He showed me his biceps and reminded me of his offer, but louder this time. And just like that, I knew that Kev was no killer. Nope, Kev was a bully-boy bullshitter trying to look hard in front of his mates. If he were going to kill me, he would have done it already. Which is why I didn't mind bedding his beloved in the back of the band van, mere metres from where he was sat sinking his seventeenth cider. She told me she thinks he's a douche as well, so it was fair karma for both of us. Our romantic liaison played out upon wobbly amps and guitar cases, with boxes of band merch falling about the place. Then, after promptly ushering a happy girl who shall not be named out of the side door, I hopped into the front seat and skidded away in a cloud of smoke. Until the next time, Kev!

Home, however, is a little less fun. It's just me again. Alone in a room. Silent. Still. Still buzzing from a night fighting and fucking zombies and unable to sleep. Yearning for something more. Something deeper. Something of meaning. I crack open the first of what I already know will be too many beers and reach for my oldest and best friend in the world... my guitar.

TOTAL WORKING HOURS: 18

SUNDAY

Brrrrrrrrring! Brrrrrrrrrrring! Even on a Sunday? You betcha. God may have rested on the seventh, the shirker, but not me. My to-do list is two sides of A4, and every day – hell, every *minute* – counts. Sunday is generally prep day for the week ahead – and what moreish rock 'n' roll delights are in store for us this week, I hear you scream? Well, for a start there's that super-exciting list of 800 Spotify curators and 2,543 radio stations to start contacting – that'll be fun, right? More album mixing, finish the album artwork, probably a pointless meeting in London or two, band rehearsal, a gig in Leicester, make a decision on the music video, start compiling press contacts for the album promo, a plethora of selfies and disposable content for social media – oh, and I almost forgot the two and a half days of day-job death dance, not to mention the five (FIVE!) rounds of Wonderwalling we've got next weekend. A truly Olympian effort.

All of this is already bouncing around my noggin as I lie in bed, semi-conscious, assessing the damage from last night's party of one. It looks like it was standard fare. The half-empty bottle of rum implies I'd cleared out all the beers and gone sniffing around the house for more at some shameful hour. It also explains why I feel like I've been shat out of the arse of hell. My guitar lies on the floor among the debris, which is a good sign. It suggests that rather than drunk-messaging people like a desperately sad bastard, I was instead playing guitar and hopefully writing some absolute bangers into the early hours. The memory of Kev's missus skims across my mind and I chuckle. Life ain't too bad. Let's get up, get some coffee, and let's do this.

A brisk jog to sweat out the booze is followed by an excitable phone chat with Rory about upcoming band plans, album progress, new gig bookings and embellished bragging about last night's sexual adventures. I feel good today. Hungover for sure, but in that happy, fuzzy, still-a-bit-pissed kind of way. And I always have this sense of new beginnings on a Sunday. Of gazing towards a week with new avenues and new wins. Happy that another week's Wonderwalling is over and eager to kick the shit out of another week on the indomitable rawk climb. I don't get the Monday morning blues like some do, because I don't live for the weekend like some do. I live for the dream. I live for the dream of living the dream. For me, Monday means another week of grafting, rolling the dice and faking it until I make it. Three coffees down and I'm jackhammering my way through the album mixing and making this Sunday count.

I remain in this half-moon position for the next eight hours until my ears can't tell what's a bass or a bassoon any more. And after subjecting my poor housemates and neighbours to a sonic waterboarding session for their entire sabbath, I've gotta tap out for the day. My head is cooked. The sun has been up, down and gone again while I've been hunching here, and as the hangover advances from benign to bastardly, I find myself conveniently at that point in the day where guiltless drinking can recommence. I've earned it, I lie. And although I may be finished 'mixing' for the day, 'finished' for the day, I am not. Far from it! My regular Sunday night livestream kicks off in an hour, where I must give my weekly offering to the digital overlords in a desperate bid to stay relevant in the algorithmic Hunger Games. This will involve singing songs, doing Q & As, lying about my week and doing tricks like a good dog. Believe me, it's painfully exhibitionist for those of us whose passion was only ever for making and performing music, not fighting for scraps of attention in the brave-new-anti-social-media colosseum. But I do as I must if I am to exist as a human – and more crucially, as an artist.

Once the deed is done, I purify my soul with a stiff whisky and confess my sins at the shrine of Zappa; I wonder what he'd have made of all this shit. By now we're pushing 10 p.m., so it's time to transition to the 'proper drinking' portion of the evening and kick back. It's been a long week. It's been a normal week. My downtime ritual for the night is a video binge of my musical heroes and getting testosteroned up watching them do their thing. That's gonna be me one day – it's *going* to happen. I've just gotta get this stupid sleep thing out of the way so I can grab Monday by the nuts and GO! Sleep has become a serious hindrance to my hustle and it needs to go. Some douche in a white coat said it's important, though, and so for a futile few hours, I toss, turn and time-check, my mind ablaze with big ideas, plans, riffs and… oh no! A really *good* riff! Now I've got to wake up, get up and record the damn thing so I don't forget it by morning. This is the true writer's curse. Not writer's block, but writer's burst. That cruel flash of genius that will only strike the second you drift towards dreamland. That 5 a.m. wake-up call is going to hurt so bad.

TOTAL WORKING HOURS: 13 (SO FAR...)

And there you have it. One week. Not a special week, just a regular week. Hopefully any idea that us musicians are a bunch of lazy slackers has now been politely elbowed in the temple? Granted, it might only be *me* that's this fucking crazy – but I doubt it. These days, the peripheral ball-aches of being a muso are more than a full-time job – they're your life. And they have to be. No longer are we fighting for air with the other bands in our town, but now we're wrestling with every other band on Planet Earth. And getting anyone to pay you the slightest of mind in today's culture of plenty is a callous task that has nothing to do with music and everything to do with survival. Artists today have to do their own production, artwork, videos, promotion, marketing, distribution, budgeting and fundraising – as well as paying rent somehow along the way. Food? Preferable. So if anyone thinks we're all hanging around the house in our pants, slapping our D strings all day, they're colossally mistaken. I mean, we'll be in our pants for sure, but we'll more likely be fretting over emails than melting any fretboards.

7.

THREE CHEERS FOR STRUGGLE

There are few eternal certainties in life, but one that stands firm alongside death and taxes is that music made by the rich will always – and I mean always – suck. It's a curious but well-proven phenomenon. Even once brilliant artists who become rich after years of grinding poverty suddenly start sucking real bad once the swimming pool gets installed. And this artistic oddity works in reverse too. Little Tarquins and Camillas may struggle for years to write music remotely resembling anything cool or inspirational – but throw in a shock parental break-up, a sudden downsize to a dingy inner-city council flat and a degrading job at the local sausage factory and they start knocking out timeless classics overnight. It's a bizarre law of nature but one that is indisputable: music created in privilege will always be obscenely devoid of the stuff that makes it rock. If you want the good stuff, you have to go to the poor. Prove me wrong.

What's behind this strange but *totally accurate* fact of science, and why does it matter? Well, I have a theory. My theory is that struggle, poverty, oppression and pain are the secret ingredients behind every major musical innovation since the dawn of time, and that being posh, privileged and pampered is to art what Tories are to joy. There are many reasons for this, which we'll get into, but for now just think about it. Folk music, punk rock, soul, hip hop, reggae, jazz, grunge, funk, heavy metal – it's all poor-people music. I mean, the blues is an entire genre of music created exclusively by people who've got the bloody blues! These are all major, history-shaking musical movements born out of social inequality, poverty, injustice and unrest. And my God, it's good. If there's one thing you can say about the cruelty of poverty, it's that it makes for some great fucking tunes. Bright-eyed, well-adjusted rich kids bumbling around with over-confident grins on their rosy-cheeked faces ain't never pioneered nada! At best they have merely copied – and even that sucked big time. Am I being harsh? Probably. But am I wrong? Am I?

The pattern is clearly ironclad, case closed, but the question remains – why? Why doesn't a gentle, stable environment filled with gushing support and the best toys money can buy create the perfect breeding ground for unrestrained, limitless musical genius? You'd think it would, right? Yet if you look at the childhoods of the biggest musical game-changers over the last century, you'd be forgiven for concluding that if you truly wanted to encourage little Timmy's dreams of rock stardom, the best thing you could do would be to *not* buy him that guitar, to *not* send him to music college, to *not* buy him food and to slap him upside the head for no reason. Michael Jackson, James Brown, Ray Charles, Chuck Berry, Jay-Z – these guys had it tough, man – and thank God they did.

But what is the link between struggle and excellence? The answer, I believe... is effort and desire. The extra effort required to overcome impossible obstacles in pursuit of your passion is the maker of greatness. We see this everywhere from sports to business to social change to art. Pressure makes diamonds, as the saying goes. And the passion to keep fighting, to keep trying, to keep getting back up, to keep hustling despite the decades of rejection, sacrifice and bruises is the mark of someone with a level of love for the craft that makes greatness inevitable. Even if not commercial success or, indeed, success in their lifetime, as was the reality for so many of history's most iconic game-changers.

The fact is, any monkey can sound good with the best drum kit in the world and a hundred effects keeping them in tune and in time. But that's the problem – it's easy. The tools are doing the work. And if it's easy, anyone can do it – which impresses no one. Hendrix had a few crappy pedals and an upside-down guitar, but he revolutionised guitar playing and music forever. Hell, Django Reinhardt only had two fucking working fingers and he could still shred better than most. Victoria Canal and Rick Allen both have one arm less than most of us but refuse to let that stop them crushing it on piano, guitar and drums. When you want something, when you *really* want it, when you *need* to scream the pain and passion out through a guitar, piano or drum kit, you'll find a way, regardless of a lack of equipment, money, comfort, support or limbs. The great do, anyway. Jimi didn't have any other means, so he forced his guitar to moan, wail and howl by jamming the strings into his mic stand, by drowning it in a flood of feedback, by setting it on fire. By whatever means necessary.

Take hip hop. These guys didn't have any instruments AT ALL, but the need to jam was so insatiable that they imitated the sounds of drums and bass with their mouths instead – creating 'beatboxing' in the process – and jamming on street corners. Or by repurposing their parents' vinyl records, creating a sonic backdrop over which they could rap about life in the projects, the police, injustice and girls. In doing so, they sparked a new culture of music, dance, fashion and art that would dominate the entire planet and change it forever. Hip hop was born on the poorest streets of America by its most brutalised and ignored citizens, and yet they ignited a revolution at a time of rampant racism where no labels would sign them, no radio would play them and the doors to most venues were closed to them. By having to circumvent their scandalous neglect by any means necessary in lustful pursuit of the beat, the bass and the truth, they overthrew the established order, created their own industries, invented a new style of music and petrified much of America in the process. With *no* fucking instruments. If DJ Kool Herc's parents had bought him a brand-new grand piano when he was eight, this world would be a very different place. It's another win for poverty.

And what about jazz? My persistent roasting of Jazzers throughout this book is merely reverential banter and musical jealousy. And I hope they know it, because when I think of jazz, I think of soul-wrenching beauty, a harmonic portal into the truth of the timeless all-that-is, of primal rhythms, a soothing sonic massage, the wondrous chaos of life improvised over delicious discord and staggering superhuman musical prowess unattainable for the rest of us. But we also think of trumpets, trombones and snare drums, right? And why were they the instruments of choice for the early pioneers of that heavenly music? They weren't. They weren't a 'choice' at all, but rather what was available. And what was available in the post-Civil War-era southern states of America was a widespread surplus of ex-military band instruments – trumpets, trombones, snare drums. Marching band stuff. But once in the hands of people – again, from mostly brutalised backgrounds – these until-then-pretty-naff instruments became the tools of musical wizardry that changed the language of the world's music forever. Poor people, crap instruments, no music school, great music. Are you seeing what I'm seeing?

Let's talk about punk, just to stamp the point home with a dirty Doc Marten. The era that spawned this gorgeous nail bomb to music, fashion and politics was one of shit-talking hippies, barbaric Thatcherite politics and comically grandiose stadium rock – music that said absolutely nothing about the growing poverty and bleak social outlook of the times. It was a culture that spoke to less and less people as the social temperature boiled to a Vesuvian level.

Something had to blow. And blow it did in a historic and radical cultural movement that forever busted the boundaries of art and how to make it. Punk not only took a defiant dump in the heart of the mass-market world of music and fashion, but it also laid a blueprint for independent art in all its forms. The DIY ethos of making your own records, magazines, clothes and record labels – in fact, the very model that most artists use today to create, release and promote their music – owes everything to the original punks. It was a true cross-cultural revolution and, just like hip hop not long after it, it scared the establishment in all its forms thoroughly shitless. Record labels, politicians, quaint middle-class society, all of them terrified of some dudes with pound-shop guitars, spray cans and a message – a message that said, 'We've had enough and we're coming to burn down your shit.' Who were these warriors, these saints of awesome? The poor, the ignored, the outcasts, the marginalised and the angry victims of a society gone sour. Punk didn't evolve; it exploded out of desperate necessity. Punk didn't come for fame and fortune; it came to destroy. And in doing so, it laid the pathway for grunge, thrash metal and a whole new spirit for rock music that was less about appeasing the industry and more about giving a middle finger to it and spitting truth at conformity through brash, distorted riffs and drums that punched holes through polite society walls. And I love everything about all of that.

I could go on. I could talk about soul, funk, Motown, folk music, reggae and metal, but I think you acquire my drift. Poor people/oppressed people/naff instruments/no instruments = world-changing music. What great musical movements have the aristocracy given us in the last two hundred years? Anyone...? Hello...? I rest my case. I guess most people can't relate to songs about fancying one's butler. So again I say, you can complain all you want about slavery, poverty and cruelty, but they make for some great fucking music. And the reason for that, as I said, is effort and desire. When you just *have* to do something, regardless of whether the only instrument you can get your hands on is a rusty old trumpet from the military band's bin or your dad's James Brown album, or whether you've never had a lesson in your life, or you don't have the money, space or limbs to even play an instrument – that's when the magic comes. Sheer determination, raw creative passion and an irrepressible need to make your music and share your truth despite the most terminal of conditions – these are the qualities that forged humanity's proudest musical triumphs. It's an error-correcting system because only the best and most worthy make it happen no matter what. The rest don't bother – and good riddance to them.

Another cheeky side effect of being a financially challenged self-taught musician – by which I mean piss-poor broke – is accidental innovation. If all the aforementioned trailblazers had had teachers, they would have been taught how to do things 'properly' and 'the way that it's always been done'. They most definitely would *not* have done them the way that they invented for themselves. 'That's not how it's *done*,' their teachers would have cried. 'Jimi, stop dry-humping the cello!' But when you don't know *how* to do something, or how it's '*supposed*' to be done, you just follow your muse. You explore, you experiment, you do it wrong and you randomly create a new style of music or unique voice of your own. Jazz broke every single rule in the book and then made roach paper out of the book. The often frustrating, confusing and lonely road of self-learning an instrument is the very cauldron that cooks up the sound that sounds like YOU and no one else. When I got my first guitar, I didn't know that the strings weren't meant to hover half an inch above the fretboard, so that's what I practised on. And I rapidly developed a muscle strength in my fingers that could wrestle The Rock. Struggle makes us stronger. Scarcity makes us sharper. Although it's also why I butcher strings faster than Google purges indie news.

And speaking of tyrannical censorship, guess what else is good for good music? That's right! Tyrants. Philistines and demonic scumbags the world over have tried (and tried) to ban, censor, curtail, remove and control music they deem to be subversive, unpatriotic or unholy. There's not a country on Earth where musicians have been safe from the blacklist, the editing razor, the jail cell or the bullet to the head. Why? Because music has the power to change the world, and the authorities know that better than most artists do. Throughout the last century alone, music has been subject to varying degrees of state control, including the editing of songs, censorship, banning of entire genres, arresting, torturing and even murdering musicians. In Afghanistan, the Taliban has practically banned music entirely, provoking underground listening parties where the mere act of listening to music is used as a beautiful form of rebellion. From the Soviet Union to Chile, China, South Africa, the USA and good ole Great Britain, real music has consistently had to fight for its life. Often literally.

But did it stop those musicians from making, recording and distributing music? Not a chance. Brave artists in the face of repressive regimes, all-pervasive state surveillance and violence don't stop doing their thing; they just get more creative. Underground distribution networks for sharing the naughty songs spread quickly along with ever more inventive ways to perform live throughout the Soviet Union after its ban on 'Western' music and any form of music deemed too decadent, rebellious or unpatriotic. In one example that I love, in Communist Bulgaria, music was heavily controlled by the state in all forms and in all places... except weddings. Those dictators are such a romantic bunch. So what became the new breeding ground for alternative and subversive music? Aunt Sofia's wedding! Right there in the dark heart of the merciless Soviet behemoth – courageous artists sticking a firm middle finger up to the law simply by calling themselves a wedding band. And hats off to all those who booked them and let them blast their seditious set list on their special day. The great and the worthy always find a way. In fact, the long-time meddling by the state in artistic works generally throughout Russia and China has inadvertently helped create a new code language for rebellious artistic expression that's popular in music and painting, but hidden in plain sight and only understandable to those who 'know' – a distinct artistic voice that still permeates the arts today. China also has a long list of musicians who are banned from even entering the country, let alone having their music played – although, at the time of writing, one of them is Justin Bieber, so I can see their point.

Don't go thinking that it's just the big, bad Communists who have beef with the tunes, though. Remember the ridiculous PMRC debacle in the US, where a bunch of politicians' wives leveraged their entirely unearned political power to have albums they didn't like covered in daft advisory stickers? Remember how it backfired big time and only served to make those very records all the more appealing to teenagers everywhere? Or the long list of songs that have been banned, edited or removed from radio in that righteous, star-spangled bastion of democracy and freedom of speech? Or what about when the BBC, the UK's state-controlled broadcaster, banned the Sex Pistols' 'God Save the Queen' from the radio, despite the song having reached number 2 in the charts? And my favourite film of all time, *The Life of Brian*, by the comedic geniuses Monty Python, was *still* banned in the Welsh town of Aberystwyth, thirty years after it was released! In a fittingly bizarre turn of events, it was only finally unbanned when a member of the cast became a local town councillor. How Pythonesque. 'God Save the Queen' and *The Life of Brian* are rightfully considered masterpieces for their bravery, cultural importance and the necessity of their message. Both bloody brilliant, both bloody banned.

In the digital age, the sinister hand of government control is even more prevalent, except that now they don't need to officially ban your song; they can just make sure no one will ever hear it. And I know. When my album *Make Anger Great Again* came out in 2020, its first single, 'The Power', was removed from YouTube after one day. My accounts were demonetised and my advertising rights were immediately revoked on Google, Facebook and Twitter. All of my social media accounts were then 'shadow-banned' (or rather, had their 'visibility limited', to use the platforms' bullshit-speak) to such a degree that they have been rendered useless still to this day. My once large and highly engaged following now sees nothing that I post, and my online reach has been largely terminated – because of a song. Different songs, different times, same enemies, same dirty tricks.

But 'real music' survives in spite of its roadblocks – maybe even because of them – because it *has* to. It has to for the artist, for society, for progress. Not even savage state thuggery can hold it back. For some artists, the fear of death or exile won't stop them doing their thing – and those are the artists we need. The true kind, not the kind that are willing puppets of power. Because while music has always been intensely monitored and challenged by state interests, it has always also been an important tool of the state. National anthems, military marches and emotional music for state ceremonies, advertising and political rallying are all vital tools in the propagandist's arsenal. Music gets the masses riled up, and it can either fill them with active revolutionary zeal or violent patriotic obedience. So to further smash home my point – what do we find when we hear such 'establishment-approved' music? Those propaganda soundtracks, advert ditties or much major-label pop – once again we find music that sucks badly. Music that smooches the ass of the powerful and jerks the chain of the machine. Music that says nothing of the evil around it and keeps the people brain-dead and oppressed with gimmickry, mindless patriotism and soft, safe, sugary jingles. State-sponsored sound – the worst kind of music there is. Made by enemies of the people and enemies of music. I will take a bullet to the brain before I serve those masters.

So as we review the many challenges faced by artists throughout the ages – poverty, prejudice, censorship, disability or the threat of torture – we can only conclude that these obstacles actually help fuel the artistic genius that survives them. For in all cases, the music frigging rocks. These conflicts are exactly what injects the music with the pain, purpose, anger, passion and raw emotion that resonates through the ages and rattles the zeitgeist off its blocks. Unlike that *other* music, that easy music, which is quite frankly bollocks. So love your suffering, my comrades, for it will be your maker.

Which makes me worry for the future. God knows musicians are under enough threat as it is. Our industry has died, most of us can't make a dime, and soon computers will be making us all redundant. But I feel we have an even bigger existential threat than all of this – one that might not kill musicians but could most definitely kill music. Good music anyway. That threat is privilege. Be wary of it, people, for it will ruin our tunes. As I've said many times, I adore the new digital music model. It's the one I've embraced my entire musical life, and without it, I simply wouldn't be here. The equalising power of modern technology to make it possible for anyone to write, record, distribute and sell their music without any dependence on the industry shysters is a truly historic moment that we should all be eternally grateful for. But too much of a good thing is a terrible thing, for it brings with it an unexpected and potentially terminal side effect: ease. That's right – dedicated musicians are at risk of being massacred... by ease. For it removes the struggles that are proven to be so essential for the creation of great art. And it further opens the floodgates to a biblical river of sludge that's already drenching the online space and ruining it for many.

Because everyone is now a musician. The great levelling of the musical playing field didn't level it for those hard-working, deserving artists who had previously been shut out under the old order of labels and kings – no, it levelled it for every douche on Earth with a laptop.

Technology has made it easy for almost anyone to make a record and release the little demon into the wild with the click of a button. Technology enables everyone to have the musical muscle of Schwarzenegger without any of the sweat, graft and effort that built it. Technology has made it easy, but where's the fucking value in that? It removes all of the resistance that makes us better, the struggle that tests our commitment, the limitations that lead to innovation, the sense of achievement in doing it for ourselves the thrill of the chase, the transcendental trip of being lost 'in flow'. And where does this ease lead us? The answer is in the tens of thousands – some say hundreds of thousands – of new songs that are uploaded to streaming platforms every day. I've listened to hundreds of these things so that you don't have to – and trust me, you don't want to. The removal of all barriers to music-making has already sent an avalanche of painfully subpar music to flood the online space, and it's only going to get worse. Please, DJ Fuckboi, just because you can do it, it doesn't mean that you should.

But how about this: maybe *this* is the very obstacle that 'real' artists these days can fight against? Maybe this is our generation's Communist Bulgaria? Maybe it won't be the scourge of poverty but the scourge of abundance that will be our grindstone of greatness. Not drowning alone under the tidal wave of low-rent, low-effort, low-talent bollocks in our beloved music space is maybe the very thing that will ignite this generation's punk rock, hip hop or jazz. Maybe *this* is the very challenge that's been sent by the gods of rock to create the next 'real guys'? No plague of locusts this time, just an epidemic of ease. Maybe, just maybe, something good can come from it after all.

There's only one way to find out. It's time for the 'real guys' to step up. Your revolution won't just be against our age-old enemies of the music industry and the state, but against your own kind who have turned to the dark side and are poisoning our most precious and magical superpower with a deluge of disposable crap. We've got to stop that, man. Music is our saviour. Music can change the world – that's why tyrants the world over have either banned the stuff or sought to control it. Music is dangerous. It moves people, inspires people, unites people, mobilises people – and that scares the holy bejeezus out of bad guys everywhere. For me, that's reason enough to keep making the stuff ever more loudly. Music is progress. Music is the way – and we have a duty to protect it.

But how? I'll tell you how. We go rogue. We learn from the best before us and we pull our ace card – greatness. That's right, it's time to make being great, great again. Those other part-time, have-a-go Johnny Wannabe's can't compete on that playing field; they simply haven't done the apprenticeship. And you already know what breeds greatness – our old friend, struggle. That tough teacher who schooled a thousand legends before us. That proven formula woven through the back story of all our heroes. Except one does not simply struggle in this new digital wonderland of endless ease. So what do we do? I'll say it again – we go rogue. When they go easy, we go hard. Meaning we're gonna have to self-impose some old-school struggle into our music.

Put some razor wire around your creative world and make it tough for yourself. Force yourself to get a great sound out of something basic. Cast away those mountains of digital FX and use an old-school guitar pedal. Use only ONE old-school guitar pedal and make that sucker do things it's never done before. Record it direct – and once it's recorded, THAT is the sound, no going back. Write a song using only one hand. Record it on an old four-track and make it sound better than the Beatles. Make the whole album for fifty quid and not a penny more. Record a song in one day and promise to release it regardless of the outcome. Record your vocals in one take on a cheap microphone – it was good enough for Aretha. Get it right at source, get it *great* at source. Limit yourself to two production effects for the whole project. Write on an instrument you've never played before. If it can't be played live, it's not going in the song. Hell, do a song with no instruments at all. Refuse to eat until you've got something world-shattering. Ban yourself from playing certain sets of chords. Make it fucking hard for yourself. Get creative with how to make it fucking hard for yourself. Your music will thank you.

The 'others' can't do that, for they are not a true sonic warrior but someone who plays one on a computer – and thus they are doomed to sound like all the rest. But by harnessing the power of pain, you can sound like none other, pioneer new sounds and maybe even create the next seismic musical movement by happy accident. So love your limitations; they are the gateway to your greatest creations. History has proven it, time and time again. So this is a call to arms. Soldiers, your time is now. The next great musical movement is on you. Your mission will be treacherous and your enemies will be many, but fight you must. You must smash the race to mediocrity, strike fear in the heart of the tyrants, dismantle the systems of artistic control and guillotine the gatekeepers. You are no longer a musician but a crusader for truth, for the right side of history, for underdogs everywhere, for music. Your struggle is your gift, your pain your muse, your rage a blessing. So go and rinse every last drop of raw passion out of that cheap-ass, beaten-up old guitar and expunge yourself of every last ounce of frustration, heartache, yearning and love. For you, for me, for us, for history. This is your duty. You have the power.

8.

HUNTER'S HALLWAY

Noel Gallagher is wrong. He's wrong about a lot of things, but he's staggeringly wrong when he claims that all a band needs to do to become successful... is have great songs. In fact, it seems to be the mantra among the mostly older (and successful) music glitterati that 'it's all about the song, man' – which, frankly, is a mountain of steaming, festering bullshit. Anyone who believes the music industry is a cuddly meritocracy needs to spend less time on the yacht. There are Godzillions of incredible songs out there but only a tiny fraction of the world's songwriters grasp anything with a faint resemblance to a career or an income from their music. I've heard songs sung in bars to five people that have torn my heart out and fed it back to me. Songs so perfect that they punch some deep, primary nerve-root in me and I get murderous knowing no one else will ever hear them, that the geniuses who penned them are likely starving and will inevitably hang up their guitars for jobs at call centres. It's unfair, it's unjust, and as we'll see... it's just the way it is.

And anyway, if good songs reign supreme, how does one explain the success of Machine Gun Kelly? Clearly, Mr Gallagher's overly confident wisdom is not nearly as dynamic as his band's ticket pricing. So before we get into what the music industry *really* is and how it functions, we must first establish what it is not. And it is *not* a place where good guys – or good songs – win. Industry snakes and our favourite rock stars will froth at the mouth in violent indignation at this, but the ugly truth is that when it comes to success in the music business... the music is largely irrelevant. Yup, irrelevant. The industry would like us to believe that artist 'X' is a global phenomenon because of the coveted talents of said industry working their exclusive wizardry and making it happen in ways that only they can. Whereas artist 'X' would rather us believe that their success is totally down to their musical genius, unrivalled work ethic and general awesomeness. And we want to believe that too, right?! We love our heroes and we willingly play along with the fiction that's fed to us by the industry, because the truth – the real truth – is a bit of a buzzkill.

Yes, our favourite artists are awesome. Yes, they deserve all the success in the world – and more! Yes, I'm happy for them – this isn't sour grapes talking here. They live the dream we all dream of – and good luck to 'em! But this isn't a comic book you're reading, and I'm not going to patronise your intelligence, sexy reader. Because the sad, boring and thoroughly un-rock 'n' roll truth is that their success has had nothing to do with their music. Zero. And neither does it have anything to do with the merits of a well-functioning industry that knows how to get shit done. There is, however, a magic ingredient that *does* fuel the music industry. A central pillar that glues the whole thing together and upon which the entire business model is stacked like a wobbly *Jenga* tower. A single element without which the industry would cease to function – and no, I'm not talking about cocaine, although if you're looking for the gasoline that *powers* the music industry, this would be it. Nope, the sole indispensable force that is the oxygen of the music business is this... drum roll... wait for it... any guesses? Ok, it's luck. Good luck, to be precise. And I'm not trying to be cute here either – luck is what the whole business model has been deliberately built around. Remove good luck and the music industry falls apart tomorrow. Fact. We'll wade into the details shortly, but basically, if you want the magic formula to success in the music industry, it's this – be lucky.

And keep being lucky over and over again. You see, it takes an impossible amount of good fortune just to be seen by the right person at the right time – that potent marriage of musical talent with the right business muscle. I guess that's why it's called a 'lucky break', eh?! A delayed train, a traffic jam, a last-minute phone call and a million other micro-events can all be the difference between making or breaking your one and only lucky shot. An A & R guy having a long line before them at the bar could mean they miss your set – or maybe you'll be the next band on and they'll catch you instead, by accident. Chance moments like these are the true genesis of all great careers. Trust me, your favourite band's discovery story will include a supersized dollop of unfathomably good luck, even if they won't admit it. Case in point: the scenario above is essentially Noel Gallagher's discovery story – nothing to do with his great songs causing fame and fortune to suspiciously drift in through the window. Ninety-nine per cent of all the artists out there doing their thing will never be so lucky and we will never know they existed. But that's just the start of it. Having your record then produced by the right producer, marketed by the right marketing team, your tour managed by the right agents and having it all financed sufficiently – that takes layers upon layers of mind-blowingly good luck. And that's just for the first album.

So many different moving parts need to be firing at the same time for your songs to reach the earlobes of the masses. And if any one of those moving parts isn't pulling its weight, it'll bring the whole engine grinding to a halt. Like, it's all very well having the song of the summer, but what if your radio plugger is crap? What if your touring agent books you an insane summer tour but your PR whizz goes on maternity leave, leaving your promo campaign to be handled by the intern? What if the main driving force championing you at the label gets laid off and now you're stuck signed to a label where no one cares? All of these things happen all of the time. Getting signed is unlikely enough, but that's only the start of it.

Because all of those moving parts also need paying for – to the tune of hundreds of thousands of pounds – so you're gonna need a label with some serious dough. Then, after mass exposure, radio rotation, TV interviews, the right festivals, support tours with bigger acts and ideally some invented controversy with no one at any point dropping the ball... only THEN is it down to whether your song is any good or not. If it is, then happy days – you might just have the fragile beginnings of a long-term career. But only if you can pull off the same masterstroke for another two or three album cycles. If you can, then you could just be the next Ed Sheeran, Metallica or... *shudders*... Coldplay. But trust me – your odds aren't good.

And don't misunderstand me here. I'm not saying that successful artists don't work their damn arses off, because they do! All those years of relentless touring, living on Pot Noodles and spending the best years of their lives in a constant state of emotional flux, high pressure, never seeing home – and all for very little reward at the start. There's a reason that extreme mental ill health and substance abuse are so prevalent at even the highest levels of this industry. It's hard. And those who make it to the top have surely earned their place there. No, I'm just saying that there are thousands of brutally hard-working artists out there with breathtaking songs, but without that elusive lightning strike of rare opportunity, we – and virtually everyone else on Earth – will never know about them. To deny that reality is to live in a dreamland.

Remember, too, that most major-label artists are only getting paid a tiny percentage of the total bucks earned, so you have to shift gazillions of units before you can make any money (let alone become rich) doing any of this. And for pretty much every band on the planet, that is just never going to happen, *regardless* of how good their songs are. So many exceptional songs have died in silence because the artist couldn't catch a break – or maybe they did but the digital department sucked so the whole campaign made a loss, leaving the artist to be dropped again. It's a cruel, cruel game and anyone who's been around this industry for more than two minutes will be able to name scores of artists who totally *should* have made it but are now working on building sites. It takes luck, man! Lots and lots of luck. Year in, year out. Our favourite artists may indeed be awesome, but my God, their luck is more impressive.

And yes, I hear you – what about those runaway unsigned success stories? That unknown bedroom artist who snags a global smash hit without a budget or a record deal in sight. Sure, they exist, but they're like seeing a shooting star – it *can* happen, but it pretty much always does not. And best of bloody luck to 'em, too. Some are able to seize their moment of astonishingly good fortune to build a long-term career for themselves, but most end up on the 'one-hit wonder' heap the second their 'beginner's luck' runs dry. The only real victory in this model is that when exceptional musical talent meets exceptional business talent, multiplied by unspeakably good luck, the world gets Nirvana, the Beatles or Queen – and we all win. But that's scarce; the graveyard of the equally deserving is so much bigger. Fortunately, however, there is now a second option for the rest of us unlucky bastards, but we'll come on to that shortly. First, do you remember that I said that luck is what the whole business model has been *deliberately* built around? Well, now that I've pissed on everyone's chips, let's discuss how the actual *business* of the music business works. Take a deep breath...

Let's start with record labels. The holy grail for many artists. These are the guys who produce, manufacture, market, sell and, most importantly, finance recorded music. They're like a bank with good contacts and extortion powers. Once you've been signed to a record label, they will pay for the recording of your songs with whichever expensive record producer has worked their way into the label's clique. They will do the same for your music videos, album artwork, touring costs, marketing and the bribing of radio stations... I mean 'radio plugging'. They will handle the physical pressing of your albums and get them into the stores, they will devise and execute your marketing campaign, blow the price of a few houses on mass promotion and haggle you onto all the major festivals that they happen to be mates with. They will hold your hand, wipe your arse, babysit you and enable – in fact, encourage – your likely self-destruction.

Or they won't. Because the truth is that nobody – especially record companies – has any clue whatsoever which artist is going to 'make it' in the marketplace, and neither *can* anyone make '*it*' happen for them. So how is it that luck is the essential ingredient without which the industry is incapable of functioning? Here's how. The record industry's official business strategy is this: 'throw shit at the wall and see what sticks' – consciously aware of the power of random chance in their business model. So for every runaway 'hit' they get, there will always be a long trail of flops that none of us ever know about. Major labels sign tons of acts each year, pump money into all of them and see which ones – for whatever reason – stick. In essence, gambling is the business model. The ones that stick, they continue to run with (until they don't stick no more), and the ones that never stuck in the first place are *adios, amigo*. What makes an artist 'stick' to that wall? That's right – it starts with 'L' and rhymes with fuck.

And here's the stinger. All the money they shell out at the casino of your career isn't a friendly freebie – it's a loan, and they want all of it back plus interest. They do this by creaming (called 'recouping') every last penny you will make as an artist until you're back in credit with the bank... I mean the label, who do everything they can to ensure that never happens. Everything that gets spent in order to 'support the artist' – promotional costs, travel, hotels, crew hire, vinyl pressing, publicity stunts, stage props, drugs, schmoozing journalists – all goes on the artist's tab. The label aren't technically 'paying' for anything; the artist is (and usually they don't even know it). Then, if all goes to plan, the artist will still be in debt by the time the next album rolls around, and the outstanding debt from the previous album will get added on top of the new debt... and on it goes. Oh, and because the label paid for the recordings and the artwork and the videos, that's all their property now, not yours. Most of our favourite artists don't even own their own recordings, and if they ever fall out with their label over a lack of fair pay (hello, Thirty Seconds to Mars), the label can simply drop them yet still continue to exploit what's rightfully theirs – the artist's recordings (hey, Taylor Swift). I know, it's mental, right?

So a record deal can be a life-changing jackpot of dreams for an artist if the label are on your side and everything is working out, but it can be a cold kiss of death if they're not. You would be stunned to know just how many artists signed to major labels are either dirt-poor broke or juggling day jobs alongside being a rock star. And I'm talking about people you've *heard* of. This forces them into a life of perpetual and gruelling touring as it's the only way they can pay their rent. Too much of this and it's not long before mental ill health, substance abuse and wild, self-destructive behaviour – which of course are all encouraged, facilitated and glamourised by the industry – become the new normal. Many bands have found themselves unable to leave a toxic record deal and remain legal hostages in a situation where their label doesn't return their calls, does absolutely nothing for them, won't let them leave and forces them to just hang in a state of invisibility for evermore – with no money coming in. Don't believe the hype – the music industry's record on casualties, burn-outs, addicts, suicides and mental ill health is one of the worst there is. Like I told you, only the *really* lucky ones make it out of this system alive, and for many artists, signing a major record deal was the worst thing that ever happened to them.

But hey, that's just the record companies! So who are some of the other savoury key players in this fine, upstanding industry? Here's my totally accurate house tour:

Music Publishers: A recording is a song but a song is not a recording. Make sense? Well, these guys make money on the song part of the recording of that song. Got it? Ok, don't worry about it.

Radio Plugger: A person who has mates that work in radio and charges a gross amount of money for access to them. Previously known for being embroiled in the famous 'payola scandals' where radio stations were caught being bribed with money, drugs, sex and use of the company plane in exchange for adding certain songs to peak-time rotation. What were you saying about it all being down to the pure, angelic, innocent song, Noel?

Booking Agents: The legends who book the tours. A good one is like gold dust, hold them close.

Music PR: Largely bullshitters who charge broke artists thousands and thousands for the pleasure of having them send an email once a fortnight. They will all absolutely 'love' your band and want to work with you, but don't be fooled – money is their one and only true love. Good ones do exist, but you probably don't need them... yet.

Artist Managers: They get 10–20 per cent of everything the artist earns, and that fact alone informs every single decision they make, whether it's in the artist's long-term interests or not.

Distributors: Companies who warehouse your physical stock, ship it to customers and haggle your album's way into the major retailers.

Major Retailers: Money-grabbing wankers. Not to be confused with the dwindling independent stores where we should all be spending more of our money.

(Money): The second most important ingredient in the music industry after luck. The third being cocaine.

Ah yes, money. For it's not the quality of one's song that gets it onto mainstream radio, Mr Gallagher, but the quantity of one's money. It's not the brilliance of one's guitar playing that gets them a support tour with Muse; it's money. And neither is it the song that's footing the bill for the tour bus, crew and the famous producer. I really do wish we all lived in the idyllic, meritocratic utopia of fairies, free drugs and great songs that Noel does, but it seems we don't. So why does Noel believe this? Well, because he's one of them! One of the lucky bastards. He knows nothing other than a music industry that's always been very good to him – which won't be your experience, trust me.

However, with all that said and despite the preceding bitchy diatribe, it would be untrue and unfair of me to pretend that there aren't some absolute heroes working within the music business. True visionaries, angels and game-changers who have slogged selflessly in this volatile and loveless industry for decades to put the artist first, put the music first, take creative leaps of faith and fight the good fight – often to their own detriment. This industry has an impressive abundance of such legends, and it's usually these courageous risk-takers we can thank for our most iconic artists. I know some of them personally, and they've devoted their lives to the cause more than anyone. It's the *model* that's flawed, not the people working within it – although literal crooks *are* everywhere in the music business. The record industry has also given the world many priceless, life-defining musical treasures. Like I said before, when that special moment happens

– when all the right stars align and exceptional artistic talent meets exceptional business talent and exceptionally good luck – we all win big. Take a bow, Pink Floyd. But its model deprives us of so much more, and so, in short and in general, if you want the honest, heartless truth, the music industry is predominantly powered by unfeasibly good luck, grotesque amounts of money, corruption... and cocaine.

So what, then, do the rest of us do? What do the 99 per cent of artists do who are never, *ever* going to be fondled by the miraculously rare hand of good fortune needed to join the major-label cartel? Well, up until a few years back... nothing. There was nothing we could do. No deal, no band. Game over; go get a day job. It's depressing to think of the generations of great artists we never got to hear because they simply couldn't get a deal and there were no other means for them to do their thing. Record a record? Impossibly expensive. And what would they do with that big-ass reel-to-reel tape anyway? Make handmade copies for their friends? Thankfully, as they always do, the nerds stepped up and completely transformed the landscape for the rest of the great unwashed. Hands up if you feel bad for bullying them in school now. Enter the Internet.

As I'm sure you're aware, no longer does one need a label for things like album production and distribution, for we can now do all of that ourselves from the discomfort of our dingy squats, thanks to the advent of home recording software, digital music and social media. Note that it wasn't the music industry who came to save its own, but the tech guys. And I know, I know – those damn tech hipsters also degraded the value of music to less than the price of a soy latte too, right? But guess what... that's *still* more than it used to be worth. You see, when we were being robbed blind for CDs and vinyl back in the day, we weren't paying for the music. Hell no! We were paying for the *ability* to hear the music. Let me rephrase that. We were paying for the plastic it was played on. We were paying for the paper and the casing and the cost of transporting it all – we were never paying for the music. The music was merely the bait that made us buy the plastic. And an artist would have to shift a hell of a lot of plastic before they saw any kind of a kickback.

But these days, every artist has the tools to, at least in theory, create a realistic and comfortable living for themselves, purely from their art – and we shouldn't be ungrateful assholes about that. It's also entirely possible for an artist recording and releasing music by themselves to make *serious* dough, paid almost instantly, for hardly any cost and with no interference or fuckery from a label or industry demon of any kind. Thanks, nerds! Sure, it only really works if said artist also happens to be a professional record producer, business mastermind and marketing genius – but it does happen, and at least the rest of us have got a few options now, dammit! At least now we can have our babies come to life and set them loose into the mad, bad world to harass the ears of others. At least now we're no longer locked out of an unfair system of gatekeepers, taste-makers and money men. At least *now* we've got a chance to fight for ourselves. And I'm all for that.

So how have the record labels responded to this seismic shift on their home turf? Well, over a few dark years, virtually all of them crashed down like dirty dominos, shutting up shop as they just couldn't (and wouldn't) adapt to the radical new way in which music was now being consumed (i.e. not on a piece of plastic). But still standing tall amid the grey, smoky debris of this dystopian wasteland are the three remaining mega-labels – that's right, I said three: Sony, Universal and Warner. And they continue their iron-fisted planetary dominance by sole virtue of the fact that they have tons (and tons) of money. They exist in an impenetrable Death Star from which they buy out, absorb or simply crush all competition, and their continued, undying existence has swiftly reinstated the old partition between major-label artists on the one side and everyone else on the other. Then, as one last dying gasp for air (read, money), they invented what's known as the infamous

'360 deal'. Under this lovely scheme, the label takes a big-ass bite out of literally *everything* the artist earns. Merch, ticket sales, sponsorships, everything. Starring in a movie? They'll have a cut of that too, thanks.

Thankfully though, the Rebel Alliance (that's us) doesn't need to care about what's happening up there in the high castle any more, cos we're armed to the teeth with the weapons to do it all ourselves – cheers again, nerds! Let 'em have their million-dollar music videos, rented mansions and questionable marketing practices – we don't care because it's down here on the streets where the musical masses stir the multi-sound melting pot. WE are the majority – and now we've got a voice. No longer is our creative existence dependent upon some industry shill deeming us worthy. Now we can do it all in-house – and know that we're not being shafted with a smile in the process. And while the major-label artists still dominate the culture (have you ever noticed how it's always the same bands playing every festival, the same artists on the radio, the same nominees at award shows?), they only dominate the *mainstream* culture, and there's a great big fucking world outside of that. And it's one where we, the mighty underdogs, roam and roar supreme.

And that's the problem. The new problem isn't that we can't cook up our voodoo and bump it out there – the new problem is that everyone else on the planet is also doing exactly the same. We've gone from being force-fed an anaemic diet of homogenous mainstream sound-alikes to drowning to death in tuneage. There is just simply too much of the damn stuff for anyone – not the artists, the listeners, the curators and certainly not the industry – to make any sense of it. I mean, it's a good problem to have, but it's a problem nonetheless. Why is it a problem? Well, if a band plays a song in a forest and there's no one around to hear it, can they still pay their gas bill? Getting heard above the cacophony of every other poet and pan-basher on Earth has become a life-or-death struggle for artists today. Making the record and releasing it? That's easy. Whether anyone will ever *hear* it is a terminal issue. We've got the platforms to circulate our call to arms to the entire world for free, but they're so oversaturated, they've become redundant.

So how do we circumvent this unchartered buzzkill? Beats me – and Mr Gallagher won't be much help on that one either. It's going to take creativity, resilience and hustle – which us modern-day music artists have got by the truckload, so that bodes well. So far, though, the current winners of the attention war are those who are less uncomfortable peddling tsunamis of cheap, clickbaity content solely designed to finger the algorithms rather than supply good tunes, good ideas and good trouble to the progress of humanity. Which doesn't bode well. And speaking of algorithms, they are going to have to evolve to a much more advanced standard if they are ever going to truly be an ally of the independent artist. At present they are merely a sock puppet with the pervy hand of the industry up its ass – you mean your 'recommendations' are all the same handful of major-label artists too? How bizarre. However we do it, getting heard above the noise is THE question to answer for any artist hoping to survive in the new utopia.

The other question that needs to be written in all caps is the one that involves GETTING PAID. As everyone knows by now, revenue from music streaming and downloads is a joke. A sick joke. A big, fat middle-finger-pushed-into-the-face-of-every-musician-on-Earth type of joke. Now, I'm not one of those mouth-breathing 'streaming is evil' clowns who thinks we should all still be riding around on horseback, but there's a desperately urgent revolution needed on the remuneration-for-artists front, and something tells me that's not going to come from the industries who benefit from it. Yes, I know the retorts – when we buy an album once, the artist gets paid once – but with streaming, the artist gets paid every single time the song gets streamed by potentially billions of people, every day, forever. And at that scale – provided a label isn't taking 90 per cent of the spoils – an artist can become very comfortable, fast. But that's the blag – the beauty of the system only works at scale. Any artist shifting less than hundreds of thousands of streams on the regular is just simply not going to make any money. And even then, once they've deducted the label's cut, the manager's cut and divvied the remaining crumbs among, the other band members, what's left is obscenely, offensively bad. Like, we're not even talking petrol money here. I'm not saying that 'streaming' is inherently bad – far from it. It's the way things are and it's here to stay. But in its current incarnation, it is the insult to the injury of independent artists the world over. So much so that even if artist shares were doubled, they'd still fall laughably short of fair, respectful or liveable, and *that*, my friends, is about as likely to happen as Roger Waters becoming my new bestie. Wish, we may. Fight, we can try – but it is simply never going to happen. So no, we need a solution more radical, more anarchic and more rebellious to finally starve out our enemies and steer our own pirate ship for good. But that's for a later chapter.

So the new model is far from perfect, but the fact remains that the shackles are now off and we've stolen the masters' tools. In theory, with a little evil cunning, you can now *make* the world hear you. For the first time ever, musicians today have a choice. Option 1 is an old-school deal with a major label, mass exposure, playing the biggest festivals and living the dream – but likely being broke, unhappy, unwell and susceptible to it all being over at any moment. Option 2 means building a solid and lifelong career for ourselves where we make the music that we want, free from commercial pressure or interference, where we are in the driving seat of our destiny and we get paid properly for our work. I made my choice a long time ago – and I'm still here.

The landscape is changing every day. As I write, the tech prophets are still pretending NFTs are the saviour of the music biz, and by the time you read this, there'll be some new thing they're banging on about. It's an exciting, dynamic time, and as a collective, we've got more power than ever before. But our historic enemies aren't gonna go down without a fight. There will be new battle lines and new martyrs lost to the struggle, but I'm confident that the direction of progress may be moving in our favour. And if there is such a thing as an eternal, universal truth, it's this: *Homo sapiens* fucking *love* music, and so long as there are ears to hear it, there will be music and there will be musicians. We're not going anywhere.

There remains, however, one enemy us artists simply cannot defeat... luck. Lady Luck is a stubborn mistress and she will continue to weave her invisible hand through our every eventuality, no matter what we do. Can we create our own luck? Can we influence our odds a little? Yes! Yes, we can. How does one do this? You keep rolling the dice. You keep learning. Keep finding creative solutions. You keep being you, keep doing you and you keep kicking ass. You adapt. You wait out the storm. You keep your bullshit radar clean, think outside of the box and *always* stay true to your art. Remember that ultimately, though, our fate is out of our hands, so just enjoy that roller coaster, man. Don't let the pursuit ruin all the good stuff that happens along the ride. Take it from me – I know. Because you also have to know when it's time to stop gambling. When the chase has robbed you of all of your money, your time, your health, your relationships and your joy, it's time to leave the casino and it's time for music to become a hobby. There is no shame in that at all – in fact, it's the sensible, honourable and sane thing to do.

Whatever we do, though, and however we do it, we all have a duty to keep this music thing moving, keep it real, keep it from the heart and keep it loud. So to my fellow noise-mongers I say, go get 'em and go get lucky! I'll see you in the trenches.

9.

THE BLUEPRINT

Do you dream of a career in music? Are you an active music artist already, out there fending for yourself in the wilderness without anchor or compass? Well, then, this one's for you. Because if there was an award for 'the most asked question in the history of the universe', this one would slay it every time: what advice can you give to artists to help them succeed in the music industry? And believe me, I've asked this question more times than most, hoping as a younger, aspiring rock star to gain the secret inside knowledge that separates the winners from the wannabes. I read all the books, watched all the documentaries, studied all the interviews and paid attention to what was happening around me. Since then, I've spent my entire life struggling, navigating, adapting, learning, failing, trying and somehow surviving (kind of) in this maddeningly volatile, unjust and ever-changing industry, and I've got the scars – and some hard-won lessons – to show for it. These days, by virtue of being an ageing 'also-ran', I now get to continue asking that very question directly to legendary music industry veterans, iconic label bosses and rock stars the world over – it's one of the few perks of my years of service. Basically, I have spent my entire life relentlessly pursuing the same dream as you and seeking the same answers.

Did I succeed? Hell no! So why on Earth should you take advice from my sorry ass? After all, I've never had a global hit record, I've never sold out Wembley, gone platinum, done coke with Ozzy, played the Super Bowl or headlined Rock in Rio, so I'm essentially irrelevant as a human and why the *fuck* should you waste your time listening to my crap?! Well, that's exactly *why* you should listen to me, because it's overwhelmingly unlikely that you will ever 'succeed' either – if success to you means anything like the above. I hate to break it to you, but your odds of commercial success in this industry are less than 1 per cent. In any other industry, if you were told you must sacrifice years of your life, all of your money, your physical and mental health, your relationships, all forms of human comfort and literal blood, sweat and tears for a 1 per cent chance of *maybe* having a momentary sniff of success and remuneration, you'd tell them to shove their job up their arse. You've got better odds at winning the lottery – and for a lot less pain. I'm just being honest with you. After many arduous decades of grind, screw-overs, breakdowns, therapy, touring, releasing albums, financing, battling and never stopping despite the horrific onslaught of injustice and unfairness, I'm pretty confident that I've done the fieldwork for you and I can give you the jewels of insight that will be relevant to the *actual* terrain you'll be navigating out there. Don't worry about success; success is easy – it's being a failure that's hard.

And here's my first insight: successful people can't tell you anything useful. Another reason you should most definitely take my advice, over that of your favourite rock star, is because every single successful musician I have ever spoken to has absolutely no clue how they got there, how the industry works or has any real understanding of what life is like when you're not a successful rock star. They can tell you nothing about how distribution works, because they've never done it. Marketing plan? The label does that. Hell, many of these guys have long forgotten how to tune their own guitars, and I am absolutely not joking when I say that. They wouldn't last one minute back in the real world where the rest of us roam without managers, assistants, drivers, guitar techs, vegan caterers and promo budgets that could feed a small country. I mean, of course they'll all *give* you advice! And it'll always be the same vague, clichéd nothingness about working hard and staying true to your vision – and what a sack of festering horse shit that is. The honest ones will simply say, 'I don't know, man, I got lucky.' If you want real-world information that's going to help you where you're at right now, that's going to help you sail the stormy, shark-infested waters ahead of you, you have to ask those fallen heroes who tried, *really* tried – not those who got crazy lucky straight out of the gates and have had huge teams of people to do everything for them ever since. Trust me, I know. I've spoken to heaps of these guys, eagerly picking their brains for *anything* useful, and you'd be staggered to discover just how little they know about how the industry works. Without their helpers, our favourite bands wouldn't last two seconds out in the wild, so please don't go blindly marching out there following the so-called advice of a multimillionaire who hasn't booked their own shows, changed their own guitar strings, financed their own recordings or had to handle their own promo in decades.

And so that's where I come in. I have personally written, performed, recorded, produced, released, promoted, financed, distributed and sold my back catalogue completely by myself. I have run my own label, my own music publishing company, placed syncs on TV shows and adverts, booked tours, spoken at music conventions, universities and the House of Lords about the music industry, taught music in schools and colleges, and had some not insignificant wins along the way. I've also made every mistake possible (several times over), wasted eye-watering amounts of money and time that I didn't have, been screwed over by every bottom-feeding ass-stain in the business and literally written the book on how *not* to do things.

So listen, when you've found success, let me know and I'll hook you up with some rock stars who can totally advise you on the pitfalls of touring the global stadium circuit. But given your odds of that ever happening, let's prepare you for the much more likely turf you'll be riding in. But before we start – a word of warning. This is a fool's errand. A kamikaze mission. Are you *sure* you want to do this? If you like free time, money, beds, food, sleep, fresh air, clean pants and relationships, then run away now! You're clearly too sane for the music industry, and God bless you! If, on the other hand, you have a perverse fetish for sleeping in smelly, cold vans, eating Pot Noodles, washing with bottled water, surviving below the poverty line, having zero job security or long-term prospects, living in constant uncertainty and emotional flux and never seeing your family or friends, then read on! If you're absolutely sure that you want to do this, then let's go – but don't say I didn't warn you.

I hereby share with you as complete an answer as possible to that most ubiquitous of questions: what advice can you give to artists to help them succeed in the music industry? Some advice is from my own personal experience and some is from what I've seen of my friends' successes and the countless conversations I've been lucky to have over the years with some great minds from within the music industry – including a good bunch of successful artists and their makers. My aim here is to finally answer that question once and for all and to give you the info you need to be victorious in the music industry as you are most likely to experience it – that is, down here with the rest of us. The kind of practical, real-world gold that no one wants to tell you because they don't want to burst your bubble and imply for a second that it's not all pixies, unicorns and million-pound record deals out there. After all, that would be to tell you the truth, and the music industry is no fan of truth.

The first rule you must be aware of is that there *are* exceptions to every rule. You might just *be* that exception but you more than most definitely will not be. Everyone thinks they will be (hello!), but almost nobody is. Ok, so your band just picked up a deal from

MegaBucks Records after only two gigs, so I'm clearly just talking trash, right? While I'm super stoked for you, get back to me in a year or two's time when they've stopped taking your calls and your album will never, ever be released because it's not your album any more. Luck is not a one-stop shop – you need a steady stream of the stuff over years to get even remotely close to glimpsing the top. Like I said, our point of reference for *success* is grossly out of touch with reality. When people talk of success, they're talking about less than 1 per cent of the artistic community. It is *they* who are the exception. The rest of us have a 99 per cent chance of not being that, so focusing your attention on how to thrive as part of the 99 per cent will set you up for way more success and happiness than failing miserably at being in the 1 per cent who got insanely lucky.

The second rule is that there are no rules. Sorry. There's no magic formula for success in this business or any other, and if that's what you were hoping for, then you're already destined to fail. Everyone's situation is different and my aim here is to give you the tools and the understanding you will need to adapt and manoeuvre your way through the jungle. So let's forget about rules and get on with it. Let's start with the basics.

WHY?

Ok, first things first. Let's get some groundwork established here. Why are you doing this? If it's for fame and fortune, give up now. Seriously. Go and get a job for some big, evil tech firm and throw the bass in the bin. If you're doing this for anything less than the crazy, irrational, unhealthy, dangerous love of music, then you're going to fall down straight outta the gates and that's where you'll end. If you're the sort of traitor who will quit the band the first time the van breaks down at 3 a.m. on a Wednesday, please leave now. If you're the kind of delicate douche who thinks a kick-drum case is not a perfectly reasonable place to call a bed for a month, your days in this game are numbered. If you're going to whinge and whine about being hungry, being tired, being lied to, being ripped off, being ill, being screwed over, missing home or being too good for this shit, get out of the way now. If your love of all things music surpasses your need for any other basic human necessity, then that's a good place to start. If you're going to embark on this noble and questionable quest, then you have to be painfully honest with yourself. Do you really want this? Are you prepared to do this for free? Forever?!

If you answered that question with a horrified 'no way', then thank you. The rest of us out here paying our dues appreciate your honesty and not taking up space. Your option at this point is to continue making and playing music purely for fun with your friends and enjoying what is actually the best part of this without the carnage that immediately ensues the second you start taking it seriously. Keep the day job, pay off the mortgage and enjoy your holidays – but don't you dare start a Facebook page or cluttering Spotify with your bedroom bangers, or we're coming for you like a pack of hyenas hungry for blood. I'm joking. A little...

If the answer to that question is a big, fat 'hell yeah!' then you may proceed to level 2. You beautiful fucking maniac.

BE GOOD

Your first commandment, above all else, is to be good. One thing this poor, struggling world does not need is any more crap music. Don't even *think* about videos, photos or quirky costumes until your band absolutely rocks. Please, we beg you. So much of your journey will be easier if your band undeniably, irresistibly, insatiably kicks ass, that you shouldn't waste a second on anything else until you've got a stack of songs written, honed, honed again and played with the conviction and force of an apocalyptic hurricane. In fact, being as great as possible, and then trying to be even better next time, should be your sole and lifelong modus operandi. This might seem obvious, and of course every band and their mum thinks their band is the best thing to ever wrestle an eardrum. But aside from not wanting to add to the infinite landfill of half-baked bedroom projects that clog up most of the internet, there is another, more subtle reason why this is so important: survival.

We'll get to more detailed shit in a minute, but honestly, if you just focus all of your attention on the music and enjoy the process, you'll inadvertently bypass a lot of the pain, disappointment and ball-ache that comes with this life simply because you've been too distracted by the craft and pleasure of the music to notice any of it. Most of your journey and success – or lack thereof – will be completely out of your control, but the one thing you can (and should) always have control of is the creation and performance of the music – the reason we all picked up an instrument in the first place. Don't ever lose sight of that. I did and it robbed me of my most precious moments, because rather than relishing in seeing the Italian sun go down as I played a seaside show with my best mates, I was twisted up in violent rage over whichever scumbag had colossally screwed us over that week. I can't even remember playing guitar, but I vividly remember the hate. The music is why we're all here, and it's the music that will ultimately get you through your darkest days on this mostly treacherous journey – so if you want to survive, just focus on the music, man.

MORE DETAILED SHIT

Ok, so you've chosen the red pill and your band is more brutal than the Hulk on coke – now what? Well, it's all downhill from here, so strap in and prepare for some stormy, stormy weather. Now, I'm not gonna tell you that next you must set up your social media accounts, get photos taken and all that stuff – if you don't know all of that already then you're gonna be dead in your boots before morning. Nope, I'm the loving drill sergeant who's here to give you the overall survival skills you will need to stand a fighting chance out there on the battlefield, so if you were hoping for an easy, handheld ride, 'go buy a colouring book, candy-ass!' It's not too late to turn back now, remember, but if you're hell-bent on self-destruction, then let's go.

FUCK YOUR COMFORT

The first thing you're going to have to do is get tough. For most, if not *all*, of your career, things are going to be rough. Real rough. You're going to have to get well acquainted with discomfort, being broke, eating crap, sleeping on steel, living in rags, washing in car parks, being emotionally and physically exhausted and running on empty all of the time. You must also be prepared for an unbelievable and never-ending onslaught of rejection, ridicule, criticism, doubt, commentary and rip-offs – and that's just from the people who know and love you. You must be ready to have no free time, no steady income, no sick pay, no holidays, no downtime, no social life, stable relationship or fixed abode. Not just for now – but for the rest of your life.

So if you suspect that the bass player is going to struggle without his scented eye mask, give him the chop now before he drags you all down with him in three weeks' time. You need soldiers out there, man, not passengers. Fuck your comfort. If you have to sleep on a guitar case, roll up a jacket and get your head down. The glamour happens on the stage; the rest is a punishing slog. Why?

MONEY

Money. Being in a band is expensive. Anywhere you can shave some shekels off the cost, do it – and if that means forfeiting personal comfort in order to keep the juggernaut rolling, then you do what must be done. Websites, T-shirts, merch, vinyl, photos, videos, recording costs, artwork, distribution costs, mastering. Not to mention the basic requirements of the 'job' like instruments, cables, strings, drumsticks, pedals, cases and stands – and that's *before* you start gigging! Petrol, a vehicle, food, somewhere to sleep (see vehicle), more petrol, tolls, fines, parking and did I mention petrol? It's savage. And you will be making exactly zero pounds while you're haemorrhaging all this dough. So anywhere you can cut costs, you absolutely must do it – and if that means trimming them from comfort, get trimming.

The other way you cut costs is by becoming a multifaceted, song-singing, guitar-swinging Swiss army knife in badass sunglasses. YOU make the artwork, you make the videos, you record the record, you build the website, you drive the van, you make the calls, you sell the merch and you carry your own shit, goddammit! You can eradicate much of the expenses by just doing it all yourself, but be warned – your guitar will gather dust and your soul will start to rust as you slowly become less of a musician and more of a secretary. A secretary who lugs an extraordinary amount of heavy equipment around the place. Personally, I recommend this route. I recommend that you do as much as you physically can by yourself – and then do more. Not only will you save essential pennies for the bottomless petrol fund, but you'll also be learning. You'll be learning how all of the different moving parts work, and you'll develop priceless new skills. Skills you can use to save money on the next video, the next album and the next tour. Doing it all in-house gives you experience, saves costs and gives you so much more knowledge and leverage for when the record labels come knocking.

'Pay for our record, you say? Well, we can do that ourselves, mate. Shoot us a swanky, needlessly expensive video in exchange for the rights to our genius for all of eternity? We've already got one, pal; we shot it on our phones and cut it ourselves for free. What else ya got for us, Mr Label Snake?' So much of what a label used to use as the bait to steal an artist's lifeline can now be done by ourselves – do not underestimate the power of that. It just takes effort, time, sweat and guts. The longer you can grow your awesome empire of metal without relying on any external players, the sweeter the deal will be when it comes – trust me. So now that your songs rock, start boning up on video editing and spreadsheets, and go make it all happen. Get creative and don't follow the established format. Embrace your lack of budget and make it part of the appeal of the video or whatever. Be punk, be a pirate, be the revolution. You can do it. And if you really can't, find someone who can and make them your minister of propaganda – who said all band members need to play an instrument?

PR

The final way you cut costs is by not wasting money on PR, playlisters and pluggers. Don't get me wrong – some of these guys are brilliant, passionate and selfless warriors for the cause. But they're few and far between, and believe me, the second that fresh blood hits the scene, the sharks come sniffing in packs. Let's start with PR. You don't need it. PR is for busy established acts who need someone to manage their press schedule and organise their interviews – you are not yet that act. PR companies don't create attention for your act; they manage attention for those who already have it. Still, a PR company will tell you very convincingly that you most definitely *do* need PR, that they are the ones to do it for you and that they love your band so, so much. But truthfully, innocent emerging bands are just keeping much of this lot topped up in Charlie while they're hustling for the next big client. Don't be a goldfish; be a piranha. Give 'em all the finger and walk away. The same goes for playlisters and radio pluggers. Now, I know *personally* of some amazing people working very hard in these areas. Real champions of the emerging artist. Good guys. They do exist, but the ones that are likely to be within your reach and budget at this point will be the other kind.

And all *those* guys do is send a press release out to a database of contacts and... nope, that's it! No chase-ups, no input, no effort, no nothing. Yet you still have to pay them even if they don't *get* you anything! It's the biggest blag since the banking system! You do not need them. You can do it all by yourself and you'll get much better results if you do. They will only bring your budget, momentum and morale down – I really can't stress this enough. Save your money, do it yourselves and know that it's getting done. When you truly need PR, you'll know. See, I told you I've got your back.

MORE MONEY

Financial prowess is not traditionally our strength as artists, is it? A bore, I know. But I've learned the tough way that unless your finances become a central part of your band's planning, you'll be at the mercy of so many setbacks, hold-ups, let-downs and screw-overs that it will categorically kill your career. Either with a swift, punishing blow or a slow, cruel torture. You have to get the absolute most out of every resource you've got – including yourselves – and protect those pennies with an almost fanatical zeal. Do not waste a single one of them.

But as well as cutting costs to their brutally bare bones, you're also gonna need money coming in – although it will never be enough. Now the classic go-tos are, of course, a rich relative, a credit card, pooling your collective pay cheques, or an investor of some kind. All of these come with problems. Money simply given by Mum and Dad will teach you nothing about how to generate or keep hold of your own dough, and most other hard-slogging artists on the circuit will rightfully see you as a scar-shy rich kid unworthy of their comradeship – and I would agree. Ultimately, you're gonna have to pay for your own shit, man. A credit card and pay-cheque pooling is for many bands their only means of seed capital for equipment, transport and fuel in the early stages, but be warned –

this can quickly become a habit that ruins all of your lives and, of course, puts a firm limit on how much money you'll ever be able to source. And investors? Forget it. I have never heard of a time when that has worked out well for the artist, and almost always ends in resentment, bad blood, court cases and band break-ups. Avoid.

That said, you're gonna need some money from somewhere, right?! Now, I'm not opposed to leaning on a credit card or everyone chipping in their own money just to get things started, but it absolutely *must* be treated as a small but necessary investment with a clear plan for how you're going to make that money back with profit. Sorry, I know this is already boring, but it'll mean the difference between still kicking ass in five years from now or drowning in debt and your band dying an early death. Ideally, you will have a second stream of income that's separate from your day job and is just for financing the band. In my previous life, my version of this was a cover band from which we all pooled the takings into a band fund that enabled us to tour Europe, hire vehicles, buy merch and sometimes even eat! But beware – that route is a steep and slippery slope into the jaws of hell. Many musicians step into that world with innocent, short-term intentions, but most do not come back out again. Today, however, there are many more options for cash creation – if you're creative and committed enough. Online content, crowdfunding, subscription platforms, instrument lessons, DJ sets, paid live streams – whatever! Basically, if you can find a way to make money that is *just* for the band and doesn't come out of your rent money, then most definitely do it. If you can't do that, then chip in – but remember what I said.

The good news is that once you've bought everything you need to get started, the band can (in theory) start making its own money. Merch being a case in point. Get some physical product to sell and get selling! Merch keeps bands on roads. And while you might have to do the infamous free shows in the early days to ingratiate your way onto the local live circuit and cut your teeth as a live band, you need to nip that shit in the bud pronto. That 'playing for exposure' blag is a toxic, exploitative piss-take – do not encourage it. Anyone telling you that they 'love your band so much' that they want you to travel for five hours to play for free at their empty shithole clearly thinks you're a chump and hates your band. If they want you there badly enough, they'll stump up some bucks.

THE CATCH

But now for the catch-22. All of these things – crowdfunding, commanding a decent gig fee, fan subscriptions – are only really an option for artists who've already got an audience. Like, sure you can crowdfund if you want to, but if you've only got three fans then you're only going to raise enough moolah to get to the petrol station and back. And herein lays the unjust truth that pervades the entire music industry from bottom to top: it's easy to win when you're a winner. For most artists, music streaming is the death blow to their ability to get paid and be heard. But if you're one of the tiny minority of artists that gets on a major playlist, then music streaming is the genie that catapults you into the ears and hearts of millions. And when you look at exactly who it is that's getting placed on the biggest playlists, what do you see? That's right – artists on major record labels. Every. Single. Time. It's the same with crowdfunding. If you've already got thousands of loyal fans, then you can raise a serious amount of cash through crowdfunding – but the sad reality is that it *takes* a serious amount of cash to make thousands of loyal fans. Likewise for social media. The algorithms mostly favour content that is already getting large spikes in activity – that is, content that *already* has a large and engaged audience. If that's not you, then you can spend as much time as you like on that selfie, but ain't no one gonna see it. And on it goes. If you're already popular, well financed and signed to a label that runs the major playlists, then yes, all of the above tools are incredibly powerful. If you're not, then those very same tools can be either irrelevant or a detrimental waste of time and resources.

PLAYING LIVE

But fear not, there *is* a solution and it is this: start local. That's right – the old classic 'think global, act local' ethos doesn't just apply to saving the planet, but to saving our sorry arses in music too. Let me explain. Let's say you live in Swansea. Well, you've got Swansea, Cardiff and Newport all within a short drive and all with their own music scenes and venue circuit. Do you:

Devote your time and energy to hammering the local circuit, which requires no hotels, no van hire, no ten-hour motorway slaughter-fest and no getting home at 5 a.m. with work in the morning? Do you hit the streets and do direct marketing and promotion regularly? Do you ingratiate yourself into the local circuit and become part of a bigger scene and community?

Think, 'No, I'm gonna hire a van, plough my life savings into the fuel tank, book rooms at an expensive inner-city hotel, take a day off work and spend all day driving to Hull on the promise of it being their "massive monthly rock night" at huge cost to everyone's time and pocket, whereupon we shall perform to the sound tech and bar staff before getting three hours' sleep and spending most of the next day driving home through hours of horrific congestion.'

Ladies and gentlemen, you are reading the words of a man who chose option 2. Not once, but over and over again. Why the actual? I hear you ask. Two reasons. The first is that I arrogantly and naively thought that I was cunningly planting my musical seed far and wide and that it would feed and water itself in my absence to eventually bloom into a sprawling nationwide mycelium of appreciation for my genius. And secondly, I was a clueless douche who didn't have an awesome book like this to tell me otherwise.

Of course you *must* think global. You *must* want to take over the world. You *must* want to play everywhere, anywhere, far and wide and get your sonic sexiness out there for all to adore. But you *must* be realistic, too. Blow all your money and work leave on your first week of gigs and you're not gonna be around very long. And if, like most bands, you're starting out with no money, no fans, no momentum and no support, the only way to start, the only way you *should* start, is to start local. Local means everyone can drive their own car to the gig, or get a lift or whatever. Local means no hotels, fuel costs, van hire or days off work. And local means that you've got an audience on your doorstep that you can nurture and build every day. Trust me, as soon as you conquer your local scene, labels, press and bookers will all come kissing your ass from far and wide. Don't downplay the power of your local scene. Start there and build your army of loyal warriors with whom you will start invading neighbouring cities together. Hammer your local scene and become a positive part of it. Get involved. Support other bands, help each other out and spark the next zeitgeist. That, my friends, is your mission and it's right there on your doorstep.

RECORDING

Well, that's all plain sailing so far, but what about recording a damn record? A great question. In the good old days when guitar solos were a thing that happened while flying over an arena in a circus harness and spandex tights – ya know, before the internet came along and ruined everyone's fun – making a record was the luxury of the chosen few. It required a mass of heavy, pricey equipment, a giant room to house it all, and a superhuman, godlike figure called a producer who possessed the secret knowledge of how to operate it and turn your widdlings into something that could be burned onto plastic at a ginormous factory many miles away and shipped by truck to other special people known as distributors, retailers and radio pluggers, who enabled people to hear your genius and make your label a mountain of money – although not from the music, but from the plastic. Thankfully, these days that entire process can be done on a basic laptop while sitting in our pants in our front room sipping a cold one. And amen to that.

That's right. If you want to make a record (and make a *good* record) you don't need any of those things any more. It's perfectly possible to make a good, commercial-sounding recording in your house or at a local studio for hardly any cost. How? If you've been paying attention, then surely you know by now what I'm about to say. Correct – you do it yourself. If needs must (and they really do), then you must do what you need. Open the doors on your wardrobe, hang a quilt over them and that's your vocal booth. Lean some mattresses against the walls, get creative with pillows and that's your sound treatment. Sure, it might mean doing the notoriously tricky (and loud) drum parts at a studio, but acoustic guitars, vocals, bass and anything electronic can 100 per cent be done at home, in your own time, in your pants. No stressing about the time or having to surrender to a take or a tone that's subpar because the clock is ticking. You can take as long as you need or you can pull some all-nighters and get the thing done. It's up to you. Your record, your rules.

I'm not in any way trying to disrespect the insanely talented, hard-working and indispensable engineers, producers and studio owners out there – you should *absolutely* work with them – but there's a lot of ways to kick an ass, and I strongly encourage you to start out by making your own recordings first. It's another skill that'll serve you in so many ways in keeping your truck a-trucking, rather than being dependent on... well, anyone. After all, what's the agenda here? To *feel* like you're making a record – ya know, like, hanging out in a big, posh studio with people serving you macchiatos? Or is it to *make* a damn record and get cracking?! And when it does come time to make records with pro producers and engineers, you'll have a much better technical understanding of the process. And, as a result, you'll be able to communicate your ideas better because you'll be able to speak their language. So it's all good, man. This is all about arming you with the skills and experience you need to get moving – and to keep moving. And the price of some second-hand microphones and recording software is an investment you will reap the rewards of over and over again. You also get the Brucie bonus of having more freedom to experiment rather than having to get it all perfect by lunchtime.

'But what if I don't know *how* to record myself?' Then you must learn. Immediately. It'll be the most liberating and empowering thing you will ever do as an artist, I promise you. And if you save money by doing as much as you can at home, then you can spend out on the mixing and mastering – which I would most definitely recommend that you do with an experienced engineer rather than by yourself. You see, I'm not writing this for the rich kids who can afford to dick around in a lavish studio being humoured by an expensive producer who gives zero real craps about you or your music. And I'm not writing it for the major-label lucky bastards either. I'm writing this for the underdogs – the street cats out there alone with no backing, support, money or guidance. If you want to set yourself up to not get eaten alive in this business at the first hurdle, you need to start thinking like a renegade. DIY all the way, baby! What's stopping you from recording yourself at home and saving your band a whack of money in the process? Money you can spend on growing your long-term empire rather than lining the pockets of whatever big-name producer you think you need. When the big dogs come greasing, *they* can pay for you to hang out at swanky studios – until then, get that hustler mode engaged and do as much as you can for yourself. And yes, that means recording, lifting, driving, lugging, designing and spreadsheeting. So get shifting that fucking mattress and start boning up on how to make a recording. It's never been easier and your career will thank you for it. And then you can thank me.

DISTRIBUTION AND RETAIL

But what of the other nefarious characters I mentioned in the old-school chain of command – distribution, retail and PR? That's simple. You sack them all off. You don't need any of them. Sure, your music needs to be on all the main streaming and digital platforms, but that's simple – there are heaps of online providers who will sort that out for you for hardly any expense and a few clicks of a button. I'm not gonna name names but that's your digital distribution sorted. Easy. Your music is now available everywhere on Earth – do not overlook the power of that. Physical distribution? Until you're shifting lorry loads of units, don't bother. The only physical product you should be shifting should be done on your merch stall or your own web pages. And shift them you should. Sure, it's cool seeing your stuff on the shelves of some big music store, but the novelty quickly wears off – and it's usually right around the time you realise that the retailer and distributor are taking all of your money for doing nothing more than storing it for you. Screw that. When you're selling so many orders that you can't physically manage it by yourself any more, that's when you get a distributor and you take the hit on your bottom line. Or you hire a mate to do it for you, and instead of giving the lion's share to some faceless company who couldn't care less about you, give a fair share to your mate or a relative and spread the love.

See, all of this stuff is a lot easier once we strip away the idea that we need a label, that we need a producer, that we need distribution, blah blah blah. We don't need any of it. All you need is a hustler spirit, a defiant fuck-you-I'm-doing-it-with-or-without-you attitude, a little creativity and lots of caffeine.

PR and pluggers we've covered already, and it's still a big fat no from me. But if you're *not* going to pay mental amounts of money to special, mystical people to promote your music using their undisclosed skills and secret magic voodoo, then how the hell are the masses ever going to know about your sick new record?! Well, *that* is the big question.

PROMOTION – AND THE BIG QUESTION

I've made every mistake possible on my treacherous journey to nowhere, but none more frequent than my haemorrhaging of vast amounts of money and time on PR. Let me spare you the same pain. But first, you have to get real. Why would you even want PR? To get a few words of validation from some magazine? While this is a nice ego rub and does add a little social proof for your music, it doesn't really *do* anything. And by next week, it's gone. The power of the music press has plummeted drastically, and many would say good riddance as yet another bastion of the old fortress has fallen down. However, there still exist two very different ways of getting shit done in this industry. One is the major-label model of throwing boatloads of cash at everything – magazines, radio, festivals, TV, tours, retailers – and forcing you into the public consciousness through unrelenting mass saturation. The other is whatever the hell we're doing over here. As explained elsewhere in this book, your odds of landing the major-label jackpot are essentially zero, and it's a lottery you certainly shouldn't wait around for. Much better to just crack on. So we need to be very honest with ourselves about what it is we're trying to achieve here. Is this 1) a vanity project to make us *look* like we're doing stuff to our friends on Facebook, or are we 2) actually trying to build a long-term career? The good news is that neither answer requires a PR agent. Every major magazine and radio station I've ever been in or on was achieved through my own efforts – and it wasn't that hard. But if you're serious about answer number 2, then read on.

What's your game plan? If we're talking promo here (and we are), then ultimately you're trying to let as many people as possible know about your braggadocious music and build a badass battalion of loyal and adoring fans who will be right along with you throughout your journey. That's the big picture – remember it. And every decision you make about promo should serve that big picture. But here's the rub. I've waxed evangelical about the many virtues of the new, independent model for a long time now – the power and the freedom to make and release our own records, how we want, when we want, and to be the masters of our own destiny – but it comes with a terminal Achilles heel. In a world where everyone now has equal access to the tools of creation (and promotion), how the hell do you get heard above the noise? And noise it is – the unrelenting blizzard of content coming at us fast and loud, every second of every day. Your band may well be in among that noise somewhere, but I didn't see it and neither did anyone else. Fuck what happened before the Big Bang – the *real* BIG question is how do we get heard above the noise, man? The answer to that perennial puzzle is the difference between a great band and a great band that someone has heard of. So how do we do it? If there was a hard and fast rule here, it would instantly become redundant as millions of people would start doing it and we'd be back to square one. So what we need are not specific actions, but some guiding principles. I propose the following:

Don't promote. That's right. We're all sick and sickly tired of people trying to ram their crap down our throats and into our ears. We're desensitised to it and we can smell it a mile off. Instead, have a conversation. Whether it's on social media, onstage or off – be human. Share your journey, with all its struggles and adventures. Share your vulnerabilities, share your process, share your doubts and your wins. So you're in a band. So what? Who cares? So is everyone these days – be a human instead and you will stand out from the yelling hordes of salespeople, attention-seekers, agitators and trolls by a thousand watts. The connection is deeper because it's real, and it will last longer than any promo campaign ever will.

Build relationships, not fans. These days, the symbiosis between artist and fan is inseparable. Fused at the heart. Without your fans, you die. Simple as. And people in this automated, dog-eat-dog, overcrowded and ever-changing digital dystopia are yearning more and more for human connection. To feel seen and be part of something meaningful, something real. That's where you come in. Are you just another asshat trying to rinse a few more pounds out of them? Or do you care, like, really care, about them as people and appreciate them as fans? Show an interest, involve them, ask questions, reply to comments, take the time. If you make looking after your fans' well-being your priority, you won't need to worry about marketing, promotion or anything else – you'll already have everything you need. You'll have the most powerful and enviable weapon in the entire industry – a legion of devoted and engaged fans.

Create a community. The obvious extension of the previous two points is to create your own community. A hive that thrives and bustles even when you're not there. A hub where your fans can find common solace, belonging and purpose among the like-minded far and wide. That's when a mere fan club becomes a movement, its own evolving organism centred around its shared love of you and your kick-ass music. That's when you have an army, and that's when the wolves at the labels will suddenly develop an insatiable 'love' for your music. And you won't need them.

So be real. Know who you are, know what you stand for, who you speak for. Find your tribe and scream your collective truth with zero fucks given. Where do you find your tribe? Wherever you can! Online, in the pub, in jail – whatever! Get creative. And get started, because it'll be a slow burner. But once you reach a tipping point, you'll have an avalanche on your hands. Maintain a direct line of communication with your tribe at all times and keep it personal. No middlemen. Just like recording the record, YOU do it. The tools are available; it just takes time, creativity and consistency. But if you don't waste time, energy and momentum on pointless PR, distribution and chasing cool magazines, you'll be a sexy little cult leader in no time. So get on it. And Godspeed.

A FINAL WORD FROM DARWIN

So that's the nuts and bolts of how to get yourself started, established and set up for a healthy, long-term conquest of the hearts and ears of the many. It requires no rip-off merchants, dodgy labels, bottom-feeders or bullshit. We haven't covered what happens after that because, well... those of you who get there won't need me anyway; you will have left my sorry ass in a cloud of dust and I'll be so fucking happy for you.

Some parting words of advice before you set forth upon your noble voyage. I said there are no rules – but I lied. There is, in fact, one rule and it's a biggie. I'll let our bro, Charles Darwin, explain:

It is not the strongest of the species that survives, nor the most intelligent; it is the one most adaptable to change.

That's right, he never said anything about stomping on your neighbours to get ahead, but did say a whole lot about the one thing you can guarantee in this life – change, constant change. In fact, by the time you read this, all our music will likely be made by robots and performed by holograms, so this will all be irrelevant anyway. But it'll still prove the point – that if there's one thing you absolutely *must* be able to do out there in the wild, it's adapt. Adapt to the never-ending torrent of new models, new platforms, new challenges and new threats – for it will be the one and only thing you can definitely guarantee. And it will be the death of most.

So be bold and be brave, fellow missionary. Challenges will be many, and rewards will be few. But it has never been easier in the history of the planet to record, release, distribute, promote and monetise your music – so please don't wait for anyone else. Get to it and shake the whole world off its axis. It's going to take its toll on your relationships, your mental health and your morale, so make sure you're there for each other, and you're there for yourself. Check in on your troops, and make sure you always remember why you're doing this: because once upon a time, you loved music with every fibre of your existence and wanted nothing more than to play it in a band with your mates. You're now doing just that, so when the going gets tough, remember what's *really* important. You've got this and I wish you all the success and good times in the world. Now go and fuck shit up.

OR SKIP ALL OF THE ABOVE AND JUST DO THIS INSTEAD

Knock out dumpster-loads of short-form, low-rent, disposable, gimmicky, forgettable and ultimately pointless bits of content and shamelessly flood the internet with them until one of them goes viral. Then you can buy a mansion, get cocky, lose everything and start again. But who really wants to be *that* dude? Not you – you're a musician. An artist. Wear it with the pride it deserves, do the work and own your battle scars. Don't be part of the plague that's turning our cultural life into a landfill; be the guerilla rebel who's making it awesome. Please. Please, do that.

X X X

Now for some popular questions...

Q&A

AM I TOO OLD?

Well, that depends on you. Lemmy was still kicking ass better than most right through into his late sixties, yet I know twenty-two-year-olds who wouldn't last three days in a van. The rules of engagement for this life are what they are, and if you're able to deliver the goods consistently without being an old, needy pain in everyone else's arse, then no, age doesn't matter one bit. We are now entering a time where the creepy obsession with youth is becoming a thing of the past – and good riddance. Whoever decided that the fountain of all creative genius and wise poetic insight was exclusive to twenty-one-year-olds was clearly a pervy old weirdo with an age complex. Thankfully, that old guard are all dying out and we're living in much more enlightened times. So get out there and show these kids how it's done.

DO I HAVE TO GO TO MUSIC COLLEGE?

No! Your best university is out there, doing it – and that campus won't leave you shackled in mountains of debt for the next thirty years. I've got nothing against music colleges; I went to one myself (which I loved) and dropped out of another (which I hated) – and there are some truly excellent courses out there run by some truly excellent and earnest people. But is it essential? Absolutely not. And if you're doing it thinking that anyone, anywhere will hire you for *any* kind of job because you've got a qualification in music, you're deluded. Neither will it give you the upper hand in joining bands, getting an internship at a studio or getting a record deal. If you've got the money to burn, then do it for the networking. If not, then the University of Hustlers' doors are always open.

ARE ALL LABELS BAD?

Well, it's a spectrum. A spectrum of evil, if you will. On the one end there's the flat-out, no-fuck-giving, loud-and-proud, artist-devouring major-label machines who will bleed you dry, thrash your physical and mental well-being beyond anything remotely humane, steal your creations, steal your money and spit you out to die hungry, never to answer your calls again. And on the other end are the bad guys. I joke. On the other end are the true heroes of the label game – the independents. There are some absolute trojans out there who do so much good for the scene, working inhuman hours with a heart full of passion, experience, talent and a genuine, selfless love for the art form. But my God, they're rare. And they'll still take the lion's share of any money you make and you won't be their only meal ticket. You'll still be subject to their deadlines, their release schedules, their budget, their priorities (which won't always be you), their decisions and their mistakes, and they can still decide to drop you at any time. And trust me, that end of the pond is also rife with scores of bad actors who will steal your money and royally shag your career up for good. Take my word for it; I've had the pleasure of 'working' with many of them. So, as I've already outlined here, the safer route is to do everything (and I mean, everything) for yourselves for as long as possible. And then when the big dogs come a-sniffing, they will have to bend to *your* demands, not the other way around. Oh, and any label that asks you for money (for anything!) – regardless of how nice they are, how much they pretend to love your music and how much they promise you – avoid, avoid, avoid. And report them. Then 'out' them online. And then tell me and I'll give them a whole chapter in the next book, the scene-trashing motherfuckers.

SHOULD I QUIT MY DAY JOB?

Hell no! Look, I've tried to be as mercilessly honest with you about the true reality that awaits you in this industry – and I wasn't doing it for dramatic effect. Be *very* wary of those who will tell you to 'throw everything into plan A and don't waste any time on a plan B'. That's kamikaze talk. I guarantee you without a shadow of doubt that whoever tells you that will either have never tried it themselves or is one of the aforementioned major-label lucky bastards, i.e. someone who got stratospherically lucky straight out of the gates and landed the golden ticket to heaven without any real time spent under enemy fire. In both cases, they'll be talking from a position of complete ignorance about how things are actually going to play out for 99 per cent of you. It sounds great, but it's bollocks. Ignore them. They won't be suffering the results of their clueless advice; you will – and they'll be just fine. There's no easy route to nirvana, and its path is strewn with the carcasses of the millions who have fallen before you. And, in the meantime, you have a life to live and food to eat. So do *not* quit that day job, my friend.

DO I NEED TO MOVE TO THE CITY?

No. But it'll help. I mean, sure, there are plenty of humongous, iconic artists who hailed from backwater dung-holes in the arse-end of swampville, but there are zero reputable record labels that have done the same. Nor agencies worth their salt, nor managers or distributors. Unfortunately, whether you relocate or do a whole lotta Megabussing, the city is where the industry is. Now, don't get me wrong – I know countless people who have moved to the city in the hope of 'making it' and the only thing they ended up making was burgers at Burger Jerk. The city can be a ruthless, cruel butcher of dreams, but like it or not, it's where the action is, and if you want a piece of that action, your hometown is likely to be doing you a deadly disservice. All of the big opportunities, production houses, labels, movers and shakers – they're based in the city. Do you need to actually *live* there? Absolutely not. But it'll help.

DO I NEED A MANAGER AND A BOOKING AGENT?

Nope and neither do you need a stylist, caterer or someone to carry your guitar for you. Managers, agents and all the rest will make themselves known to you when the time is right. Until then, just get out there, do your thing, do it well and do it local. A good manager and a good booking agent are worth their weight in platinum and can open many locked doors for you – but chasing them just distracts from the main mission, which is to build your tribe. Focus on that and the rest will follow. You've got everything you need already – so get out there and don't take any fucking prisoners.

10.

TOP TEN

A person's music collection is a window into their soul. When visiting someone's home for the first time, I will immediately seek out the record collection. Then the books. It's my version of a dog sniffing their behind – I'm sussing them out. Within minutes I can detect whether my fellow canine is a misfit, a heavy thinker, a dreamer, a stoner or is entirely bereft of any cultural or philosophical capacity. I can tell straight away if they're likely to be 'my kind of dude'. I'm not saying we have to like the same music – and if it's mostly stuff there that I've never heard of, then even better – but if all they own is *The Best of Phil Collins*, then I know it's going to be a long, long night. And the worst-case scenario is being held socially captive at the home of someone who has *no* record or book collection at all – a frankly unpardonable sin.

This endeavour has been made somewhat more difficult in the digital age, wherein a person's entire cultural and intellectual identity is now hidden away inside their phone – their bare bookshelves now a display for plastic plants, a rare printed photo and the occasional travel book. And I get it. Why have a load of dusty old plastic discs filling up the place when you can have all the music in the known universe sat neatly inside your pocket? But for me, having the physical album isn't *just* because I'm old – it's for the reasons I outlined above. The albums I love are my identity; they're an extension of me; they're my history; they made me who I am; they define the gang that I represent – and I want the physical thing. The physical album makes it real, not some disposable sound in the ether. The physical album is a monument to artistic genius, a memento of heartbreaks and good times past, a moment in time – a time when things felt a little more 'real'. And the act of playing that record is a ritual, something that requires a little effort on our part, a little participation in the process.

It's a beautiful thing. Especially if you're going to listen to that bad boy through actual speakers and not some tiny tinny headphones that butcher the bass and massacre the mix. A physical manifestation of an artist's work in your hands, relished out loud through the airwaves, the way it was always intended. The change in our society's focus from the communal to the individual is perfectly revealed in our music listening habits. We've gone from the shared, social experience of blasting good tunes through speakers to the solitary experience of a personal playlist piped directly into one's ears as they sit oblivious to the other equally atomised animals around them.

Well, tonight we're going old school and sharing a listen together. We're dusting off the vinyl, kicking back with a bourbon, with the speakers up and the phones turned off, doing it like we did it in the nineties – the whole album, from start to finish. Now, I think it's fair to say that one of the hardest questions ever posed by humanity is: 'What are your top ten albums?' I have pondered this eternal paradox for decades and I can never settle on the same answer twice – there is simply too much great music, dammit! So for our purposes here, I've had to make some devastating decisions. Out of all of the many incredible albums that have touched and moulded my life, I have opted to choose a small selection that are good representatives of all the others that couldn't fit into a grossly unfair top ten. Hell, I could fill at least five spots with Pink Floyd but then there'd be no room for the twelve Zappa records that have to go in! Compiling this has been a headfuck for sure. Compromises have been made, corners cut, losses swallowed and timeless classics tossed asunder (hence the honourable mentions later on).

So, if music is the window to one's soul, then I am hereby welcoming you to take a snoop around my festering edifice, but please don't touch anything – it might be contagious. These are the albums that have made me who I am. That have defined my life and my music. The albums that I always come back to and I know that I always will. The albums made by artists that I could never thank enough for the life-affirming friendship, guidance, inspiration and good times that these masterpieces have given me. As you will see, I have been sculpted by the hands of the expressionists, the rebels, the dreamers and the punks. They say you never forget your first love – well, here are ten of mine. There is no way that I could ever put these in any kind of order or hierarchy, for they are all equally perfect to me. So while this list may be a top ten of sorts, it is not in any order of preference – come on, man, that's just impossible. Ok, let's get the tunes on.

JEFF BUCKLEY – *GRACE*

Pure, divine beauty from start to finish. This album speaks to a primal spirit deep within me and connects me to the eternal. Delicate, haunting, visceral, spiritual, transcendent – there is *nothing* like it. This album had a profound effect on me as a teenager hearing it for the first time and it has been a mainstay of my life ever since. You can hear its influence in my music, my singing, my guitar tones, and I am still as fascinated and transfixed by this extraordinary masterwork as the first time those ghostly falsettos gently crept into my ears.

I still remember my first time. It was one of a bunch of CDs that I stole from a music store when I was a student too poor to afford the grotesque asking price of the times. I didn't know who this Jeff Buckley bloke was, but it was a wild-card steal among my other more solid lootings of Rage Against the Machine and Smashing Pumpkins. Back at my mate's parents' house, we surveyed our treasures and opted to start with this one. By the time it finished, neither of us had spoken a word – we just sat there with our mouths open, changed forever. The album quickly became an obsession. I'd never heard anything like it. Music at that time was mostly smothered in fuzzy guitars with everything cranked to eleven (which I loved, of course) – but here was an album by a *new* artist that had dramatic dynamics, pristine clean guitars, beautifully eerie music... and that voice. What can one even say about the voice of Jeff Buckley? Heavenly? Paranormal? Sublime? There are no words. But Jeff's focus on vocal expression, impeccable layering, wild gymnastics and raw passion were like nothing else at the time and inspired generations of singers who followed him, still to this day. Sadly, following Jeff's accidental death not long after, this album stands as his one and only commercial release – something that makes it even more special. As if Jeff were sent here by God to deliver this gift to humanity and then promptly return back to the heavenly choir from whence he came. It is perfection. The music, the production, the performances, the musicianship – everything. It is simply a masterpiece. And I have it on vinyl.

RADIOHEAD – *OK COMPUTER*

A game-changer. For me, for guitar music and for Radiohead. This is the band's finest moment. The sizzling sweet spot bridging the songwriting prowess of their previous albums and the experimental anarchy to follow. Hearing this album was like falling head first into a Pandora's box of limitless possibility as to what could be done with a rock band, a rock song and, most certainly, with a guitar. Overnight I went from practising my speed-shredding to exploring modulated delay pedals and dissonant guitar chords. For me, this was a guitar band at the height of their creative powers. I'd just never heard guitars do this stuff before. Not a flashy solo in sight, but the creative layering of clean sounds, spaceman atmospherics and sonic wizardry opened up a world of wonder for me that I just hadn't heard in any of the heavier music I was into at the time. The guitar work throughout this album is revolutionary, but so is the production – filtered drums, robot voices, ethereal keys, musique concrète, percussion, strings, a fucking choir! And which other rock band in the nineties had a hit single with a song that was slow, fragile, painfully beautiful and whose main riff was played on a glockenspiel? Not to mention the flawless streak of songs, viscerally inventive musicianship and Thom Yorke's vocals on top form, wailing about alienation, politics and existentialism. Still, to this day, lying back and letting this album wash over me is like being teleported into space – a strange, dystopian space. As a young musician developing my own musical identity, *OK Computer* smashed every notion of what was allowed in rock music into tiny irrelevant pieces. I stand firm that it's the band's finest work and one of the defining albums of the genre. Did I mention the guitar work?

FRANK ZAPPA – *WE'RE ONLY IN IT FOR THE MONEY*

And speaking of blowing musical boundaries into tiny, irrelevant pieces, no artist in the history of music has done this so consistently, so perversely or to such an extreme as Frank Zappa. Fact. Let's just get this established right away: Frank Zappa was a genius. Like, an actual genius – not the type of genius we call everyone these days whose new song we like for a week, but an actual genius. The type of genius who, in his lifetime, released over sixty albums with nearly seventy more released posthumously as of the time of writing. The type of genius who, despite this colossal output, died leaving a vast, underground, temperature-controlled vault full of thousands of tapes of EVEN MORE music. The type of genius who on several occasions released more than ten albums in one year. The type of genius whose musical output included rock, jazz, orchestral, musique concrète and a thousand piss-takes of pop, punk, disco, country, the blues and whatever else – sometimes within the same song. This unstoppable musical fearlessness was matched only by his scathing commentary on politics, society, the music industry, censorship, religion, sex and, well... pretty much everything else. Blending comedy with fierce social critique and some of the most complex musical compositions ever written, Frank Zappa is one of the most unique and fascinating figures in modern music.

So, with such a prolific catalogue, why this album? Because it sums up the spirit of everything I love about Frank. It's dark, it's thought-provoking, it's hilarious and it's musically fucking mind-blowing. Released in 1968, the album starts taking shots before you've even pressed play. Its original cover art was demoted to the inside sleeve by the record label for its brutal satirising of *Sgt Pepper's Lonely Hearts Club Band*, but the punches didn't stop there. Throughout the album, released within a year of the Summer of Love, Zappa delivered icy blows to hippies, middle-class America, the police, racists, politicians and other musicians – and he did so in a strange, just-sucked-a-helium-balloon type of voice throughout, because of course he did. There's jazz, there's rock, there's backwards tape, random digressions into bizarre musique concrète and parodies of country, ragtime and hippie rock. When I first heard it, it was an awakening. The prison bars of musical convention were bent open and the universe opened up wide. So there are NO rules?! I don't have to keep my love of rock or my love of electronic music separate? I can throw all of my wildly eclectic musical tastes at the wall, Jackson Pollock style – *and* slag people off at the same time? Frank showed me the way and I followed. Displaying absolutely zero regard for song structure, commercial appeal or the listener's comfort, this is not an album – this is art. Important, radical, pioneering art that held up a mirror to the society of the times while redefining what rock music could be at the same time. If only Frank Zappa were alive today.

PINK FLOYD – *THE WALL*

I'll confess, I did wrestle between this one and *The Dark Side of the Moon* – and I'm still wrestling as I write. What kind of twisted injustice is this where someone has to choose between two of the most iconic albums ever made in order to save space in a stupid fucking top ten? By now, everyone on earth knows that *Dark Side* is a perfect album. One of the best albums of all time. An example of humanity at its highest artistic potential. An album from another dimension. A transformative album. And one of the most cherished albums in my life. But I'm not here to talk about that. I'm here to talk about *The Wall.* So why have I made the choice I've made? Oh, I don't know, perhaps it's just songs like 'Mother', 'Nobody Home', 'Another Brick in the Wall', 'One of My Turns', 'The Trial' and 'Comfortably Numb'. Do you see my point? Well, I have another confession to make: Roger Waters makes me cry like a baby. Yep, it's true. As a man raised in a culture where under *no* circumstances shall a man *ever* shed a tear, the music of Roger Waters has me in a blubbering mess every time. I am powerless to it. And it's not just this album – anything from *The Final Cut* or *Amused to Death* will do it too. If you ever find me uncontrollably gushing with tears, shaking, snotty, inconsolable, that'll just be me listening to Roger Waters. Good tears though. The ones that need to come out sometimes. I don't know what it is, but there is something in this music that just drop-kicks me in the heart every single time. Is it the drama? The raw emotional intensity?

The words that speak to the human struggles within all of us? The honesty of the performance? It's all of it – delivered through the medium of some of the best songwriting ever to grace the earth.

It is physically impossible to listen to this historic work, about the walls we all build around ourselves throughout our lives and the evils that can fester inside them, without it panging a nerve at some point – unless your heart is made of bricks, of course. Through the music, his words and his delivery, Roger Waters hacks into the innocent purity that still lays within us and sets it free like a religious rebirth. And *The Wall* shows the man at the pinnacle of his powers. Waters's lyrical wordplay is at its finest throughout as he explores the journey from good to evil through the invisible steps we all take in life, while also critiquing war, education, fascism, love, parenting, society, celebrity and more. It's a wild ride for sure, and whole books have been written on this album so I won't labour the point, but there are a million reasons why *The Wall* is rightly considered to be one of the greatest albums ever made. As you'd expect, Dave Gilmour's guitar work throughout is exceptional, tasteful, innovative, and some of his most iconic guitar solos can be found here on tracks like 'Mother' and the legendary 'Comfortably Numb'. I could talk about *The Wall* all day – and I will, if allowed – but given that practically everyone on Earth already knows this magnum opus well, I'll bow out now. I love this album deeply and, yes, I still cry like a baby when I hear it.

WHITE NOISE – *AN ELECTRIC STORM*

Ready to get weird? Chances are you haven't heard this album. You probably haven't even heard *of* this album. And you wouldn't be alone, as this rare, difficult and very niche work of evil genius was a complete commercial failure and promptly disappeared out of circulation not long after its release. It is, however, rightly hailed as a classic among insiders and had a profound influence on electronic music. Whether you've heard of her or not, you all know the work of Delia Derbyshire, for she was the co-creator of the original *Doctor Who* theme music in all of its spacey, theremin-popularising glory. She is a superstar of early electronic music. White Noise was a one-off project between Delia, David Vorhaus and several other musicians, with *An Electric Storm* being their only release together in 1969. Produced just prior to the arrival of synthesisers, every single musical sound on this crazy album was produced by the manipulation of recorded tape. Old-school style. No computers here. With a gazillion tape cuts – literally cutting bits of tape by hand with a razor and splicing them together to create new sequences of sounds – or by speeding up a bass to sound like a violin, slowing down a drum cymbal to make an unsettling whooshing noise or by loading the tape backwards to create bizarre, otherworldly sounds until then unheard of, the painstaking technical wizardry on display here still beggars belief to this day. The musicians of this album are tin cans, car beeps, bouncing balls and an array of random household sounds, bangs, crashes and wallops.

Sounds like fun, right? Well, then what *does* the album sound like? Like being stranded in a deranged hellscape of depraved ghosts and impending madness. In the best way possible. In short, it's dark. So dark that I can't really 'go there' any more after way too many times of being, shall we say, chemically assisted while having this satanic symphony piped into my poor, defenceless brain. It's like the soundtrack to a nightmare that's so good you just can't turn it off, despite it being deeply unsettling. Twisted, brooding soundscapes; maniacal, blipping bouncing noises; menacing textures of ever-looming torment; demonic howls; crying; an orgy! And those creepy fucking singers, too – even the melodies are demented! And that's why you have to hear it. Ideally through headphones. There's nothing like it, and if you make it to the end, it'll be an experience you'll never forget, no matter how hard you try. It will leave its demonic imprint on you forever. Anyone who has heard my album *9.i.P* will see the influence of this stunningly horrific work of art woven all through it. It's an alien of an album. It came from the future to blow our heads wide open and then disappeared. With its handmade technical prowess of an era long gone and eerie music that could never have been made any other way, it stands alone – there is nothing else like it. And I like that.

ICE-T – *HOME INVASION*

I was thirteen years old when this one hit the streets. I say 'streets' not to sound gangster but because nobody I knew actually owned an original copy from an actual shop. You see, albums like this weren't borrowed from your dad's record collection; they were smuggled between friends on home-copied cassettes and listened to in secret while keeping a paranoid eye out for parents and teachers. Because if the elders ever caught you listening to this album, especially at my age, the tape would have been spooled out, cut into bits and set on fire. Although not by my parents. My parents were so rock 'n' roll, they even took me to see the controversial rapper live and gleefully sang along to 'Cop Killer' while me and my brother quietly died inside. But still, I felt pretty damn naughty listening to this late at night through headphones and chuckling at the non-stop torrent of fucks, motherfuckers and more motherfuckers. And that was just the intro. In a legendary response to the newly enacted stickering of certain albums with parental warnings, Ice went one further in service of the cause and added a spoken word intro to the album, wherein he warned the listener that there would be much swearing forthcoming. He then shouted every swear word imaginable out as a helpful little example of what was to follow. To us, it was like crack. We couldn't get enough of it and we shared that cassette around like we were trafficking class As. I once gave it to our school bus driver who, in a decent effort to be cool with us kids, agreed to play it and cranked it up. After thirty seconds the tape was out, the driver was pissed off and I'd become a village icon.

But teenage daftness aside, this is a serious album. And at the time, a dangerous album by a dangerous artist – back when there *were* such things as dangerous albums and dangerous artists. The album came out hot on the heels of the infamous 'Cop Killer' by Ice-T's other project, the rap/metal band Body Count – a song that even the president was publicly involved in squashing. And the subsequent issues with the record label and censorship led Ice to set up his own label and release *Home Invasion* independently. This meant he was now free to say whatever the hell he wanted, and boy, did he go for it. Dropping as many truth-bombs as he did F-bombs (and that's a LOT), Ice takes no prisoners when tackling the media, the police, the music industry, racism, gangs, drugs and deploring us all to stop fighting among ourselves, realise we're being played and unite against our common enemy – the government and the powers that be. No one got away unscathed from Ice's hyperreal take-down of everything that was fake, fraudulent and fucked. For thirteen-year-old me, it was an education. It was a pep talk from Uncle Ice, a blueprint for independence and an example of what to do when power tries to shut you down – you come back even harder. I love it for being independent, when he could have stayed with a major label, taken the money and toed the line. I love it for coming back guns a-blazing when he could easily have retreated after all of the controversy and attempts at silencing him from the music labels, the radio stations, the retailers and the government. This album is defiance on disc. Intelligent, wise, compassionate and ruthless in delivering the harsh truths that society so badly needed to hear. I think we could with a bit more of that about now. Don't you?

QUEEN – *A NIGHT AT THE OPERA*

I mean, do I even have to say anything? 'Bohemian Rhapsody' is on this fucking thing! If ever there was a band who knew exactly who they were and were completely unapologetic in being exactly that, it was Queen. And thank God. Ah, Queen, the only royalty I recognise or will ever raise a glass to. Picking just one album by the monarchy of rock is impossible, and I was tempted to cop out entirely and go with *Greatest Hits* (the first one, obviously), but that ain't the rules of the game, kiddo. Such an incredible band, so many incredible songs, so many incredible albums – so why this one? For me, this is their crowning moment. Ok, yes, 'Bohemian Rhapsody' will always be the star of the show here, but let us not overlook the brilliant 'Death on Two Legs', 'You're My Best Friend' and, of course, the stunning 'Love of My Life'. Classics, man! Queen were such an eclectic and versatile band that it's impossible to truly describe their sound in any way other than... well, it's Queen! And this album has got all of the quintessential Queen-isms that we all know and love – master-craftsman songwriting, thousands of pitch-perfect vocal layers, a flurry of different musical genres from opera to jazz, rock, country and musical theatre. It's camp, it's heavy, it flexes the full muscle of their musicianship and, most importantly, it's damn good fun.

Listening to bands like Queen growing up instilled in me the notion that it was perfectly ok to have songs in radically different genres to each other throughout an album. That it was totally acceptable to explore your love of classical music right in the middle of a rock record if you wanted to. That smothering your songs in a Queenzillion overdubs was fair game if it sounded good. While I have always been drawn to the power of rock music and the attitude of punk, I've also found both to be too tightly limited in what is acceptable within the genre. Like, if you added some Radiohead-esque guitar atmospheres to a metal track, it wasn't really *metal* any more; it was something else. Metal and punk were guitar, bass, drums and vocals – and that was it! Anything more and you were being pretentious. Queen didn't give a shit about that and so neither did I. This was a band that would play songs like 'Stone Cold Crazy' and 'Don't Stop Me Now' in the same show. At once both completely over the top, flamboyant and indulgent, but also understated and tastefully restrained. I mean, the band's musicianship is insane, but it all sounds so musical, so effortless, so tasteful, so fun and so inimitably cool. And they achieved that rare status chased by so many artists: respect among their peers *and* enormous global success. With tongue always planted firmly in cheek, Queen were fearless, unbound by genre and completely at ease with who they were as a band. The fact that they are as relevant today as they always were is testament to the longevity in sincerity – and writing epic, epic songs. Copious amounts of all of the above are found on the brilliant *A Night at the Opera*. God save Queen.

NIRVANA – *IN UTERO*

Surely you saw this one coming! Don't let my baby face fool you; I was actually *alive* when Nirvana were doing their thing, and if you remember that time too, then you know what lucky bastards we are. For any Gen Zedders who might be wondering, yes, for a teenager, the nineties was a good a time to be alive – especially if you liked music. This was the golden era when MTV actually played music videos and then hit you with some *Beavis and Butthead*. That was our regular daytime TV, man! There was no Spotify, no Apple – hell, there was no internet! There was vastly more time to spend properly digesting much fewer things, so we got to get *really* into a handful of bands. I'm so glad I got to witness that last hurrah of the old music industry before it all got complicated – and to witness it as a music-loving teenager was a priceless privilege. The grunge era, landing as it did, just as I entered my formative teenage years, really was a gift from the gods. The ridiculous hair rock of the late eighties was hard to take seriously, and endless songs about whisky, strippers, being a bad boy in lipstick and the adventures of one's penis didn't really do it for me. Bungees, spandex, pyros and make-up were all preposterous to me and I continued to gravitate towards the grittier and much more authentic punk and hard rock of the seventies, though it was all before my time. And then grunge came along and put a rusty bullet in the head of all the pretty-boy poser bands and ignited a musical revolution the world desperately needed. We were back to focusing less on daft acrobatics and more on great songwriting and lyrics that meant something, with an updated seventies aesthetic.

Grunge spoke to me. It was real. It was grimy. It was the long-lost bastard son of punk. It was needed. These guys were broke. They wore dirty, ripped jeans and cardigans with holes in them. They played second-hand guitars and stamped on crappy, cheapo guitar pedals with dirty Converse high-tops. They were depressed. And teenage me loved all of that. Grunge was the soundtrack to my teens, and it's always *those* bands that stay with you forever. Soundgarden, Pearl Jam, Stone Temple Pilots, Alice in Chains, Smashing Pumpkins and the biggest band on the planet... Nirvana. What a time to be alive. In many ways, I could have chosen records by any of those bands to be in this place because I worshipped all of them, but I guess *In Utero* is a solid representation of everything I loved about that period. So, speaking here on behalf of all of grunge, I give this spot to *In Utero* by the eternally explosive Nirvana.

But why not the classic? Why not *Nevermind*? I feel enough has already been written about that timeless monument of a generation – and rightly so – but I always preferred *In Utero* and feel that it was unfairly overshadowed by its older, cooler brother. It's grittier, darker, more visceral and rougher around the edges. It's a band aggressively reclaiming their grunginess after accidentally becoming the darlings of the music world. And this brittle, angry, fuzz-smothered scream of a band lashing out at their own success couldn't have been captured by a more perfect person behind the glass. The production on this beast is ginormous and there are no frills, no fancy studio tricks, no gloss, no smokescreen – just Nirvana sounding like the best version of Nirvana. That drum sound feels like it was crafted with God's own hands – because it was. The music world lost an irreplaceable force with the recent passing of pioneering producer, musician and all-round badass, Steve Albini – a true rock 'n' roll superhero. A man whose uncompromising dedication to raw authenticity and artistic integrity has few equals – and, for me, this album is one of his finest moments. Walls of feedback burst out of the cracks between spiky guitars, pained vocals and thunderous drums as the album charges through banger after perfect banger – 'Heart-Shaped Box', 'Rape Me', 'Pennyroyal Tea', 'Tourette's', 'All Apologies' – songs that spoke to a generation. Masterful songwriting, noise, chaos, beauty, truth and a 100 per cent rawness of delivery – the album crystallises a moment in history. A time when shit was still real. Rest in power, Mr Albini, sir – I hope you're giving them hell up there!

When I began making my own recordings ten years later, it was this album that guided me. Despite my lean towards the avant-garde, electronic elements and 'clever music', when it came to making a record, *this* was the inspiration for the overall aesthetic. I failed drastically, but irrespective of the complex and heavily layered music I was making on my first few albums, I always wanted it to sound like a band in a room doing its thing, sans bullshit. Warts 'n' all. I wanted to hear the click of the fuzz pedal. I wanted to hear the bathroom reverb. Real and raw. Just like *In Utero*. This was my road map. I'm so glad that it was grunge that was the sound of my youth and not Def fucking Leppard – and seeing teenagers today wearing mass-market Nirvana T-shirts from high-street chain stores doesn't induce cynical, middle-aged eye-rolling in me; I think it's pretty bloody awesome. They're keeping that precious era alive, and in the age of Insta filters, music streaming and AI, having a bit of filthy, old-school grunge in your life is a beautiful and important thing.

THE CLASH – *LONDON CALLING*

Whenever one chooses this album for a top ten, people will always say two things. First, they'll throw their head back in orgasmic bliss before wailing 'awww, CHOICE!' – and then immediately follow it with the question... 'But what's wrong with *Never Mind the Bollocks*?' To which the answer is, 'Nothing, absolutely nothing.' In any throwdown between the titans of punk, it will always eventually come down to a tussle between these two. And for good reason. So having to choose one over the other is a very rough predicament to be in, but choose I must. So let me place my flag down right away – I'm more of a Clash guy. Calm down, calm down – I LOVE *Never Mind the Bollocks* and I LOVE the Pistols. How can any self-respecting adult not?! But punk is a broad church, and if I have to pick a pew in it somewhere, I'm gonna sit with Strummer. Which always leads to more and more questions, inevitably settling at the biggie: what is punk?

Is punk Johnny Rotten spitting anarchic venom at the Queen and EMI? Yes. Is punk Mick Jones gently reflecting on alienation and consumerism over clean guitars and melodic bass? Also yes. It seems the two are not of the same seed. But they are. For punk is not a narrow style of music; punk is not a fashion, a hairstyle, safety pins or gobbing on each other – punk is an attitude. Punk is an ethos, an outlook, a general spirit. You can *be* punk and still look like an accountant. Punk is either in your heart and in your blood or it's not – no hairstyle can change that. So for The Clash to cast aside the shackles of a sound and throw reggae, dub, rockabilly and pop into punk's seething cauldron – that was a punk move. Eschewing the expectations of what punks think is punk – that was a punk move. That's the point about punk – you're not supposed to give two shits about what people think, even punks. So when The Clash came out with this total curveball of a double album, lobbing a Molotov cocktail of fresh new sounds into the mix, it set a new dawn for punk. Pianos, brass, keyboards and percussion were hardly standard fare in punk until this mammoth of an album came along. It was the Big Bang that would ignite punk's evolution and ongoing longevity. It also kicked open the doors for the rest of society to join forces within its graffitied walls. Now the genre was no longer just the bullhorn of angry white youth, but the venting ground for everyone else.

With songs like 'London Calling', 'Spanish Bombs', 'Hateful', 'The Guns of Brixton', 'Lost in the Supermarket' and 'Clampdown', The Clash tackled corruption, hypocrisy, war, drugs, the police, poverty, consumerism and apathy with uncompromising, sharp, intelligent flair. In a genre notorious for just gobbing off at the world, The Clash were smart. Joe Strummer's wordplay through the album is a masterclass in saying a lot without saying too much, and his words are just as relevant today as they were in 1979 – which should worry us all. And they *looked* so goddamn cool too. Everyone could take a spray can to an old T-shirt, scrawl slogans across the front of it and instantly be like The Clash. They had it all – the music, the look, the message.

For me, they epitomise the punk spirit. Rebellious, fearless, inventive, dangerous – they spoke for the underdog and stuck it to the man. And they did it with swagger, style and great fucking tunes. Long live The Clash – and we haven't even *mentioned* the album cover...

RAGE AGAINST THE MACHINE – *RAGE AGAINST THE MACHINE*

Chunky riffs. Pummelling drums. Bowel-rattling bass. Politics. Hard rock. AND HIP HOP? Yes please and supersize me. As with Ice-T's *Home Invasion*, my first exposure to this game-changing album came in the form of a home-copied cassette handed to me discreetly by a friend in hushed tones and paranoid looks over the shoulder. Listen to it through headphones, he said, before disappearing into the shadows. I was thirteen. At that time I lived in a tiny, secluded village in the middle of 'where the fuck is everything?' No shops, no post office, no nothing except fields and more fields. As I did my daily hour-long trek through some of those fields in order to meet my mates at the neighbouring village that *did* have a shop, I popped the tape into my Walkman – yes, I said Walkman. Long story short, I never made it to the next village. After stopping dead in my tracks to stand dumbstruck in a cow field for ten minutes as 'Killing in the Name' played out, I knew this was urgent business that needed my full attention, so I laid down in the grass and listened to the whole album from start to finish – and then did it again. With cows gently chomping around me and the milky Welsh clouds mutating above, my inner world was in the chaos of a violent revolution. I had never heard *anything* like it. Now, it's heartening to see that RATM are still relevant and much loved by the youth of today, but at the time it came out, this album was a carpet-bombing that reshaped the terrain forever. The unapologetic smashing of hard rock, funk, punk and hip hop, laced with overt political messaging and revolutionary zeal, was unlike anything I'd ever experienced, and it gave me goosebumps to the core. And of course, there was the swearing. Zack de la Rocha screaming 'Fuck you, I won't do what you tell me' sixteen times in a row and then following it with a 'Motherfuckeeeeeer' was the best thing I had ever heard in my thirteen years on Earth. I felt like I was in the possession of some illicit cargo, and that as soon as parents, teachers or the government found out that I had this subversive weapon in my possession, that'd be my arse. But I did my duty to further the cause and secretly made copies to distribute among my friends. Most guys my age were doing this with grainy VHS tapes of crappy old pornos, but I felt that what I had was far more explosive and punishable.

For a young guitar shredder diligently practising my scales, what Tom Morello was doing on his six-string was pure black magic. Brilliantly hip-hopifying his guitar parts with insane sample-isms, whammy pedal madness and distorted deck-scratches was truly pioneering and became the subject of fevered debate among my friends – how the hell is he *doing* that?! Add a rhythm section that could knock down houses, throw in some rap, funk and rock, a large dose of anger and the use of repetitive, rebel-rousing political chanting, and they achieved what most do not – a sound that was unreplicable. Even if you don't know the song, you know immediately which band you're listening to. They made politics cool. They gave a voice to the frustration I was carrying. They came with a sound that was both fresh and irresistible. They informed, they inspired and they mobilised. There was no one who didn't love them – rockers, metallers, hip-hoppers, punks – and no one could deny their musical authenticity and delicious subversiveness. The band were radical – politically, musically, onstage and off. There was no one like them and there hasn't been since. So many songs on this album are now considered protest anthems, and they are still inspiring and igniting the rebel spirit in new generations over thirty years after its release. I don't know what happened to that original home-made cassette, but the moment of its first hearing in a cow field in Wales is burned forever into my being – it was a life-changing moment. I now own that essential piece of musical history on vinyl and it still gets my blood up every single time.

✕ ✕ ✕

When I look at this collection of albums, I guess what they've all got in common is their bravery, their fearlessness in standing alone musically and in challenging the social norms of the times or in trying to explain the universal human condition. They're emotionally honest, innovative, authentic, rebellious, eclectic and unique. None of these albums sought to conform and toe the established line, and all are now considered classics and important artistic milestones. So what does that tell us? All have words that mean something, that speak truth to power, inspire the rebel spirit in us or take us closer to the eternal truth within all of us – with music that fucking rocks. These albums didn't just rock my world, provide the soundtrack to my formative years and inspire my music; they informed my world-view, my value set and my anti-conformist attitude. These albums were my education and I am an eternally grateful student.

Now, of course, singling it down to just ten albums is an impossibly unfair endeavour. Unfair on me and unfair on all those other artists who had a monumental impact on me as a fledgling musician and lyricist, so we've got to at least give a shout-out to those other legends and geniuses who broke the rules, changed the game, blew our minds and kicked our asses. Don't get me wrong; I listen to barrels of new stuff, too. But these are some of the other artists I was immersed in as a kid and as a young musician soaking up a world of influences while my brain was still squidgy and spongy. You will find all of these on my record shelves, and all of them have in some way or other influenced my musicianship, my songwriting, my artistic aesthetic, my lyrics, my arrangements and my general attitude towards music-making and life. So if you were wondering who to blame for all of that, then here goes...

Prince, Portishead, Squarepusher, The Wildhearts, Björk, Kate Bush, Melt Banana, Massive Attack, Stone Temple Pilots, Miles Davis, Public Enemy, Eric Satie, Steve Vai, Soundgarden, Stravinsky, Allan Holdsworth, Parliament, Sex Pistols, the Bulgarian State Television Female Vocal Choir, John Coltrane, Stevie Wonder, Sepultura, Django Reinhardt, Jimi Hendrix, Debussy, Jay-Z, Stan Getz, Pantera, Ennio Morricone, David Bowie, Eric Dolphy, Immortal Technique, Dave Brubeck, Smashing Pumpkins, the Beatles, The Prodigy, James Brown, Suede, NWA, Ravel, Ivo Papazov, Bob Marley, Sparks, Charles Mingus, BB King, The Beach

Boys, Michael Jackson, Alice in Chains, Pat Martino, Led Zeppelin, György Ligeti, Manic Street Preachers, Tod Dockstader, Stevie Ray Vaughan, The Doors, Bob Dylan, Aretha Franklin, Iannis Xenakis, Talking Heads… you get the picture.

So now that you've perused my record collection and taken a good whiff of my canine posterior, what are ya saying? Could we hang?

11.

THE TRIBE

Fan: *an enthusiastic follower, admirer or devotee of a sport, artist, pastime, etc.*

Sounds a bit limp, doesn't it? Hardly sums up how I feel about Pink Floyd. I am no mere 'admirer' of the artists I love – I am a religious disciple, a foot soldier, a cult member entranced in reverence and awe, ready to die for the cause. To me, my favourite artists are no mere mortals but demigods possessing ancient powers of awesomeness, sent to deliver us all from evil and live forever in the hearts and minds of millions. And yet, even though the word derives from 'fanatic', I've always been conflicted over the term 'fan'. As an artist, it just doesn't fully encapsulate or give due props to everything that a 'fan' means to us. The word is shamefully inadequate. Fans are the people who voluntarily support, encourage and enable us to do the thing we love the most. They don't have to. There's plenty of other things they could spend their time, passion and money on rather than helping us live as some kind of gothic Peter Pan all our lives. They're fucking heroes, really. Angels. I think of my fanbase more as a community of friends, comrades, an extended family. And I feel woefully disrespectful addressing them as fans. But then I'm also a 'fan', so I get it. I'm happy, in fact, *proud* to be a 'fan' of the artists I love. I get that that's the word we use, so let's just run with it. But the blanket term is misleading, however, for there is, as with most things, a broad variety of species throughout the fan kingdom, with many overlaps and blurred lines between them. Allow me to explain.

At the top of the pyramid you've got the super-fans. Every band knows who these legends are. They'll be at every show – and they'll be at the front, with a banner. They'll travel around the world to be there. They'll be the first to buy your new merch the second it's out and they'll buy it all again when the deluxe hardly-any-different-to-the-last-version-but-hey-it's-got-a-different-colour-disc reissue comes out for twice the price. They know all the words, the back stories, the personal lives, the names of your pets, and will bring handmade gifts to your shows, sit on the pavement for hours to see you, have you tattooed on their body and support you no matter what heinous crime you have been found guilty of.

And God bless 'em. Until they turn psycho. You see, 99 per cent of these dudes are absolutely incredible. The literal lifeline that keeps bands doing their thing, keeps morale high and brings the fun, the love, the special memories and the deep mutual connection that lasts a lifetime. But then there's that 1 per cent. One wrong move with this lot, one unreplied message, one email missed, one minute longer spent talking to some other 'bitch' than them – and you're toast. Plus they know where you live, of course. And so a once beautiful and fun relationship can rapidly descend into darkness. Stalking, abuse, hate campaigns, physical violence, spreading the type of lies that can not only kill your career but put you behind bars, suicide and even murder – nothing is off limits to a super-fan scorned.

But lunatics aside, super-fans sit proudly at the top of the fan hierarchy, and please do not under-estimate how much we love you guys. We see you, I promise. Hot on their heels are 'the fans'.

This majority group is where most of the rest of the fan kingdom reside – and it's a broad church. Ranging from 'kinda liking that one song you did', to 'I'll see you live if you play in my town but I ain't catching a bus for you', right up to 'actively following everything you do and supporting as much as possible but never to the point of wanting to bludgeon your girlfriend because hidden messages in your lyrics told me to'. I guess this is the group most people think of when they think of 'fans'. And artists need as many of these troopers as possible, but they've got to work to keep them. It's a two-way street. A level-one fan (that is, at the top of the fan pyramid bordering on super-fan) can easily slide down to a level-five fan (at the murky bottom of the pile bordering on hater) if you release that divisive curveball album, start talking about politics or go away for too long. And I know because I've still not forgiven Radiohead for *Kid A*. These guys keep you on your toes. They keep you working, they keep you growing and, if you handle things right, they'll stick by you all the way. Stop looking after them, however, and there'll always be someone else waiting in the wings ready to steal your fans. Treat them with the respect they deserve – for we are nothing without them.

Haters. Why are the haters not at the bottom of the list – and why are they on the list at all? Well, it's because haters – the real passionate ones anyway – function more like fans than they'd ever admit to. They follow all your pages online (so they can fuel their hatred of you), they engage with every single news article about you (to call you a wanker), they share your latest videos on all of their social media pages (so they can show everyone how laughable it is), they'll spend time learning to play your songs on the guitar (so they can show their friends how easy it is) and they will buy tickets to your shows (so they can stand at the front and shout 'you suck' repeatedly). I even had someone once tell me that they'd bought my entire back catalogue so they could burn it all. I can only assume that they're also reading this and, if so, I have a brand-new deluxe hardly-any-different-to-the-last-version-but-hey-it's-got-a-different-colour-disc reissue coming out soon that you're just gonna LOVE to hate. The first 100 sold come with their own matches and, yes, you can pay by card. So haters, we love you. Please continue doing the essential work of hating us so diligently and we'll keep giving you stuff to hate.

Then there's the bottom-feeders. These guys just want some free shit. And they aren't prepared to do anything in exchange for it, not even hate you. You'll be their favourite band in the world once you've given them a free T-shirt, but you will then be forever forgotten. These are the guys who'd love to come to your show tonight but don't have any money for entry, or a beer, or a ride home afterwards. Once on the guest list, they'll spend all night outside drinking *your* beers before conveniently 'missing' the last train and needing you to give them a lift home. These chode chuggers exist, believe me. I chauffeured and watered several in my early days, keen to build a fanbase, and the second the freebies stop, they're gone – soon to be seen scavenging around another band's merch stand. And while one band's bottom-feeder can indeed be another band's super-fan, your chances of converting one into *your* fan, let alone a super-fan, are a grand total of zero, so don't waste your time on these parasites and keep their grubby hands off your merch.

Finally, there is everyone else. That is, the rest of the world who don't know you and don't care. Yet!

Whichever stratum we're talking about though, the indisputable truth is that it is fans that make or break artists – not labels, not luck, not nothing, but fans. I mean, sure, luck is essential, as I've emphasised throughout this entire damn book – but luck can only bring you 'lucky breaks'; it can't sustain a career. To do that, you need fans. Lots of them. And these days, where most artists are releasing music independently and managing their own careers without the support of a record label, the role of the fan is more crucial than ever before. Most music today is not even funded by record labels; it's funded by fans – to be sold to other fans. It is fans who blow up our content online and spread the word to others. It is fans who chip in to crowdfunding campaigns, who let us sleep on their sofas, who nag radio stations to play our songs, who write reviews and blogs, who buy tickets and merch and sing their heart out from the front row. For an artist, it all begins and ends with our fans. Our fans are our label, our investors and our PR team – do not fucking disrespect them.

Too few artists truly grasp this fact, however, and too many fans still don't understand the immense power they possess, so let's run over the essentials and lay it all out. Your role as a fan can be monumentally life-changing, so what exactly can you do to help your favourite artists? Who doesn't love a checklist?

GO TO THEIR SHOWS.

This is a biggie, especially for emerging, independent artists. It's well known that artists have to have more song streams than there are stars in the known universe before they can buy a sandwich, so playing live is still how most artists eat. By supporting indie artists this way, you'll also be supporting endangered grass-roots venues and vice versa. And you'll have a far superior time than sitting in the stalls of a stadium squinting at ants. Buy a ticket, get to the front and dance your ass off. There's nothing like it in the world. And *always* watch the support bands.

BUY THEIR MERCH.

Most bands make more on their merch than they do on their music, which, let's face it, is free now – so think of it as a T-shirt tariff. The money you spend on the merch store, whether online or at a show, goes directly into the artist's fund and keeps them in food and petrol. Plus you get a super-sexy shirt to strut around in, showing basics everywhere just how profoundly cool you are.

CHIP IN TO CROWDFUNDERS.

This is how it's done now. It used to be that a label, bank or sugar daddy would pay for our recordings and we would owe them our ass for all eternity. Now, thanks to you guys, there's a better path, and it's called crowdfunding. Many people are still confused about what it is, but it's real simple. You're buying an album, or a T-shirt, or a house concert, or a video message, or whatever it is – you're simply paying for it in advance so that the artist has the funds available to make the thing in the first place. And then we owe our ass to you instead, which we're all totally fine with. Recording an album, printing merch, going on tour – it all costs a jaw-dropping amount of money that artists just don't have up front. So, by buying it in advance, you're making the whole thing possible. People still mistake crowdfunding for 'fundraising' – it is not fundraising! You are not donating money; you are buying the thing you want – just paying for it early. Got it? Awesome. Please support artist crowdfunders. Without your backing, artists simply can't afford to make your next favourite album.

FOLLOW THEM ON SOCIAL MEDIA AND ENGAGE, SHARE AND COMMENT.

This is an easy one, surely? It's just clicking buttons, man! In order to stay relevant from one nanosecond to the next in this crazy new world of hyper-speed content and miniscule attention spans, musicians these days have to be graphic designers, video makers, lighting techs, models, TV presenters and Hollywood movie directors in order to constantly flood us with throwaway content, as well as finding time to breathe and stuff. All you have to do, in exchange for all this time-intensive and ultimately pointless content that we're all addicted to, is click the freaking button. Sending a 'like', a 'comment' or a 'share' to an artist's post not only gives them some kind of validation for the effort, but more importantly, it feeds the hungry algorithm monster. The algorithm monster is a popularity junkie. It cares not for quality. It giveth no shits for art. All it wants to know is 'what's trending'. If people seem to be interested in this over here, it'll push it out to more people who might be interested over there. And on it goes. That's how things go viral. The streaming platforms work the same way. All they want to push is what's cool, what's hot RIGHT NOW, this very second – blink and it's gone! And with a user base of billions at their disposal, having the algorithm pumping in your favour is a damned handy thing. Social media and the streaming platforms have the power to launch an unknown artist onto the screens of millions – and it all starts with you pressing those buttons, man. So get sharing, get 'liking', get involved. It's so easy, you can do it in your pants while bingeing on cartoons. Get clicking.

JOIN THEIR MAILING LIST.

Despite everything I just said, social media sucks. What were once profoundly empowering platforms for artists have mostly become a wasteland of short-form pointlessness, trolls, propaganda, spam, adverts and mindless distraction. Sure, there may still be some good ones out there, but that can change at any moment – and when it does, whatever audience was built there gets lost forever. And aren't you sick of one multibillionaire or other deciding what ends up in your newsfeed? Sick of censorship by algorithm? Sick of ads? With a few exceptions, engagement rates on most of the biggest platforms are now lower than 1 per cent, meaning we're seeing hardly anything from the pages we've chosen to follow. This breeds frustration among artists who feel they could be spending their time much better than making content for no one to see. So they stop bothering, which isn't much better. What *is* much better is to join their mailing list and have them jump direct to your inbox, free from the meddling hand of evil tech villains and arseholes. Stop missing out on tour news, secret shows, new releases and selfies – join their mailing list. Join mine!

SPREAD THE WORD!

No matter how much things have changed, word of mouth is still the most powerful weapon on Earth – and it always will be. People trust their friends. I'm a thousand times more likely to check out a band if a mate bangs on about how amazing they are than if the band pops up randomly in my newsfeed when I'm trying to watch videos of monkeys breakdancing. No matter how good the song, no matter how slick the video – don't you dare interrupt the chimps, pal. So be an ambassador, an evangelist, a taste-maker, a trend-setter, a messenger of the one true message to all who will hear it – that *this* band will change the lives of all who are graced by their presence. Don't keep us to yourself; spread the word.

GET CREATIVE.

Have fun with it. How about a banner? Why not set up a fan club? Does *your* town have 'James Kennedy and The Underdogs' graffitied across the roof of your local MP's office? Why the hell not?! The world is your canvas; go as wild as Cocaine Bear.

GET INVOLVED.

Wanna get even more involved? Offer your services – they will be eagerly welcomed. Fancy manning the merch stall? That would be a colossal help, and the band will doubtless give you free merch and free entry too. Take pictures of the show and send them to the band to use on their pages. They will love you for it. Offer a sofa, offer a lift or just offer a hand and, trust me, you will become an instant legend in the eyes of your favourite band, who will move you from fan status to one of the family. And you'll have a great time doing it! However, understand and respect that solo female artists, for example, are highly unlikely to accept sofas or lifts from randos, however well meaning you might be. Similarly, all of this is top-tier-fandom-type stuff and you have zero obligation to do any of it – by supporting the band online and showing up at shows you are already making dreams happen, you absolute fucking Jedi.

Fans wield immense power, as you can see. And when a fanbase becomes a tribe, working together for one cause, it can become a movement. Don't underestimate your strength as a 'fan' – the capacity to change lives, make history, break records and have the time of your life doing it is already in your hands. And on behalf of artists everywhere, I'd like to say this – thank you. Really. You will never know how much you mean to us. Sadly, it's not always easy for us to show it amid the chaos of a live show and having to race off, unable to spend any real time with the people who matter the most – you. But I hope you know that *we* know that without you, we're nothing and that this beautiful ride ends tomorrow.

For believing in us when no one else did – thank you. For supporting us when we had little to give back – thank you. For showing up, hanging out and coming back – thank you. For the kind words in tough times – thank you. For the sofas, food, beers and parties – thank you. For waiting – thank you. For sticking by us, no matter what – thank you. For bringing the noise, the good times, the passion and the madness – thank you. For the tears, both happy and sad – thank you. For making us better – thank you. For the moments we will never forget – thank you.

Thank you, for everything. Now let's do it all again.

12.

QUANTUM JAZZ

You'd have to be a monumental wasteman to suggest that Pythagoras was anything less than the King Kong of clever dudes. Hailing from the country that *literally* invented the musical scales that have been the basis of all Western music for the last 2,000 years (something he had an integral role in), our man in the robe also played a prodigious part in the development of mathematics, music theory, philosophy, geometry, and even has his own theorem. Have you got a theorem? Or a badass robe? I didn't think so. P-man's theorem is still used today in geometry, architecture, engineering, electronics and navigation, so not bad for a bloke who died in 495 BC – which was *long* before calculators, YouTube academics and ChatGPT. So Big P was indeed one clever dude.

But our man from Greece was also wrong. In his 'Music of the Spheres', the success went to his head, he changed his name to a symbol and claimed that the planets above us produced music through their movements in space. With the benefit of a two-thousand-year upper hand, we now know outer space to be a vacuum, where sound cannot travel – and when the universe does produce sound of any kind, it sounds bloody awful. Not so much music as terrifying soundscapes of demented torment and death.

Fans of Japanese noisecore would love it. So Big Daddy P dropped the ball on that one. But hey, it *was* 400 BC, so let's cut a brother a break. And, as it turns out, he wasn't entirely off the mark, but we'll come on to that.

You see, ever since the ancient Greeks invented everything, scientists have been searching in one way or another for a unified theory of everything. An immutable, universal law of nature that unites all the other laws of nature in one, tidy and cohesive mic drop. A long-time physics migraine, for example, has been how to unify quantum mechanics with Einstein's theory of relativity – both heavyweights at the top of the physics Champions League that still remain in conflict.

Now, you're probably wondering where I'm going with all this, so I'm just gonna throw it out there. For the rest of this chapter, I'm going to attempt to convince you that the building blocks of all matter, the behaviour of the universe and the nature of life itself can all be explained and unified by one singular force – music. I'm about to throw forth my own theory of *musica universalis* and dive boots first into particle physics, relativity, evolution and the great gig in the sky.

Side note for any scientists reading this, or in fact anyone with a basic high-school education – this chapter is about to infuriate you with a reckless romp through half-read theories, misunderstood concepts and a perverted violation of scientific terminology. But hear me out and come sit with me on a largely tongue-in-cheek joyride through space and time via the medium of rock.

Our journey begins, rather fittingly, in Greece. Maybe there's something in the air down there. Perhaps there's a philosophical aroma to the place that lingers on all these years after the great minds roamed around stroking their beards in the Mediterranean sun. As I laid there watching the gentle lapping of the turquoise sea, with the enchanting improvisational gymnastics of John Coltrane tooting in my ear, casually pondering the mysteries of the universe, as one does, it hit me – waves. Then it hit me again – entropy, order, relativity, frequency, randomness and harmony. I felt a profound union between the music in my ears and the awe-inspiring nature around me, and I saw a parallel in their construct. The waves on the shore got me thinking about sound waves in music, in quantum physics, in the omnipresent nature of all things to consist of dualities, whether it's the peaks and troughs of a wave, the light and the dark, the positive and negative charges inside an atom, sound and silence or life and death – and that got me thinking about spirituality. Then the structured improvisation of the music had me thinking about evolution, ecosystems and the orbit of planets. I guess I'd missed the point of being on holiday.

But let's not get ahead of ourselves. If I am to get close to the lofty goal of convincing you that the force that governs our universe and everything in it is, in fact, our beloved music, then we'd better take this one step at a time. Let's start with those waves I watched gently stroking the beach. Waves are everything. The sounds you hear, the colours you see, the light you see them with and all matter itself, at the subatomic level at least, are made of waves. Everything you can see, touch, smell, taste and hear is actually made of waves – this book in your hand, the chair you're sitting on, even yourself and the cells that make you. Once we zoom in far enough past the atomic level, what was once thought of as a solid particle is, in fact, a vibrating waveform. The speed and strength with which each waveform vibrates determines the properties that are manifested in what we experience as a solid particle. But it's not; it's a wave... and a particle... at the same time. Yeah, I know.

Let's explore this with a guitar. When I twang, say, a thin E (you know, the one that always breaks), we all hear one pitch, called an E note. But if I put my finger on fret five of the same string, we get an A note. Fret thirteen, a high F. By shortening the length of the string by dunking my finger on it, I am changing the vibrational *frequency* of the string and, as a result, the physical property it produces – in this case, a pitch. A shorter, tighter string vibrates faster, giving us a higher pitch. A long, thick, slack string vibrates at a slower frequency and therefore produces a lower-sounding pitch – hello to the bass players. Similarly, different wave frequencies down in the quantum realm are what define all of the properties further up the atomic food chain. And, because of that, they ultimately produce everything that's tangible for us up here in the real world too. Whether it's a pitch we hear on an instrument or the properties within an atom, it's all about the frequency of those waves, man.

Remember when I said a few paragraphs back that mainstream science has battled for decades to find a theory that can harmonise (pun intended) the conflicting theories of quantum mechanics with Einstein's relativity? Well, today they have a strong contender for that theory. The 'Theory of Everything', they're calling it, which is a badass name. It's at the cutting edge of modern physics and is, at the time of writing, one of the main contestants for understanding the universe and everything in it. Do you know what it's called? It's called string theory. That's right, 'string' as in a fucking guitar string! And for the very same reason that I just laid out – that at the subatomic level, reality functions like the pitches on our trusty guitar string. Whereas my string produces musical notes, other forms of vibration produce the building blocks that end up as plants, planets and politicians. Same process, different 'strings' vibrating at different frequencies. Everything in the known universe is made from vibrating waves – the ingredients of music appear to be the life force that animates our universe and everything in it. And I'm not speaking metaphorically here either.

But here's the brain wreck. That E string of mine isn't just producing the E pitch we all know and love. Nope, it's also – and at the exact same time – producing a stack of other pitches called 'harmonics'. The note we hear is called the 'fundamental' – an E, in this case. But, unbeknown to our ears, that very same string is simultaneously producing a potentially infinite amount of these harmonics – the first one at twice the frequency of the fundamental, the second one at three times the fundamental and so on, ad infinitum. We don't 'hear' these little baby notes, as such – but it's these harmonics that decorate the fundamental pitch and create its unique 'tone'. That's why the same note played on a guitar or a trumpet sounds so different – it's because this harmonic colouring gives each instrument its distinctive sound. Ever phoned someone and had that robotic 'engaged' tone come back at you? That's what the world sounds like without these invisible harmonics making it beautiful and awesome. A quick shout-out to our man Pythagoras again here, for he worked all this stuff out thousands of years ago, the cocky bastard. So to summarise: every note of a plucked string, every chime of a struck bell, every toot of a trumpet not only produces the note we hear but also a vast range of additional 'harmonics' that we *don't* hear as a note but are essential to colouring the pitch with its unique character. Back at the wave level, what we're talking about here is an infinite stack of waves that exist as varying multiples of the 'fundamental'. Capisce?

Ok, let's take a breather from physics class and bathe in the warm waters of spirituality for a minute. Because the ancient Hindus believed that the universe was founded upon a sound – a primordial sound from which all reality was born. They called this sound 'om'. Now, in musical terms, 'om' could be considered the 'fundamental' note – the divine note – from which all other things materialise. And from the miniscule waves that power our particles to the enormous forces that orchestrate our universe, all other reality could be considered, with some merit, to be the 'harmonics' of that one 'fundamental' note, the om. All energy, light, motion, planets and corrupt bankers existing as the end result of the myriad 'harmonics' produced by that first twang of the universal E string – all a part of what gives this universe its unique 'tone'. Now, for the physicists among us who might be getting a little shuffly here, chill out and smoke this, for Planck's sake, cos we're not done yet.

So if that's the case we're running with (and I am) – that all energy, matter, motion and life exists as a result of the harmonics twanged into existence with the one divine note – then who plucked the cosmic guitar string? Who kicked off the great gig in the sky? I mean, a Big Bang sure does sound like the start of a rock concert, right? Boom, fireworks, a burst of space dust, the big E chord and the knowing head nod. Could it be that the moment the universe reached 'peak breaking point', just before the Big Bang, the pressure provided the first strike of the gong of existence, inflating the universe outwards in the longest 'standing wave' unimaginable? Well, without getting all religious on your ass, it seems we still don't know who or what kicked off proceedings at the best show in the universe, but we do know that what's happened since has essentially been the longest jam session in history.

Through endless mutations, interactions and evolution, the universe has been morphing through different states for billions of years as a result of waves, frequencies, velocities, cycles, feedback loops and harmony – standard tools for musicians everywhere. And I know there'll be those bore-ons who'll gleefully point out that I've got it arse-backwards – that it is not the universe that follows the laws of music but in fact music that follows the laws of physics. But I can't hear them because the music's too loud, so let's continue with my brilliant theory, which is that just like a band jamming aimlessly and going wherever the music leads them – sometimes loud, sometimes soft, sometimes noisy, sometimes harmonious or destroying itself in a cacophony of dissonance – the universe has also been in a state of improvisation since the dawn of time (but never, *ever* stopping for a joint).

Which leads me to a conclusion that I absolutely hate to admit: if there is a god, they're most definitely a Jazzer. Can you imagine the elite level of smugness that will ooze from every jazz head on the planet were that ever to be proven? It doesn't bear thinking about. Why do I say that? I say it because as we look around us – the universe, nature, society, the cells in our body, the cycle of life – we see what mostly looks like the outcome of randomness. No matter how hard we look, there doesn't seem to be any reason or meaning to any of it. Cells in healthy people randomly mutate into cancer cells; life erupts into being for no apparent reason and continues to evolve relative to an ever-changing set of entangled stimuli, which is itself the outcome of collective chaos when looked at as a whole; and Coldplay are famous while Crass are not. From the bizarre world of quantum physics, to the cells in our bodies and the behaviour of our social systems, randomness rules, it seems. Not entirely, of course, for there *are* very rigid and fixed laws of nature, just as there must be in music – but within those frameworks, chaos and improvisation seems to reign supreme.

Which is why God must be a Jazzer. Think about it. Much like a jazz piece, it seems the universe adheres to a strict set of established laws (a chord sequence, if you will), but outside of that it's mostly in a state of free-form improvisation, forever jamming, mutating and evolving. And musical improvisation, much like evolution – whether of solar systems or living things – is a group activity. Because nothing evolves in a straight, unaffected line; all things evolve due to the influence of their environment. And yet, that environment is also evolving under the impact of everything within and around it. Just like a piece of music being improvised by the interplay of its band members reacting to each other within the confines of a set chord structure, everything within this awesome rock show in the stars is the product of holistic improvised evolution. Quantum jazz, if you will. All things are entangled with all other things and are, whether alive or inanimate, evolving together and *because* of each other in a universe-sized Bitches Brew. All reality is born of the harmonics from the best power chord ever strummed, and we are all part of the great cosmic jam session kick-started by the Big Bang – or perhaps we should say the twang of that big note, the 'om' from which all else has sprung.

Like all jam sessions, however, there's always the risk of descending into free-form carnage and the whole thing collapsing in on itself and disappearing into the black hole of its own arse. The drum solo, in other words. What is needed in such a wank-fest is a little bit of 'harmony' to pull it all together. That's right, musicality to the rescue again – for without harmony, there would be nothing. No atoms, no solar systems and certainly no life. Whether it's a magnetic force, a planet, gravity, the particles within atoms, the natural balance of ecosystems, the formation of solar systems and everything else, it is the power of harmony, or a harmonious synergy between different entities, that binds this whole damn universe together. Sure, there's a hellish dollop of delicious chaos all around us too (the aforementioned quantum jazz), but without harmony holding it all together at the seams, all would be black. It is the harmony between the opposing forces within an atom that keeps it spinning. It is the harmony between gravitational pull and motion that holds our solar systems together. It is the harmony between predator and prey that stops our ecosystems from collapsing. Just like a good jazz piece, the chaos is where the fun is. The chaos is where the thrill is, where the danger is and often where the innovation is – but without some kind of harmonic gravity glueing the thing together, it all falls apart. Supernovas, extinction events, hurricanes, new species, diseases, meteors, volcanic eruptions and ice ages are all good old chaos letting rip, yet still all things end up held together again, rather miraculously, by a form of cosmic harmony apparent in all things. Chaos and order – a fundamental duality.

Still with me, you crazy bastards? Cool, then let's get crazier. We'll finish up back on that beach in Greece with those stunning waves. Because waves personify another sacred feature that has some sexy implications for the sciencey-spiritual-stoner trip we're on right now – I just mentioned it... duality. That is, that a wave's existence is essentially a fluctuation between two opposing states – call them up and down, peak and trough, on and off, in and out, positive and negative, whatever. Without one, you do not have the other, and the wave ceases to be a wave. We see such dualities everywhere we look in nature and our daily life. The positive and negative charges within an atom, light and dark, life and death, the ebb and flow of the tides, good and evil, hot and cold. All reality as we know it seems to reflect the nature of the basic wave function. Ancient cultures seemed to grasp this intuitively – what do you think yin and yang are all about?

Exactly: the codependent dance of opposites. Encapsulated within the beauty of a simple wave is the genesis of all things, from the literal (magnetic charges, atomic properties) to the symbolic (life and death, good and evil) – dualities in all their forms. Reality as we know it so far has been the story of singularity to duality. All things can only exist because of their opposite – a truth that is simply and elegantly evident in our humble wave.

It's been said that learning to ride the wave is what it's all about. That while we may all be but a momentary ripple on life's ocean, we'll forever be a part of what makes that ocean – our ocean being the infinite universe. But hey, that's a conversation for another spliff break sometime.

So when we look at the universe and how it is the product of harmony, tension, waves, dualities and improvisation, we can see that Pythagoras wasn't wrong after all. The universe really is a celestial symphony birthed and maintained by the magical ingredients of music. How it manifests itself as the outcome of these ingredients isn't – as Pythagoras thought – *literally* musical in the sense that it makes audible music, but rather that the music of the universe exists in the form of planets, atoms, magnetic forces, motion and you and me. This is the divine jam session that we and everything else are a part of.

Thanks for sticking with me on that bumpy expedition through quantum physics, string theory, Eastern spirituality and jazz – I do hope I've made some converts to the new cult I'm starting. And so what does all of this mean for musicians? Well, I suppose that if waves, harmony and improvisation are the primal language of the universe, then us musicians are the noble alchemists of the sacred force itself. Handle it with care. Perhaps that's why music is considered to be the 'universal' language. It sings to something in all of us that is woven into the very fabric of all that exists. It is ethereal. You can't put it in a jar and look at it; you can't grab it with your hands – it just is, and it rattles the primordial space dust inside all of us.

Humanity has been seeking its creator since the dawn of thought. There have been many candidates, but if I were going to put your money on anything, I'd say we've found our maker. We can see it animating the waveforms that are the genesis to all things – those infinite harmonic variations of the one big note that kick-started the longest space-jam session ever. We can see it in the ubiquitous balance of dualities through which the existence of all things is held together by unique tensions between harmony and discord. We can see the work of a cosmic band-leader everywhere – and they're clearly a Jazzer. If we seek a heavenly guardian to lead us through the uncertainties and struggles of life, there is none better than music. Music doesn't judge; it doesn't punish. It might suck sometimes, but there's always another tune on the way. Trust the music. The music is the way.

So what's my religion? You know the answer. I worship at the temple of the noise. The divine force that breathes life into every particle, every cell and every soul ever to be strummed into existence. First there was the sound, and then there was the symphony – the cosmic symphony of all that is. God is music. Music is God – and I am its prophet. Anyone who disagrees is a blasphemer. Now kneel before me and give me all your money.

13.

DON'T BE THAT DOUCHE

Ok, let's break for some catharsis – God knows we need it. Catharsis for you, for me, for freelancers of all kinds and, of course, for the musicians among us. The following can also be considered a public service for our relatives, well-meaning members of the public and dickheads in pubs, so that they don't put their foot in one of the absolute wangers that follow. It's time to finally get it all out on the table, have the fight and then make up. Now, it might seem like a cheap issue, but the existence of the subsequent conversational landmines highlight that the great divide in society over creatives and freelancers, generally, is still alive and smelly. Many, it would appear, still see us as alien creatures whose lives they can neither fathom nor encourage, and I think it's because we haven't cleared up the confusion. So how about we put a bullet in some of these age-old misunderstandings once and for all?

It's important to let people know, for they have no idea of the impact their words can have on our confidence, feelings of belonging and validation. So I'm gonna say it so that you don't have to – even if it's just to make us feel better. Am I about to get bitchy? You betcha! And I hope my fellow creatives will relish the vitriol I am about to unload on some of the stupidest shit we have to put up with on an almost daily basis. The gloves are off. This is our bite-back.

What follows is a collection of things one should never say to a musician, creative or freelancer. Let's start with the classic. Nothing makes our blood freeze quite as quickly as this absolute pearler, this icon of ignorance, this timeless monument to the moronic. Ladies and gentlemen, I present to you, the friendship killer:

'STILL TRYING THEN, ARE YOU?'

The musicians here will know this one all too well – and it hurts, doesn't it?! How many times have you wanted to respond with:

'*Ok, Trev, listen up. Firstly, I'm not "trying" to do anything except make music. The assumption that in doing so, I'm therefore "trying" to become rich and famous says more about you than it does about me. You've blindly conformed to the shallow idea that something is only worth doing if it makes money. You know nothing of passion, the pride of seeing your creations come to life, of adventure, of risk, the commitment that goes into learning a craft, of wanting to be part of something more meaningful than a fucking bill-payer.*'

Those who mumble this mindless mantra, without any mind given to the judgey rudeness and social gracelessness of it, would be red with righteous rage if we said the same to them. Luckily for them, us creatives are well practised in criticism, and we'll usually say something polite and vague in response – but now it's our turn. So let's turn that skid mark of words around and see how *they* feel:

'*Oh, still at the day job, are you, Trev? How many years you been there now? Fifteen!! Bloody hell, mate, still "trying" then, are you?! You mean you're not running the entire global company yet? You're still just working in HR? Wow, well, how about I unfairly compare you to the most successful business person I can think of in order to imply that you are a sad little failure in contrast. How about Richard Branson?! He's been in business as long as you have, mate, and look at him! Yet you're still "trying"! Let's all continue to talk about this in front of you as if you're not here.'*

Trev, mate, imagine, if you can, that every time you went out, some arsehole was holding you to judgement over your job? Always asking whether you'd 'made it' yet and comparing you to others. It'd piss you off, right? A job that you've worked hard at for years, pay your bills with and are perfectly happy doing. Well, you'd think it was rude, wouldn't you? You'd want to say to them: 'Who the fuck are *you* to judge me?' or 'Mind your own business, you cheeky bastard.' And you'd be right to do so, Trev. But for some unexplained reason, creative freelancers need to be held in perpetual comparison to the top 1 per cent of their industry – Ed Sheeran or whoever – and then made to feel like a total loser because they're not 'there' yet. Well, how about this – maybe we're not *trying* to become famous. Maybe we're just trying to survive in a tough industry and pursue the noble goal of creating something new and living our passions. You don't need to 'get it', Trev, but you do need to shut your mouth.

'DON'T YOU WANT TO GET A REAL JOB?'

Another classic. Casually offered over a pint, without a second's thought as to the implications of what's being said or whether it might be offensive. As if it's just universally agreed that being a creative is not a 'real job'.

'So what is a real job then, Trev? Let me guess... oh, you mean like your job! Of course.'

How about we try to demonstrate to poor, defenceless Trev over here why that line stings so much? Not only because it denigrates our beautiful craft into the realm of a hobby or a passing phase, but also because it grossly disrespects the effort, sacrifice, risk and skill we've put into it. I wonder how Trev would feel if we belittled his job, his choices and his values in the same way?

'A real job like yours, eh, Trev? So, going to the same place every day, doing the same repetitive thing with the same people in the same clothes, being bossed around by some douche who tells you when you can go on holiday or have lunch for the rest of your one and only life, in the hope that one day – one day – you'll be free to finally enjoy life a little before it's all over? To devote your best years to paying off a house you're never in because you're always out working to pay for it? To be buried under a mountain of debt for all those things you bought thinking they'd make you happy? Nah, I'm good, thanks, Trev. I'll take "skint and free" any day of the week, mate.'

If you or I said any of that to Trev, or indeed anyone, we would be a colossal dickbag – so why is it so acceptable for people to say the equivalent to us? Just because creatives and freelancers have chosen a different path in life, it doesn't make it ok to talk about us as if we're impaling babies on spikes for a hobby – we play music; it's not *that* strange. We just have a different set of things that are important to us. What Trev sees as security, we see as chains. For us, freedom, creativity, flexibility, spontaneity, passion and adventure are more important than security, routine and safety. Sure, it comes with financial instability, emotional burn-out and general life uncertainty, but that's our choice and our problem to deal with. Our job brings different riches into our life – like travel, freedom, creativity, meaning and being our own boss. We might complain about it from time to time, but doesn't everyone? Do we pay our bills? Yes. Then keep that 'real job' shit to yourself, Trevor boy.

'WHY DON'T YOU GO ON *THE VOICE*?'

This is usually meant as a well-meaning compliment, so we'll go easy on this one. What people are saying when they say this is: 'Wow, you're so good, you should go on *The Voice* and they'll make you famous' – and I'm sure none of us can take offence at that. But here's the truth. Firstly, as we've established, most creatives are not trying to be famous; they're just trying to make their living from their chosen craft. Secondly, most musicians that I know despise these TV music shows with a dizzying, blood-curdling venom, so the idea that we would actually go *on* one is preposterous. It's like telling a well-seasoned lawyer that they could make easier money shaking their arse on OnlyFans.

The Voice and all the other shows like it are TV shows – they exist to make good TV, not good music, and to make a yacht-load of money for the show, not the artists. They don't give a crap about the contestants, their talent, their future or their dreams – that's just the bait they suck them in with so they can be mercilessly exploited into supplying the show with free drama. When they say 'there can only be one winner', they mean themselves – the show wins every time. With *very* few exceptions, the only people getting famous from these shows are the judges. As for the singers – firstly, can anyone even remember most of the winners? And secondly, do you know where they are now? They're back doing the club circuit. No shame in that, but if being on a hugely popular global TV series in front of millions of viewers and buddying up to the world's music elite can't secure you some kind of foothold in the music business without having to immediately go back to playing the social clubs, then that should tell us everything we need to know about the stupidity of the music industry, the true purpose of TV music shows and the fickle, fleeting interest of the public. Here today, gone tomorrow. So personally, I'd rather spare myself the six months of gruelling TV schedules, make-up, promo, travel and humiliation so that I can be a momentary dancing monkey for the public's *schadenfreude* and a TV producer's yacht. It's a circus. An old-school freak show. An exploitative, tightly orchestrated production in which the public are led to vote for the show's chosen favourite through blatant editing of clips designed to make them look good and the others not good enough. This is not where stars are made. Stars are made on the stages of our rapidly dwindling grass-roots music venues, so if well-meaning people really want to help an artist to 'get out there', they should go to their gigs instead and stop watching *The Voice*.

'I ALWAYS KNEW YOU'D MAKE IT.'

Uh oh, Trev again.

'*No, you didn't, Trev. I'd never even seen you at a gig until I started playing shows with people you think are famous. Now that I'm rubbing shoulders with names you recognise from TV, now you want to come to the show? And you want to come in for free because now I'm your best mate? We go waaaay back, we do – you always supported me from the very start and you always knew I'd "make it", right? Piss off, Trev, and go join that long line of recently discovered besties and lifelong supporters. You see, we don't need your support when we're successful; we need it when we're struggling, when we're broke and desperate and working our arses off against all the odds – that's when we need your support. It's easy to back the winner. But you didn't want to champion what might be a losing horse – and more than likely quietly prayed for my failure. Well, if you can't stand by me when I've got nothing, you can't stand by me at all, Trev. And no I won't ask Kelly Jones to send you a video. Piss off, Trev.*'

'I'M DYING OF CANCER; CAN YOU HOOK ME UP WITH OZZY?'

Most people would be rightfully shocked to discover how common this is, but believe me, it happens – a lot! We're talking here of course about people who most definitely are *not* dying of cancer, just to be clear. Ask any member of a successful artist's entourage and they'll tell you of the daily onslaught of messages from people who will stoop beyond the lowest levels to upset you into giving them what they want – and what generally can't be delivered. Like, if artists said yes to every stranger on social media who asked for a free ticket, free merch or a backstage pass, they'd all be on the fucking dole. And it's not just famous artists either. This shit starts the second you're out of the gates. Here are some of mine. 'My sister is a huge fan but she's too ill to come to the show, so will you travel to our house seventeen hours away and perform a personal concert for her for free because she's dying? She's free on Sunday.'

I'm not even joking.

'If you don't start replying to my endless messages nagging you to do (and give me) free stuff, I'm going to kill myself.'

I mean, who pulls shit like that?!

'Hey, my dad is a huge fan of yours...' – wait for it – '...but he's too ill to come to the show cos he's dying of cancer, so will you instead come to Leicester and bring some free merch to his bedside? He's free on Sunday.'

Wow, all of these huge fans I never knew I had and they're all dying of cancer. It's brutal, but once you've fallen for it a few times, you get hardened to it real quick. Fucked up, isn't it?

The sick outcome of this is that on those occasions when it's actually true and that meeting their hero really would help someone who's struggling, it just gets written off as more twisted, weirdo blagging. Decent, well-meaning people living with awful life-threatening illnesses get automatically lumped in with the liars, the entitled, the hangers-on, the unhinged and the dangerous. It's why many artists are so damn hard to contact – they just can't handle the daily emotional blackmail and heart-wrenching bribery any more. The whole 'I'm dying, so give me free stuff' scam is sick and appallingly distasteful. And anyway, if I only had six weeks left to live, the last thing I'd give a shit about would be meeting Roger Waters. Actually, scratch that – I'm gonna guilt-message his roadie again now.

'WE CAN'T PAY YOU BUT THERE'LL BE FOOD AND DRINK.'

'What am I, a Dobermann? If it's for charity, fine. But if it's for your event and the event is making money, the venue is making money, the sponsor is making money and the bar is making money, then pay the fucking artist, Trev! And in money, not food. Believe it or not, we've already got food, thanks. And beers too.'

No one has yet been able to explain to me what it is about the mention of 'free beers' that some people think has such a mystical and irresistible power over musicians. Beer is everywhere. I've got a fridgeful already. It's just people trying (once again) to get artists to work for free, and they think that by merely mentioning 'beer' we will fall into some magical trance and agree to absolutely anything in pursuit of that mythical and scarce delicacy. Or they hit you with the absolute zinger – exposure. I know it's a cliché, but it still happens; it happens *all* the time, as any fellow creatives, graphic designers, photographers, writers, actors or freelancers will confirm. Promoters, event managers, charities – they all still pull the 'exposure' card, as if playing their crappy event is going to somehow catapult us to global-rock-god status. They say it like they're actually doing us a favour. Like they're gifting us this great opportunity to finally realise our dreams. Like, they're angels, really – we just need to stop being so obscenely ungrateful and appreciate what they're offering us here: the chance to finally play on the world stage *and* be given free food and beer. All of this if we just give Aberballache FC a mere day of our time. Ok, well, let me just check if my energy supplier will accept next month's payment in exposure, food and beers and I'll get right back to you, Trev...

'WHAT YOU WANT TO DO IS...'

Ooh, I love this one. Enter the experts. Us musicians seem to attract a lot of these. Our job is public, see – it's a spectator sport. But unlike in actual sport, we can be easily approached at the bar after the show and be bored to tears by some bloke going on and on about 1) our guitar tone, 2) our set list, 3) the 'sound out front', or 4) his mate 'Paul', who seems to be an even bigger beacon of all knowledge. Unbeknown to this self-proclaimed guru of all things, we're at that stage of the night now that is all about drinking, dicking around and chatting people up. Being cornered by some fella repeating that 'what you want to do is get a Les Paul', 'what you want to do is work on your mic technique', 'what you want to do is work on the sound out front', 'what you want to do is have a chat with my mate, Paul'. Ad fucking nauseam. Kill me now. What I *want* to do is scream:

'Bro, I've just done a show. I'm hot and sweaty and I'll tell you what I want to do: I want to drink a cold beer, have a laugh and chat up the supermodel who was waiting to speak with me but is now walking out the door with the drummer from the support band. Please, mate, I beg you – I didn't come here to learn; I came here to rock. I do appreciate your wealth of whisky wisdom, screamed in my ear over the music I'd rather be partying to – but if I want to know about guitars, I'll ask Steve Vai, not your mate Paul. And I'll ask him tomorrow, not now. Thanks and bye.'

'WELL, I'VE NEVER HEARD OF YOU.'

Oh no, I'm devastated! Trev at the local pub says he's never heard of my band and seemed to take great delight in saying it, too. The implication here is that if *he* hasn't heard of my band, then my band must be shite. Delivered with a smugness of tone and body language typical of an arsehole who believes he's delivering a fatal blow with a genius line that has never before been uttered, Trev seems happy that my ego has been fully shat upon. Well, of course Trev hasn't heard of my band; he looks like a man who thinks Rod Stewart is hard rock. I'm glad he hasn't heard of us. It's not the arrogance or general cockishness with this one that bothers me, but the logical absurdity inherent in the idea that in order for something to be good, Trev from The Dick and Duck has to have heard of it – for Trev is clearly a man of the cultural elite. I'm guessing ole Trev *has* heard of Joseph Stalin. So does that mean, by Trev's bizarre metric, that the moustachioed mass murderer has some kind of credibility to him? Because Trev at The Dick and Duck... has *heard* of him. The internet is full of Trevs. Share an opinion on social media and out he comes: 'Who are you to say Eric Clapton is overrated? At least I've *heard* of him. I've never even *heard* of you,' as if that is somehow a valid counter-argument to your point. But for Trev, making sense doesn't matter – all that matters is that there are things he's heard of and things he hasn't. I wonder what else our man Trev hasn't heard of – let's ask him. Sia? Never heard of her. Polyphia? Never heard of her. Nova Twins? Never heard of her. Fucking Skindred? Nope. Hmm, ok, it's starting to look like the list of people that Trev *has* heard of is depressingly small, and I think I'm happier being in the camp of people that this little bellend *hasn't* heard of after all.

'MUSIC, MUSIC, MUSIC, MUSIC.'

Oftentimes when people talk to musicians, they think that the only thing we can talk about and *want* to talk about is music. Again, this is meant with the sweetest of intentions – an attempt to bond, to speak our language, to make us feel welcome – and to all of the beautiful humans out there who do this, we thank you sincerely. But you can relax, because generally us musicians are thankful for the opportunity to talk about anything *other* than music! We spend our entire lives dealing with music and music-related stuff. What began as a wild fantasy somehow became our job and, just like any job, it's nice to leave the work at the office sometimes. Musicians are just as into sport, politics, TV, fitness, books and local gossip as anyone else, and since music became our job, many of us have gotten non-music-related hobbies that we're often more passionate in talking about. So to whom it concerns, please don't feel pressured into *having* to talk music with us all night, but you're an angel for trying to do so.

'PLAY "WONDERWALL".'

Substitute with 'Mr Brightside', 'Belter' or 'Sweet Caroline'. Surely I don't need to explain this one.

14.

WE NEED TO TALK

It could all be over in five minutes. Maybe less. I just need to follow through this time. Don't think about it and just do it. It's time. I can't bear the weight of the pain, shame, regret, anger, resentment, frustration, failure and grind for another day. It's killing me and I need to eject. I can't fight any more. I've got everything I need right here – a belt, a bathtub, a blade, a bottle, a window. It's time. Don't think about it; just do it this time. One swift action and it's all over. Silence. Black. Freedom. The end. Just thinking about it fills me with a warm, soothing sense of profound peace. Peace at last. Rest in peace. The demon is out of his cage tonight, running amok, fuelled by alcohol and whatever else I could pump into him, and is talking his usual talk:

'Do it, you fuck up. Do it. No one will miss you. If anything, they'll all be better off without you, you waster. If you love them, do it.'

Some nights I frighten myself with how rational and sensible it all seems. This is no fleeting flight of fantasy but a calmly considered solution to a problem. The problem of being alive. It's not how they describe it. It's not sadness or hopelessness or brain fog. It's an existence fog. It's a thick, impenetrable black shadow that engulfs my daily life, devouring all that is good. Everything is struggle. Getting out of bed, people, eating, a phone call. Much better to just sleep. Sleep forever. Is this the price we pay for the artistic gift? Is this deep existential nihilism just part of the artist package – the blessing and the curse? Or is it the inevitable result of too many years spent on the wrong side of this toxic, unjust, cruel, nepotistic shithouse of an industry and the subhuman living conditions we're forced to suffer while chasing it – only to fail catastrophically in almost all cases, with absolutely nothing to show for the effort except for debt, scars and a shattered heart?

I'm done. Just so fucking tired of it all. I've fought – like, really fought – this battle longer and harder than most, but still I've lost. Lost the fight, lost the best years of my life trying and lost the will. It's time. There's nothing left to lose. Except the shame, the rejection, the stress, the destitution, the unfairness of it all and the creeping schizophrenia. It's enough to kill the best of us. And it does.

X X X

We have a problem in the music industry. A shocking, shameful and not-so-secret problem – despite the attempts at burying it beneath a facade of glamour, adventure, riches and wild abandon. A problem so tenacious it ruins the successful as much as the struggling, the rich as much as the poor and the old as much as the young. Prepare yourself for some truly appalling facts: 80 per cent of musicians admit to struggling with some form of mental ill health – 80 per cent! And suicide rates, substance abuse and mental health issues are almost *twice* as high among musicians as they are in the general public. I'm gonna repeat that: suicide rates, substance abuse and mental health issues are almost *twice* as high among musicians as they are in the general public. In the list of industries that have the worst track record for inflicting states of mental illness, suicide and substance abuse, you will find the military, front-line health workers… and the music industry.

Yet the myth that's still peddled by the industry, the media, the artists themselves, and lapped up by the public, is one of millionaires living carefree lives of parties, adoration, travel and groupies. But let me tell you what they won't: there is an epidemic at the dark heart of this industry that is literally killing its own.

And it has been for as long as it's been here. For as far back as the records allow, we see a disturbing pattern. Whether we're looking at the 1930s, the 1950s or 2025, the picture's the same: depression, poverty, exploitation, substance abuse and suicide are all ever-present – and in much the same proportion as today. It seems we've made zero progress. And, as I said, it doesn't seem to matter if you're successful, unsuccessful, signed or unsigned – the uninjured stand as a rare and intriguing minority in this sick industry. Need we remind ourselves of the A-listers who, despite millions in sales, millions in pounds and, by most people's metric, a life of living the best dream there is to live, chose to end their precious lives way too young – Kurt Cobain, Avicii, Keith Flint, Ian Curtis, Chester Bennington, Chris Cornell, Pete Ham. And add to that the tragic victims of self-abuse, addiction, neglect, burn-out and the rampant excess that's considered normal in this business – Taylor Hawkins, Amy Winehouse, Jimi Hendrix, DMX, Michael Jackson, Sid Vicious, Phil Lynott, Scott Weiland, Stuart Cable, Elvis Presley, Jim Morrison, John Bonham, Whitney Houston – you know the list. It's a list of fucking icons.

And these are the guys on the winning team, so fear for the rest of us. Those of us whose suicides, overdoses, self-harm, hunger and hospitalisation will never make the headlines. Those of us out there in the wild without agents, assistants, labels, rehab or support of any kind, desperately fighting a daily battle against exploitation, poverty, instability, with a dire lack of any of the rewards of success for the effort. It's not just the madness of fame that breaks the few, but the degrading lack of basic humanity that breaks the many. Things like routine, financial security, emotional stability, fair pay, downtime, home time, respect and balance. If you're a musician, you can forget those things. Much has already been told about our damaged, fallen heroes. Movies have been made and many a salacious bestseller is driven by the ever more extreme tales of depravity and despair suffered by its author. And we love that stuff, don't we? We don't want our rock stars healthy and happy; we want them jacked up on heroin and booze, driving cars through hotels, wrecking their lives, and ultimately, we want them dead. Preferably violently, miserably, disgustingly dead. It's a cruel and telling irony when the first time an unsigned artist receives mass media exposure is after one of them opens their veins in a cheap hotel room somewhere. Overnight they become the media's darlings, all hail their tortured, artistic genius and you can't find anyone who doesn't claim to have been their biggest lifelong fan. For a few days, anyway. I've seen it too many times. It's clear that we prefer our rock stars to suffer. Or even better, we prefer them dead. Those of us who have yet to surrender to the ultimate escape route are doomed to live invisible. There's a lot of us out there, and it's a tough place to be. So what's the deal? Why does this sickness plague this particular industry so intensely? Here are just some of the reasons:

THE REALITY OF FAME AND 'SUCCESS'.

It really ain't what it seems. It can be isolating, inhuman and ruin the real relationships you once had. It's a rigidly regimented life dictated by relentless schedules, always being in transit, ever in demand, and often mind-numbingly boring. Don't believe the hype; celebrities are products, and products exist to make money – usually for somebody else. Cut off from any real connection to the outside world, existing only in identical stadium car parks and faraway hotel rooms, barely seeing home and family for months at a time, surrounded by a stream of interchangeable sycophants, hangers-on and sharks, and slogged beyond human ability to keep the circus rolling on a never-ending treadmill of shows, promo, travel, repeat. It is a lonely, detached world where stalkers, death threats, failed marriages, paparazzi, resentful offspring and screaming strangers are considered normal. It's enough to drive anyone insane. Which is where the drugs come in. And the wild, erratic behaviour that's born out of frustration, monotony and yearning. For some, the unrealistic pressure of it all becomes too much. For others, the excess takes them while they sleep. And those who make it out of that insanity alive do so with a plethora of scars, dysfunction and therapy to show for it.

THE REALITY OF A *LACK* OF FAME AND 'SUCCESS'.

Much the same as the above but with the added insult of poverty, rejection and a heavy sense of failure while slumming like a rat in a van from club to club with zero reward for the struggle. Juggling degrading day jobs and a hundred other roles in order to merely stay afloat, thrashing your nervous system beyond repair and living with the knowledge that you will likely have to continue living like this for evermore. Forever 'trying', hoping and hustling, almost always to be met with nothing but disappointment, more lies, rip-offs and still not being good enough. This is the reality for many musicians – the ones who are taking it seriously anyway. The ones who put all their chips down on this music thing long ago and now there's no plan B. Don't believe their Instagram, for it's bad rock 'n' roll manners to complain, expose the industry or admit that you're borderline penniless, have a side hustle at Burger Boys, are being brutally rinsed by labels and managers and are barely getting by. None of us want to admit it, but it's the truth.

THE BLESSING AND THE CURSE OF CREATIVITY.

The notorious tortured artist syndrome. Sure, this is real, but it's not what we're talking about here. The bulk of this industry's mental health crisis is institutional – not everyone who comes here arrives with damaged goods, but almost everyone leaves with some. There's no denying, though, that great art is often the unfortunate outlet of tormented souls and broken angels. The curious, the sensitive, the heavy, the outcasts, the misfits, the victims and the ignored. As artists, we have a unique lens through which we understand the world, which is both our greatest gift and our most painful burden. A burden we're willing to suffer for the privilege of a craft, a passion and a voice. But one that can also destroy us in a thousand different ways. And while it's true that many people come into the music industry with their demons right alongside them, the industry has still got essentially nothing in place to protect its main asset: its artists. And that is gross negligence on a scandalous scale.

THE CULTURE AND THE FICTION OF THE MUSIC INDUSTRY.

You know, where self-destructive, abusive, dangerous, reckless abandon is normalised, encouraged, enabled and expected. Where being legless on vodka at 10 a.m. is seen as hilarious and it'd be disappointing if you weren't. Where gouging your body with shards of glass onstage is seen as a bloody good show and not a worrying sign of encroaching madness. Where sexual predators are heralded as triumphant sportsmen. Where you will be plied with whatever cornucopia of pills, powders or booze your aching heart desires so long as you keep getting on that damn stage. Where dysfunction is standard, self-abuse celebrated, destruction expected and any mention of duty of care for artists is met with an eye-roll. It serves a convenient function too, for it's easier to exploit and control artists who are too drunk to read their contract and will do anything to keep the coke habit funded. From that angle, we can see some labels as nothing more than pimps, with their artists being the drug-addled, coerced, controlled and manipulated prostitutes working for their owner's profit and unable to leave. It's all rock 'n' roll, baby, until someone dies – and then it's even better. The rock 'n' roll cliché is toxic, outdated, unnecessary and anti-artist, and if anyone thinks that's boring, they can fuck off.

So the music industry is stacked up in such a way that it makes mental illness almost inevitable. Yes, some people may have been damaged when they got here, but the vast majority are damaged by the process – and that's a shocking indictment of an industry that delivers so much joy to the world. Regardless of where you are in the pecking order, the common themes are clear: financial insecurity, perpetual emotional flux, a lack of respect or security, the ever-present threat of being dropped or becoming irrelevant with no safety net, and a business model that is principally governed by luck. There are several reasons why this absurd system has survived for so long, but most of it comes down to a thing I call the 'fiction business' – a deception that we artists actively participate in. The fiction business is multilayered, all-pervasive and immensely powerful. Let's get into it.

The fiction business is record labels owning all the major streaming playlists, filling them with their own artists and then saying with feigned surprise: 'Wow, congrats to Devil Dick on topping the Official Metal Playlist on Spotifake.' Or worse, when they have the gall to control a playlist called 'Emerging Talent' or 'Rock Rising' when it's packed exclusively with major-label artists and is very firmly closed to any kind of emerging, rising or unsigned talent. Back in the day, labels would buy their own records so they could force them higher up the charts; these days they do it by inflating streaming activity, monopolising all of the main playlists, shoving boatloads of money into social media boosting, which raises the price of ads for the rest of us beyond what we can afford, using click farms to make videos 'trend' and having armies of creatives around the world saturating the online space with variations of their content. It's gangster tactics. It's commercial bullying. It's bullshit. And you can do a lot of it when you've got the money. Just wait till they ramp up the AI.

But the fiction business runs deeper than mere numbers-fixing and dirty dealings – fiction is the very essence of the music industry. It's in the idea that everyone here is having a great time, all the time, happy faces all around. That everyone here cares deeply about music, art and artists – and that any money is a nice, but incidental, side effect. That the money being carved up in ways that guarantee the artist barely gets any of it always seems to be someone else's fault – someone who's always in a meeting. The fiction business is in the idea that artists never get tired, never get sick and fucking tired of touring, never want a break from doing press and engaging with fans, and never get ill, depressed, anxious or lonely. Happy faces all round. The fiction business is in artists pretending to love all of 'the life' all of the time, never complaining, never demanding more or better, only sharing the glamour, the travel, the parties, the famous friends but never the gruelling motorways, the endless waiting, the lack of sleep, the broken hearts, the dysfunction, the rip-offs and the failures. It's when bands claim to be independent because it makes them look cool, when really they're signed to a massive independent label, which is a very different thing. The fiction business is in the mythology of the rock 'n' roll lifestyle – a smokescreen that intentionally obscures the exploitation, corruption and sickness behind it.

On our part, some of it is the old 'fake-it-till-you-make-it' trick. Some of it is denial. Some of it is ego and some of it is a reluctance to tell the truth because, guess what... the public are in the fiction business too. The public have bought into the fiction that every muso on Earth is a multimillionaire, jetting the globe on private planes, with Chris Martin on speed dial, selling millions of records to legions of adoring fans, partying all the time with a superhuman tolerance for narcotics and supermodels queueing up to have sex with them. And who could ever complain about a job like that?! Some people have got 'real jobs', and mincing around the world with your rich mates and playing music is *not* considered a 'real job'. So speaking honestly about it being anything less than the greatest ride on Earth seems ungrateful, entitled and extremely un-fun. Well, us artists *are* entitled – we're entitled to the same basic human needs as everyone else, but for the most part it seems that we'd rather just play pretend instead because it's easier than accepting how terminally fucked we are. Much easier to have another drink.

Outside of the fiction business, outside of the cartoonery peddled by the music industry and their lackeys in the media, outside of the mythology and wishful thinking of artists and fans alike, lies a stark and crushing truth. And the truth is that many artists are financially desperate, are in a poor state of mental health, are under an intense amount of pressure and anxiety, lack any form of stability and feel they have no one they can speak to honestly about their situation because of the collective lie we've all bought into. Far from living the dream, for many, it's a nightmare.

But the first step to recovery begins with acceptance. Only when we cut the crap that we all so badly want to believe in will we be able to confront the other issues that feed the disease within this business – such as fair remuneration for artists, a duty of care for artists' mental and physical well-being, realistic working schedules, fair and honest working practices, an end to the major-label monopolies, the same social and financial safeguards enjoyed by practically everyone else, government policies that support the arts, and public floggings for anyone who consciously exploits a member of my beloved community. We know all the solutions already; we just need to stand together and fight for them – and the first blow is honesty. Unashamed, impolite, loud and proud honesty. We must harness our enormous collective power as artists and demand that we be treated as human beings – human beings that bring so much light to the world and deserve a little respect. Anything less is just more fiction business, and it's time for that shit to die a speedy death. It's time for us all to be brutally honest about our daily realities, our industry, our struggles, our enemies and our illnesses. Let's fucking shame this industry into changing. But mostly, it's time for us to be honest with ourselves, for the cold truth is that the music industry is not a place of decadence, glory, glamour and riches – a place where talent and hard work prevails. Far from it. This is a place where 80 per cent of the community have become mentally ill as a direct result of being here. Where the rate of suicide and substance abuse is twice as high as the general population. It's time to cut the crap. We all play a part in either keeping the fiction business in business – or burning it down. So why don't I get the petrol and you bring the flame...?

X X X

On Facebook, my life was awesome. A daily brag-fest of new countries, adventures, kick-ass gigs, parties, booze and six-pack abs. It was the only part of the story I wanted to share, and it was the only part of the story that anyone wanted to hear. Messages flooded my inbox about how thrilled they were to see me finally 'making it' and how they'd always known I was gonna 'go places' – mostly from people I hadn't heard from in years. Now they were the best mates I never knew I had (hi, Trev), and I was happy for them to believe it, because I wanted to believe it too.

Because outside of Facebook, it was a very different story. I was under nine stone in weight, an insomniac, drinking to blackout most nights, penniless, single (again), sleeping in a van, depressed, bitter, frustrated, resentful and, despite being surrounded by people 24/7, intensely lonely. The enjoyment of it all had long been eroded by years of rejection, rip-offs, burn-out and struggling on the poverty line. And far from making any money doing this, let alone riches, it was costing me money – money I didn't have. To be in a band, every other aspect of my life had to suffer, and by now, the fabric of my soul had been sandpapered down to a brittle, angry, nihilistic middle finger, one gentle nudge away from destroying anything that moved. Mostly I longed to destroy myself. To just escape it all with a cocktail of booze, a bath and a blade. I'd become addicted to the casino of 'trying' and was, by now, the gaunt and desperate addict abusing himself for just 'one more chance', 'one more shot', one more 'this is the one'. Which made me easy prey for the vultures – and, boy, they came out in packs. My body, mind and soul had been screaming out for sustenance for years, but I'd become deaf to all but the demands of my toxic relationship with music.

And then it happened. I snapped. I shattered. I just couldn't hold it together any more. All of the constructs I'd built over the years of me as a band guy, a musician, a rock 'n' roll nomad, an artist – they all came crashing down in one explosive, uncontrolled demolition. Laying bare the vulnerable, exhausted shell of a man that had been hiding behind it all for so, so long. And by now, I just couldn't care. The breakdown was beyond my control. Mostly, I was sick and tired of pretending. Pretending I was ok, pretending my career was doing better than it was, pretending that this next opportunity definitely sounded legit, pretending I'd spend more time with my family once this tour was over, pretending it was all worth it. Having the weight of my personal fiction business lifted was a sense of liberation and rebirth that I could physically feel in my body. Beneath those fragile constructs lay me as a person – a human being – and for the first time in my life, I yearned to just be that and nothing more. This was beyond ego, reputation, artistic dreams or legacy; it was a primitive necessity that I was unable to deny any longer. Having the walls crash down around me was painful and terrifying – *who was I* without those identities? – but it was out of my control. It just happened, whether I liked it or not. And now here I was amid the rubble of my former self, exposed, defenceless, irrelevant. And it felt incredible.

For the first time in a long time, I began living life – unashamedly and unapologetically. I went on things called 'holidays' – something I hadn't done in over a decade. I started earning money, I caught up with family and friends, I got back with my girlfriend, I ate nice food, I put on weight, went teetotal and, by some bizarre twist of fate, I even started enjoying music again. I started listening to it and playing the stuff purely for fun again, and man, it felt good. Did I release any new music? None. Did I tour? No chance! But I sure played my guitar a hell of a lot more than I ever did back when the only time it saw daylight was when I had a show to do. Needless to say, it wasn't long before my band broke up. A healthy, happy human is of no use to the hungry needs of music industry junkies. But this new feeling of human connection and liberation trumped everything I'd associated with 'the life' and I missed it significantly less than I'd ever imagined I would.

For a while, anyway. Of course, the ole blessing and the curse didn't lay dormant forever, and it was only a matter of time before new songs were flooding out of me and the lust to play them on a stage somewhere started yanking at my heartstrings again. Like I've said, man, it's in the blood. And it wasn't too long before I was back recording, touring and releasing new music, but since that personal great reset, it's all been... different. No longer do I burn the candle at both ends and in the middle too. No longer will I sacrifice my personal well-being, health or happiness at the bloody altar of rock. No more will I endure toxic people or exploitative practices. I say no to things. I maintain a work– life– chill– fun balance where music plays an essential part but doesn't devour every other aspect of my life like a voracious cancer. I cancel things if I need to and I don't accept meetings with industry cannibals because I simply don't desire anything they have to offer me now. I put my health, family and my experience of the full tapestry of life first – the music industry comes a very distant second, if it's on the list at all.

I guess what I'm saying is that I just don't take any of it that seriously any more. The highs or the lows. I just roll with it all, eyes wide open to what's *really* important in life and in music. And what's important for me in life is health, family, happiness and enjoying the miracle that it is to be alive – I've spent enough time in the back of a van, thanks. What's important in music is getting back to where it all started before ego, ambition, pressure and dickheads polluted it all. Tapping back into that childlike feeling of innocent wonder and awe. The cleansing meditation of losing myself for hours on my instrument. Of being a fan again and the buzz of discovering new sounds. Of playing just for the sake of it. Getting back to... the music. The industry will blacken your soul, your passion and your health. For some, it may even kill you. But music? Music was always my saviour, my friend, my happy place – and it still is. After the scaffolding of my life's work and identity crashed down around me, what did I do? I played my guitar. Not to write a song this time, but because I needed to. It was automatic. Just as I did when I was a shy kid being bullied in a strange new school. Or when I got my heart broken for the first time or felt the rush of falling in love. Music was always there for me.

Music never made me ill. Music is, and will always be, the best friend we could ever have. Music only ever had a positive effect on my mental health. It gave me confidence, an identity, strength, inspiration, hope and thrill – and it can do it again and again. Reconnecting with that is what will save us as artists. Approaching the music industry with a clear-headed commitment to what really matters in life and music will protect us from the many poisons that are dumped in our waters. Seeing it all for what it truly is and just focusing on the music. That's what will get us through the rest.

As well as Mother Music, here are some things I've discovered from years of first-hand, expensive trial and error that also work, for me at least, in keeping this crazy bastard on a relatively even keel. Man, I've tried it all – sobriety, therapy, medication, hypnosis, breathwork, fasting, tapping, acupuncture, going vegan, going keto, yoga, exercise, sound baths, ice baths, meditation, smashing shit up, hiking, you name it – in a quest to find ways to calm my frazzled nervous system and reconnect my body and mind with something resembling pre-music-industry normality. Many didn't work for me; some did and do. So let's talk first about sobriety. I did three and a half years without a single drop of alcohol, after more than a decade of heavy daily drinking. And I fell in love with it immediately. My days were longer, I had more energy, my head was clearer, I made better decisions, I was happier, healthier, calmer, I slept better and I realised how thoroughly toxic and boring some of the people in my orbit were without the trickery of booze. There was nothing negative about it at all, only positives, and I would strongly recommend everyone try going alcohol-free – even if just for a while. Why, then, did I start drinking again? Simply put... because I like it. For many, I know that 'going back' is just not possible, and their only option is total and final abstinence, but luckily, I'm now able to enjoy a friendship with booze that's more... shall we say... grown up. Because for me, a cold beer or a neat bourbon is one of the great nectars of life – except now I'm not drinking them to drown my sadness, ease my fears or numb my shame. And that makes a big difference. I'm also not drinking myself into a coma every time a drop passes my lips. My time with sobriety confirmed for me, though, that nothing good can come to us while we're under the tyranny of these traitorous substances. Drugs and booze are not really our friends, and removing their power over us is the catalyst to an avalanche of positivity in our lives. Easier said than done, I know. But I also know that it's possible. If substances are your crutch, you *can* free yourself of them. Help is widely available – please, please, please use it. It'll be the best thing you ever do.

Some of the other things I've learned in my sweatpant-wearing journey into recovery I'm almost gutted to share with you because it means admitting that the hippies may have been right about a thing or two. I am no lover of hippies. Especially the ones with expensive SUVs. But... as much as it burns me to admit it, they're right about a few things. Granted, they stole most of it from the ancient East, but they've been instrumental in spreading it over here for the rest of us, and for that, I begrudgingly thank them. I'm talking of course, about meditation and yoga. I know, I know. Pass me the fucking twinkly bells. But let me be straight here: this stuff *works*, man. I'd go so far as to say that meditation is a superpower. It ain't easy – far from it – but twenty minutes under its gentle blanket can change your entire day for the better. It took me a long time to stop being a cynical jackass and give these things a fair shout, but I'm glad that I did, for I soon unearthed a whole new chamber to my being that I'd long forgotten was there – the human part. The part that had been buried beneath layers of stress, tension, anxiety, speed and adrenaline. The pureness that exists beyond the noise, the struggle, the demons. Through meditation and breathing exercises, I'm able to instantly slice through the bullshit and reconnect with reality any time I need to – and that is a potent power, my friends. By harnessing these powers, I've learned that my anxiety, panic, anger and depression *can* be moderated, and I've enjoyed depths of peace and calm that I thought beyond the reach of my poor, frazzled-out nervous system. After just a short time on the hippie programme, my sleep improved dramatically – which is a miracle for an insomniac – and sleep... well, sleep is the biggie. The number one, most important *pièce de résistance* in the whole goddamn wellness arsenal. Get sleep under control and everything gets better. Real sleep though, not the kind that needs a bag of bennies and a bottle of bourbon. The hippies have given us powerful gifts that cost nothing, can be done anywhere and need no equipment. Bells, incense and tie-dye are not required. So thank you, hippies. I'm still gonna take the piss out of them any chance I get though.

Something else that caught me totally by surprise was the profound benefits to be found in quitting sugar. Trust me, I was a sugar fiend hard-wired into the glucose roller coaster and loving every sweet second of it. But just like booze before it, once I quit sugar and pushed through the very real cold turkey of sugar withdrawal, I felt amazing, fast. My highly charged nerves settled down, my panic attacks mostly disappeared, I had way more energy, no more sluggishness and a mental clarity I hadn't felt in years. I'm actually quite bitter at sugar for being such a sneaky player in my ill health for so long. Why is it that all the things that are the worst for us are always the most fun?

Other things that work for me, and are free and easy, include breathwork for anxiety, spending time in nature, unplugging periodically from the rat race, doing something I love just for the fun of it and spending time with friends and family. Like, ya know, all the normal human stuff. Does this mean I'm cured? Hell no! This is a lifelong battle, but it's one I'm willing to fight. And for the introverts among us, of which there are many, myself included, we need to get our 'me time'. 'Introvert burn-out' is a very real thing, believe me. If I don't get at least one night a week to myself to shut out the persistent pounding of other people, my head starts to crack. I *need* my alone time; it's imperative. Us creatives need our time to dream, to think, to recharge, to be inspired and to plot our next masterpiece. So I enforce that 'alone time' with an iron fist – I *need* it. It can be nigh on impossible on tour when you're imprisoned with the same bunch of mentalists 24/7, but a big part of keeping the show on the road is taking care of ourselves and our personal needs. If we want to be the best – and we do – we must take some breathers from the crazy train now and again.

We need to write new rules. We need to update the rock 'n' roll cliché to one where it IS possible to be a badass rock star and a healthy, happy, well-treated and well-adjusted human at the same time. And if that means other things have to suffer, like the labels' demands for more and more shows, then tough shit. Artists first. There's no music in a dead musician. There are also some incredible organisations out there doing heroic work for our community, providing free support in mental health, hearing health, financial help, career guidance and much more. If you're an artist, please reach out to them, and if not, please support their brilliant work.

Our biggest breakthroughs can come from our darkest battles, and when I look back at those times when I was at my lowest – an emaciated, broke, alcohol-dependent insomniac fantasising about ending it all – I see them now as the moments that ultimately saved me. Not so much the end, but a new beautiful beginning. And so, to the artists reading, I say this. My fellow shaman of sound, you are awesome. You are an artist; you are pure; you bring magic to the world; you change lives; you change the times. You are part of a noble craft and a sprawling, respectable, enviable community. Don't ever forget that, and don't ever feel that you're on your own. If studies prove that 80 per cent of us here feel exactly the same, then you are certainly not alone. We're all in this together. Reach out. You are needed, you are vital and you are loved. The light is right around the corner. You have been blessed with a gift – don't you dare throw it away. Your work here is far from over. If I can do it, you can do it. One day at a time.

15.

HIDDEN HEROES

I get it. It's all about the 'main guys', isn't it? The godlike dudes and dudettes towering over us on a stage, haloed in lights, their voice bellowing down from the heavens in reverb – that's who we're there to see after all, isn't it? So far, this book has focused exclusively on those exalted strata of the music world – their trials, tribulations, adventures and true realities. But behind the stage there is a whole other community of mysterious figures who lurk behind heavy equipment, rush around with large fistfuls of keys, lift stuff, climb stuff, fix stuff and shout at people. And it is these shadowy characters that we're going to study in this chapter like an anthropological field study. Who are they? Do they only come out at night? Should you approach them? We're going to shine the spotlight on the monstrously talented, insanely hard-working and absolutely essential members of the extended family who make the show happen, yet receive none of the glory or recognition.

Granted, we've been talking thus far only about those everyday underdog artists whose 'crew' is comically non-existent, but these guys are underdogs too – the unsinging and the unsung – and they don't grace the pages of music books anywhere near enough. Without these guys there would be no show. Literally. No sound tech – no sound. No lighting tech – no lights. Just a bunch of posers on stage silently flailing around in the darkness. And that goes for the drivers, merch guys, backstage crew, security, promoters, cleaners and runners too. All of them are there long before the artists arrive and leave long after the fun is over. They work more hours than exist in a day, survive on little sunlight or sustenance and rarely see their families or homes – all so that *we* can have the best night of our lives. They're long overdue a shout-out. So let's meet some of them, but approach them slowly and don't look them directly in the eye.

THE TOUR MANAGER

> ***As the TM, I have to be the first one there and the last to leave,***

says Lee Davies, tour manager and merch for bands like Punk Rock Factory, Motionless in White and Atreyu, and a fellow Pontypool boy. That's because a tour manager's job is to oversee and orchestrate all of the many other moving parts, which can range from a relatively lean touring operation, with a driver, sound tech and merch dude perhaps, to a fully fledged army of set designers, backline techs, lighting engineers, fleet of trucks, catering, wardrobe, riggers, pyro dudes and local crews for a larger touring artist. Holding the whole maelstrom together and making sure that everyone gets to where they're needed, on time, is the superhuman tour manager. And it's not just people-herding that falls under the TM's vast jurisdiction, but hotels, flights, budgets, planning, paperwork, payments, travel and the putting out of fires both figurative and literal. The key to it all... is the 'advance'.

> ***The better the advance, the easier the road,***

Lee told me. If you don't know, an advance is a document that lays out every detail of the tour plans for every member of the touring party in *advance* of you all leaving. It can include travel routing, arrival times, accommodation details, contact numbers, stage layouts, parking, food, set-up times, health and safety, insurance, equipment requirements, risk assessments and every possible eventuality that may or may not be likely to bite you on the arse two weeks into the tour. Every member of the touring party gets a copy of the advance, and so long as no one goes rogue and all follow its meticulous itinerary, all should (in theory) go smoothly.

> ***Most of what holds a tour together happens before the tour has even started. It's basically loads and loads of admin work, preparation, spreadsheets... and a little babysitting.***

Babysitting because someone has to get those pesky artists on stage somehow – and sometimes that can mean having to *find* them. You can put as much planning as you like into crafting the perfect advance, but one thing you can't plan for, or control, is those damn artists swanning off to see the local sights and losing track of time. But, generally speaking, the power of the advance is strong. And when it's not, all eyes will fall upon the TM to fix it – and fix it fast.

> ***You want to minimise the amount and the severity of the fires – which there will always be – but if you've got a really good advance and a good team, it can be relatively painless. It's about knowing how to deal with things when they happen, and that can be anything***

> ***from unpredictable artists to weather issues, venue issues, equipment issues – and being able to make those decisions quickly.***

One of your vans has gone AWOL and you're soundchecking in two hours? Singer of the band decides last minute that they're too ill to do the show? The venue had a flood last night? Flights all cancelled? These and a limitless supply of totally-not-stressful curveballs will all be in the remit of the TM to sort out on the spot while in the middle of a tour with a gang of hairy musicians and crew members all staring at them. No pressure then. Which is why your advance should be so watertight that the only things that could possibly trip you up mid-voyage are acts of God.

Lee walked me through an average day on tour. He told me of the 8 a.m. start and the need to be the first one at the venue to make sure everything is running as it should. One small, innocent hiccup in the itinerary could create a shitshow of biblical proportions and it is the TM who will have to deal with it.

> ***It can be something as tiny as access time. If you turn up at a venue to find the doors closed, that half hour of trying to get hold of someone to come and open them up can set the whole sequence of events back in a domino effect. So you have to run a tight ship.***

Once in the venue, Lee will oversee the arrival of whichever local crew has been hired to unload the trucks and assist with stage setting. A local crew is exactly what it says on the tin – a gang of lifters, luggers and techies local to the venue who are hired for that one show. Using local crews means fewer people to house on tour buses for the entire tour. While the local crew are doing their thing, Lee will liaise with security, the backstage crew and venue staff to ensure that all are on the same page and that any unexpected issues with stage dimensions or technical requirements are ironed out fast. And then someone has to find the band and make sure they're onstage for the afternoon soundcheck on time – that someone is the TM. Food may or may not occur around this point, and then once soundcheck is wrapped up, it's all about the show, baby! In a mere few hours, it's game time and every moving part that makes the show happen needs to be moving as one, well-oiled T. rex. Merch, sound tech, lighting tech, backstage crew, security, venue staff, the band – everyone needs to be at their station and ready to give you, the lucky ticket holder, the show to end all shows!

If all goes as it should, the collective juggernaut does you proud and you filter out into the streets with the thrill in your blood, love in your heart and a charge in your soul. Onwards to beers, food and sex. Not so for the crew. Someone's gotta pack everything back down again, stack it into vans or trucks and start dragging it all to the next venue to do it all again tomorrow. Coordinating this manic scramble is our new bestie, the TM. The seconds are everything. People need to sleep; it's been a long day, with another one tomorrow. As the crews do their thing, the TM's final port of call is to settle up with the venue. Ticket sales, costings, splits and profits are divvied up and then – and only then – can the TM crawl onto the bus, squeeze into their bunk and get a few hours' shut-eye before it all begins again. A typical bedtime of around 2 a.m. meaning a standard working day of around eighteen non-stop hours. All hail the mighty TM!

BACKLINE CREW

Enter Eddie Marsh. My good friend Mr Marsh is not only an outstanding multi-instrumentalist, a brilliant songwriter and one of the loveliest blokes on Earth, but he's put in decades of graft behind the scenes for small up-and-coming artists like Bullet for My Valentine, Black Sabbath, Devin Townsend and his main family at Iron Maiden – you may have heard of them? However, all of this is overshadowed by his time playing bass for the legendary James Kennedy and The Underdogs – yep, he's *that* Eddie Marsh. Hailing from Newport, just twenty minutes down the road from Lee, you will see throughout this chapter that Wales produces some of the best crews in the world. Eddie pulls the strings (literally) for one of the biggest bands on the planet as Janick Gers's long-time guitar tech. I know, pretty cool, huh?

So what exactly does a guitar tech like Eddie do? Absolutely everything other than play the actual guitar parts. Do you really think Janick is gonna spend his day tuning and pruning his fucking guitars? Hell no. So Eddie's job includes restringing, tuning, repairing, setting up the guitar rig, modifying, re-valving amps, sourcing spares, tweaking tones, soundchecking, doing the running-onstage-with-a-new-guitar-in-hand routine and being stage-side throughout the entire show to deal with broken strings, broken straps and broken guitars quicker than you can say 'Run to the Hills'.

> ***For a band like Maiden, the techies do all of the pedal changes for the band during the show too,***

the aptly named Eddie told me, and *that*, my friend, sounds like something I need in my life. Tap-dancing, as us guitar players call it, is what we're doing with our feet throughout a concert – operating an array of effects pedals on the floor that we probably don't need but, my God, they're just too irresistible. Except they cause us to be stuck to the spot during the gig, so having someone else do it for you remotely from the shadows while you posture and swagger your way around the place must be pretty damn cool – I wouldn't know. Just one of the many jobs our secret hero is juggling from behind that curtain.

> ***And if something goes wrong, the show cannot stop. You know the old saying, 'The show must go on'? Well, also, the show***

> ***mustn't stop. If something goes wrong, you have to keep it moving by whatever means. If a lead breaks, a guitar breaks, an amp blows – you have to be prepared for that and be ready to immediately replace and repair without a beat. So you have to think on your feet. The show cannot stop!***

Sure, Iron Maiden only perform in front of, like, a million people each night, so I can't imagine an entire guitar rig going down mid-song puts much sweat on one's brow?

> ***The band's entire rig is doubled, so if something goes down, it's immediately replaceable. But then that means you don't have a spare.***

Which is why a guitar tech must be a master of the high-speed repair, on the spot, backstage, mid-show and in the dark. It's intense, high pressure and multifaceted work with 100,000 fanatical fans dependent upon you keeping the solos soaring. So, while the band are running around onstage and the crowd are bouncing in the hall, an entire factory line is working like an orchestra behind the curtain, ensuring that the show goes on – and does not stop.

> ***The call us The Country Club. The riggers who've been there since 2 a.m. building the stage – they call us The Country Club because us techies don't arrive until around 10 a.m. But we don't get back on the bus until gone 2 a.m., and we're working pretty much non-stop during that time.***

Upon arrival at the venue, Eddie explains that it begins immediately. The local crews will offload everything into the middle of the venue while the stage is being built, where the techs can begin their repairing, restringing and re-valving ready for tonight's battle. And once everything is moved again and assembled stage-side, it is the techs who will soundcheck it all for the band. A brief food break and time for last-minute tweaks and checks, and before you know it... it's show time! And thus beginneth the blinding whirlwind of pedal switching, guitar changing and on-the-fly firefighting that will undoubtedly happen during a gargantuan rock 'n' roll extravaganza like Iron Maiden's.

If all goes well (and with your hidden heroes behind you, you can rest assured that it will), the gods are onside, all goes off without a hitch and the night of a lifetime is had by all. But sometimes – just sometimes – catastrophic shit happens. If you think about it, it's pretty mind-blowing that it doesn't happen more often given the ludicrous amount of moving parts, people, equipment and variables that can go wrong, but it's thanks to legends like Eddie that they don't. Sometimes, though, it's just not your night. The last thing you want at a rock show is a sudden silence, and while it can be something as innocuous as a small connector cable that's given up the ghost somewhere in the chain, it can kill the entire operation. For a band like Maiden, where there is just too much investment, too many paying customers and too many livelihoods on the line, this is just not an option – the show *cannot* stop. And that's when you see them – the techies. That's when you catch a rare glimpse of these skinny-jeaned superheroes bursting out of the shadows to sprint onstage and frantically poke and pull at things and work their show-saving magic so that rocking can continue in record speed. And then... in a flash, they're gone again. Concert saved. Without the backline crew, the band would be screwed – and so would the audience. Simple as. Thankfully, due to the diligence and professionalism of dudes like Eddie and Lee, major disasters are mostly a thing of folklore these days: speakers falling on people, stages collapsing, singers catching fire – you know, the fun stuff. But shit very much does still happen, and when it does, the backline crew are ready to pounce.

In a blur, it's all over, and as the band saunter off in their sweaty glory, the breathless backline techs enter the next segment of the working day. Oh, you thought it was all over and they'd be sharing victorious drinks and groupies at a party somewhere? You've been reading the wrong music books, my friend.

We call it the push,

Eddie told me. It's a race to get everything packed down, dismantled and onto trucks in record time so they can start making moves towards the next show as quickly as possible. It's a high-energy military operation undertaken by soldiers who've been on the battlefield since the early hours already. All departments are keen to get to their bunk for a few hours' respite, so the push is the final heave to get a stadium's worth of equipment packed away as quickly as is inhumanely possible. I told you these guys are heroes. If the push is smooth, everyone can be back on the bus by 2 a.m. for some badly needed shut-eye before it all begins again in a few hours. Average daily working hours: sixteen. And they're the fucking Country Club!

THE PROMOTER

Meet Aled Lewis – that's right, another Welshie. Aled runs the amazing Big Day Productions, a promotions company who have hosted shows by Gun, Massive Wagons, Phil Campbell and the Bastard Sons, Kris Barras and many others.

Simply put, I'm the person who organises the gigs,

says Aled, which is a respectably humble way of describing what is actually a very challenging, multifaceted and risky job. You see, when you go to a show at, say, TramShed in Cardiff, someone has had to hire the venue, hire the security staff, hire the sound and lighting techs, pay the band, pay for their rider and also pay for all of the costs and materials involved in promoting the show – a show that, at that point, has sold zero tickets. It's a brave financial risk in an industry that has become synonymous with starving artists, closed venues, growing ticket prices and people not getting paid. A titanic gamble. But for a show to exist in the first place, someone has to roll the dice and put their money where their mouth is – that person is the promoter and God fucking bless them. Nothing shows love for the cause like putting a stack of your own money up front to support music, artists and bringing the good times to your town. And if no one buys a ticket, it's the promoter, and the promoter alone, who is out of pocket. Fair play to them.

So how does it work? Essentially a promoter is the link between venue and artist. At Aled's level, things are a little less risky now that he's mostly working with bands with a reliable audience draw, but in essence it goes like this:

> ***We get regular gig offers from booking agents for artists they've got touring, and our decision to book them comes from research into whether the ticket price point will be right for the area, what else is happening in the area that night, what the band's draw has been in recent history and whether we can afford to put the show on.***

If an offer comes in that a promoter feels they can make work, they accept it and take full responsibility for the show – hiring, financing, organising and promoting. Bear in mind that at any one time, a promoter could have a whole bunch of shows that they're backing.

It's a massive fucking risk. And people not buying tickets in advance, for a promoter, it's hell.

Ah yes, we need to talk about that. Brief digression. Guys, please just buy your damn tickets already! You know you're going, so just buy the things. Promoters and artists really need to know how things are looking for the show. Do we need to 'up' the promo effort for the Liverpool show? Do we need a bigger venue? Should we cut our losses, cancel and save the extra expense? Are we going to break even or prepare to lose a stack of money on the Swansea show? The thing is, while the promoter may have footed the up-front costs for everything, bands still have to travel to the show, eat, maybe stay over and travel back – and bands, as I hope we've established by now, are broke. As in piss-poor, poverty-line broke. They'll be taking a day off from paid work to come to your town and dragging thousands of pounds' worth of heavy equipment with them in an expensive hire van and eating stale sandwiches all day on the off-chance that you motherfuckers *might* grace them with your presence at the show – or you might not. Don't mess us around; if you're coming to the show, let us know by putting your money where *your* mouth is and buying a ticket. Don't do the last-minute 'walk-up' – please buy your tickets in advance and as soon as possible so we can all plan and amend accordingly. Thank you.

Anyway, so the promoter agrees to take on a show and thus begins the spending. Costs include renting a suitable venue, hiring tech staff, and creating and distributing promotional materials. The promoter will then be the ongoing band liaison for the show so it's a job that requires a wild mix of marketing prowess, networking, having a finger on the pulse of the local music scene, artist handling, data crunching, educated risk-taking, blame-taking and *lots* of emails. Aled says:

> ***I don't sleep. I work with bands from all around the world, so sometimes I'm having to arrange something at four in the morning. And I like to go to every show that I'm promoting, so I'll get up, catch up on emails and calls and then get to the venue. I'll be there for soundcheck and the hanging around for fucking hours eating sandwiches. Then we'll do the show, come home and do it all again tomorrow.***

Long hours and a lack of sleep are common themes in this business, if you hadn't noticed. But if the stars align, the tickets sell, the band rocks, the gamble pays off, the promoter makes some money and we all get a killer show, then the whole machine can keep turning and live music lives on. And all because of the initial vision and good faith of our courageous promoter. Thankfully, for Aled, this is the norm more often than not, but for new promoters working mostly with new, unestablished bands in smaller venues, the pain is all too real. We've all seen it. Five dudes scattered across an otherwise empty room as the next Nirvana play their heart out for a crate of beer. For the band, it's all part of the apprenticeship – everyone has to start there and every band has their proud 'one man and a dog' gig story. But no one ever sheds a tear for the valiant promoter – the poor bastard who footed the bill for the show and still had to pay for the venue hire, sound tech, door staff, tickets and advertising costs. They say it's tough at the top – it's even tougher at the bottom. And it's harder now than ever. The dominance of social media, the lack of money in the business, grass-roots venues closing down, the growing cost of everything – it all makes a difficult, uncertain job a hell of a lot tougher and means that people on all sides of the transaction are much less likely to take risks.

> ***Social media is phenomenal; it's a brilliant thing for us all – but it's given people a lot of choice, so it's much harder to promote like we used to and it's made it too easy for people to think that they've promoted a show by clicking a button. Before social media, you'd basically flyer every show. We'd print thousands of flyers for each show, put posters up around town, running down the road with a bucket of wallpaper paste and the police chasing you. And I think that led to a far better scene then. There were less things happening and you could really fucking hammer each show and we had a really good community working together.***

He's not wrong. It's harder now for everyone – for bands to get noticed, for venues to fill their floors and for promoters to promote. So how about a huge, hearty pat on the back for the few people left in this industry who are willing to try and deliver us all from evil by putting their own money in and giving local bands a chance, sometimes at a bitter loss to themselves – the promoters. I asked Aled why the hell he does it.

> ***I just love being outside a venue seeing people coming out smiling. Because that's my job, to make people happy. And when I see that, my job is done – whether I've made or lost money.***

And there it is – he does it for the love of it. Not the money, not the glory. But the love of music and making people happy. It's the same reason we all do it. I can't imagine Ticketmaster or Sony saying the same thing, so please support the love fest. Support your local bands, support your local venues. Coldplay are doing just fine. And please, please, please buy those tickets in advance.

THE SOUND TECH

Aaah, the sound tech. God knows I've screamed at a few, but without these guys and gals we'd all be royally screwed. They are the difference between sound and silence. They are the difference between 'the best gig of the tour' and spending the entire gig fighting the urge to smash everything to fucking pieces. The difference between having a heavenly mix of audio coming at you, where you sound your best and can play your best, or sounding like a muffled bucket of lumpy crap all night – and knowing it. Quite simply, they can make or break a gig – for the band and for the audience. Do not piss them off.

Cardiff boy Dan Wooles is a sound tech who has worked with the likes of Skunk Anansie, Stiff Little Fingers, Those Damn Crows and some bloke called James Kennedy. I've got questions, lots of questions. Like the other legends before him in this chapter, Dan tells me that an average day for him (if there is such a thing) goes something like this:

> ***Let's say we arrive around 10 a.m. The first thing everyone does – and no one mentions this – is run for the toilet, because tour bus toilets only allow for a number one, not a number two, and unless the driver stops at a service station at some point, you just have to wait until you reach the next venue.***

The pain is real. Tour buses are not much fun, and neither are motorways, city traffic, diversions, gridlocks, narrow claustrophobic bunks, snoring drummers, farty guitar techs and holding in the need to drop a deuce until Dundee. Once the deed is done, work can commence. You guessed it – it begins with the loading in of comically heavy and expensive audio equipment, and Dan then immediately gets to getting everything set up, plugged in and tested before the band arrives for soundcheck. Time is everything. If there are problems, you need to be fixing them now and not five minutes before the first band is set to start. Remember, these guys are the difference between sound and silence – and no one is coming to the gig to listen to silence. Every venue is different, has different acoustics, a different layout and set-up, so this initial prep time is paramount to ensuring a smooth rest of the day.

If nothing bites you on the arse, the band will arrive in a few hours, you do a soundcheck, everyone's happy and you can hopefully nip out, have a bite to eat and catch your breath before the show starts. The reality, however, is that you'll probably still be tweaking by the time the doors open, especially if you're dealing with one of those pretentious prats who wants:

a little less high end on the vocal reverb

ooh no, now a little more, please

no, that's too much, a little less, please

nearly there, just a touch more

Ok, let's go with that *for now*. Now can we spend an hour checking the Mongolian skin flute that I use on one fucking song? Thanks.

Believe me, I've seen it and it hurts to watch. If crap like this chews into time, then you can be stuck behind the mixing desk until the doors open – and then, of course, you're doing the show. Which means no food and no toilet break. So there's little rest for the wicked and another reason to prioritise that early morning offering to the porcelain gods. This is almost always true for the poor 'in-house' sound engineers you'll see at smaller venues who are mixing the sound for several bands a night that they've never worked with before. These often all require different set-ups and audio mixes, which the tech will mostly be doing on the fly after already working non-stop since midday – all for some prima donna like me to have the gall to give them shit when the vocal monitor isn't quite perfect on the first song.

> ***Nobody notices sound engineers when everything goes right; they only notice them when something goes wrong,***

Dan told me, and he's not wrong. So please show your sound tech some love, guys! They work hard, and they're responsible for *your* sound, so tell them 'thanks for the sound, mate, it sounds incredible up here' and then get the hell off the stage before you start wondering if that reverb really does need just a little more high end. Don't be that dickhead. And if you *are* that dickhead – ya know, barking orders at them throughout the show – our ever-stoic sound techs have got a little something for you. It's called the DFA channel.

Truthfully, I almost don't want to tell you about this out of respect for my long-suffering sound tech brethren and sistren. But for the musicians reading this who have always wondered (and I know you have) whether the sound tech is actually doing anything in response to your never-relenting requests for 'more me, more me' in the monitors, then let me tell you... you're right. They may be seen to move a fader on the mixing desk. They may give you the 'hows that?' look and the thumbs up to imply that they've sorted it. What they've done, dear reader, is turn up the DFA channel – with DFA standing for Does Fuck All. Yep, it's true. I mean, we always kinda knew that might be the case, but now Dan has confirmed it for me and, yes, all sound techs are in on the blag. I love that. I love that we've all been getting DFA'd good and proper all this time and most likely deserved it. That's a cheeky win for bedraggled sound techs the world over.

Anyway, food break or not, the doors are open before you know it and the sound tech will spend the rest of the night hunched over that mixing desk making sure that both band and audience get the best sound possible. By this time, they've already been there for nine hours and haven't seen daylight. And unlike the backline crew and band, the sound tech is often stationed right out there in the middle of the hyena's lair – by which I mean the general public – and that's a whole other load of head-cooking to deal with.

> ***I've had to knock people's pints off my mixing desk before now. I've actually had people put full pints on top of a forty-five-grand mixing console.***

Yup, those fuckers be crazy. I'm not surprised in the slightest. If our poor sound tech makes it to the end of the show relatively unscathed by demanding artists, technical challenges and a drunken, spewing, fighting public, then they've made it through round two! I'll give you three guesses as to what round three entails. Nope, not beers, not parties, not bed, but packing it all away again before the doors close and they can crawl back on that bus. Daily working hours: approximately fourteen. It's tough being a sound tech, but it's also the one role that absolutely every gig at every level has to have, or else... silence. So, next time you see a burnt-out, grey-skinned sound tech, tell them how much their sound rocked tonight, that you can see how hard they've worked, and do not, under any circumstances *ever* put your fucking beer on their mixing desk.

X X X

Now before we go any further, how about a rapturous, roof-rattling racket of applause for every driver, rigger, sound tech, cleaner, tour manager, backline tech, promoter, security guard, set designer, lugger, lighting engineer, merch dude and all of the hard-working, talented, selfless, patient and downright bloody awesome crew members the world over who keep this industry kicking. Without them, we'd be nothing. There would be no music. There would be no live shows. It's as simple as that. So let's drag them all out onstage, ramp up the stage lights and let 'em know we appreciate them. That their indispensable brilliance does not go unnoticed.

For they are the true heroes of rock and we salute each and every one of them.

And if you want to join the ranks of these legends and be a rock 'n' roll superhero like Lee, Eddie, Aled and Dan, they've got some priceless words of advice for you.

> ***Start with a local crew and get involved with the tours coming through your town. Get your hands dirty, get to know the moving parts. Meet people. Earn your stripes. Be the merch guy. Lift some shit. Help out. And then find the part that you love the most and specialise in it,***

says Lee in a sentiment almost identically echoed by Eddie:

> ***Find your local tour-crewing company and offer your hands. You'll start doing the dirty work – lifting, fixing, running errands – but you'll learn the ropes and you'll get yourself in the circle. Learn as much as you can and then pick what most interests you and then specialise in that. At the start you won't get much money, but you'll learn, make contacts, get experience.***

Sound advice that applies whether you're interested in sound-teching, promoting, doing merch, rigging, driving, whatever – get involved in your local scene, do the work, meet people, learn the ropes, earn the stripes, get started. Offer yourself as an assistant or helper to some local dudes and learn from them. One day, they'll be ill and you'll get your first job – that's how it works. Dan points out that these are all skills that are easily applicable in other industries too. Like, you don't have to be a sound tech for a sweaty rock 'n' roll band – there is a very comfortable and well-paid living to be made doing the sound for corporate events or theatre, for example. You can be a tour manager, techie or set designer for a theatre production or celebrity chef on tour. And the opposite is also true. On a tour the scale of Iron Maiden's, there are countless roles involved that don't require heavy lifting or loud noises. Eddie tells me:

> ***Being in a touring party, you don't necessarily even need to be musically talented as there are set designers, drivers, clothes designers, seamstresses, make-up – so if you like travelling and like the idea of being on a tour package, there are loads of roles you can get into – and get paid!***

It's a great point. But whichever way it goes down, there is one thing that there's no escaping from… the travel.

> ***The hardest thing – unlike bands who do a tour and then go home, crews will jump from one tour to another, so you have to be ok with being away from home for most of the time. You miss birthdays, you miss funerals, you miss births, you miss Christmases, you miss everything. There's a lot of sacrifice in it. So you have to love it. If you don't love it, don't do it – you will not last,***

says Lee, with whom all agree about the one, universal downside of 'the life'.

> ***Being away from home, definitely! And staying healthy on the road is also really difficult,***

adds Dan, with a heartbreaking elaboration from Eddie:

> ***The hardest part is being away from home, missing your kids and family so much – while being on this whirlwind, rock 'n' roll jaunt around the world, trying to hold this rock 'n' roll extravaganza together, and then your seven-year-old daughter says:***
>
> ***'Daddy, when are you coming home? I really miss you.'***

He continues:

> ***The travelling can also be brutal – even at the Maiden level. Whether it's a transit van or a bunk on a pro-level tour bus, cabin fever is cabin fever and a motorway is a motorway. Planes still get cancelled, buses still break down. And you can be on a bus for twenty-three hours, stopping only twice to relieve yourselves.***
>
> ***But the travelling can also be the best part as you're spending time with your extended family who've all had very interesting lives, so you're sharing stories from your various previous tours and experiences, having a laugh and being there for each other.***

And amen to that! But what about all the wild, disgusting, excess, filth, drug bingeing and partying that we've been told happens every night with every band who ever lived? Surely that passes a few hours? Well, Aled is here to burst a bubble:

> ***The rock 'n' roll lifestyle is well and truly a fantasy. People think that touring is all being pissed backstage, girls and lines everywhere, having a laugh. Wrong. We're all sitting around bored as fuck with a cup of tea, waiting for something to happen for five hours.***

Lee agrees:

> ***I hate to disappoint you, but honest to God, it's not as rock 'n' roll as it used to be. If you walk down Bunk Alley at six in the morning, everyone's in bed.***

I hate to say I told you so. The times have changed. Or have they? It's been remarked by veteran industry insiders that less than half of what we've been told about the good-time shenanigans of the music biz is based on anything resembling truth. The rest, as they say, is a big pile of steaming horse shit – and always was. Modern economics, however, have ensured that the nail stays well and truly in that coffin – which is another way of saying that these days there's simply not enough money to pay for anyone's stupid shit, so 'pro up' or go home. Lee explains:

> ***People are making nowhere near the money they used to in this industry – and it costs SO much more now to put on these shows. Plus livelihoods are at stake, so if a show gets cancelled or is subpar because of some bullshit, everyone in the whole touring party is affected. No one can afford that.***

It's an interesting parallel with what's happening *on* the stage too – for in the same way that musicians now have to double as graphic designers, producers, admin clerks and web developers in order to save costs, roles among crew members are also merging because of budgetary constraints. Eddie told me:

> ***Things are getting smaller instead of bigger because everything now costs so much more, and everyone is getting paid less because there's less money in the business – so you're seeing sound techs also now being the driver and the tour manager. But that puts more pressure on everyone, which takes a toll on people's mental and physical health.***

Lee confirms this to be the case and says it only leads to looser ships, lower quality, more pressure and more burn-out. Am I trying to turn you off? Hell no! I'm just being honest because I want you to dive in with your eyes open and your boots on. All of these guys continue to work, love and thrive in the barricades and say they wouldn't have it any other way. Seeing the world, meeting amazing people, hanging with the stars, escaping the suck of the day job, using your talent to make magic happen for adoring fans every night and getting *paid* for it... well, it sounds pretty cool to me! I'll let Aled have the final word on it:

> ***I love it, mate. I just love it. I've been doing this thirty-five years and I'll stop when I'm dead. I have no idea how to do anything else. This is me and I love it. No matter how corrupt it is, no matter how dodgy it is, I love the industry.***

Concordo, Mr Lewis, *concordo*. I need say no more. To the legions of honourable supermen and women the world over who devote their lives to keeping us all stocked up in the good stuff, we thank you. You guys fucking rock.

16.

KILL THE MACHINES

The times they are a-changin', so, before we proceed, let's raise a glass to the past. And as we hurtle towards the future, bleary-eyed and bewildered, I wish you good luck – because you're gonna need it, my friend. Shit is about to get weird. Really weird. And neither you nor I are even remotely prepared for it.

Picture the scene. A breathtaking, spine-tingling, tear-wrenching opera performed with such soul-trembling perfection that you're transported to other dimensions from your centre-stage seat at La Scala opera house, Milan. An overwhelming emotional charge swirls through every cell in your body. It's transcendent, primal, religious – and you're not even religious. This is music. The way it's meant to be. Live, human, physical, communal, divine.

Except it's not. You're not in Milan. You're in Swansea, sitting in your pants on the sofa shovelling crisps into your face – but VR technology is now so advanced that it makes actual reality seem... well... a bit crap. So next stop is Singapore for the Queen concert with an actual Freddie Mercury on vocals! And who can blame you for that?

The musicians performing these immaculate conceptions are true-to-life avatars, unconstrained by age, energy, illness, bad days or rehab, who can be in 195 countries at the same time, performing 24/7, perfectly every time. That voice though? Oh, that's just one of the many voice licences now owned by the giant major-label-and-big-tech mergers who have bought up the rights to every iconic singer ever known. Because that's how it works now. You see, no one really *does* singing any more; they just sell the rights to their voice and a machine does the legwork for them. Wanna watch Adele singing with Jimi Hendrix and Beethoven on drums? You've got it, but you'll have to pay for it – and who gets the money? That's right – Gooliath UniVerse. One of three companies who now control all the content on Planet Earth.

Music fans love it. Tech nerds love it. Everybody loves it – and the music labels *really* love it. Musicians? Ah well, they're extinct now. Irrelevant. A quaint relic from an ancient past when mere mortals had to do things, like... in reality. Man, how that must have sucked! I'm speaking, of course, about the rapidly encroaching invasion of artificial intelligence into our worryingly unprepared and unprotected music space – and it's closer than you might think.

Now, by virtue of me being ancient, I can remember a time when things were very different. Hear me out – I'm not about to get all 'back in my day' on your ass – far from it. But I'm old enough to remember a time when there were no mobile phones... or even Internet. Wrap your head around *that* one, Gen Zedders! It was a time when music could only be consumed on chunky lumps of plastic and played through even chunkier lumps of plastic called hi-fi systems. It was an expensive addiction. Major labels dominated, artists got screwed and the music fan got what they were given. And no one knew otherwise.

Soon, the Internet came along and life got a lot quicker. Suddenly music could be consumed through the air and streamed through a tiny device that connected us at all times to more information and more content than it would ever be possible to fathom, consume, retain or navigate. Major labels dominated, artists got screwed, the music fan got what they were given. And no one knew otherwise.

Then came the robots. Unhindered by human limitations, these motherfuckers churned out bangers by the thousands – all day, every day. It was a massacre. Us poor bastards with our wooden caveman instruments were obliterated overnight. They called it Music 2.0 – we called it Music Game Over. Major labels dominated, artists got screwed, the music fan got what they were given. And no one knew otherwise...

So what's my point? My point is that while we're not there yet, we're disturbingly close to the beginning of Music Game Over, and that all of us have an urgent role to play in applying the lessons of the very recent past to minimise the damage. I'll explain. Record companies exist to make money. Lots and lots of money. Their love for music exists so long as music is lining their pockets and filling their nostrils. They care not for art, artists or culture – and they play a significant role in the destruction of all three. Let's call them Enemy Number One.

Enemy Number Two is the tech companies. These fresh-faced hipster nerds should not be trusted. They are not our friends; do not be fooled. They also exist for a range of nefarious reasons that include collecting data on our every desire, weakness and perversion, influencing our political leanings, censorship, spreading disinformation and advertising – oh, and making *shit* tons of money.

And Enemy Number Three... is us. Our historic compliance in being happily shepherded into our own subservience suggests a pattern that isn't likely to help us much when the robots come a-knocking. And that, my friends, is an unholy trinity that could be the death blow for music as we know it and the sexy humans who write and perform it for us. These are powerful enemies, and at the moment, we're all too busy marvelling at the gadgets and gimmicks to spot the artificial ass-whipping that's gaining on us. Am I being paranoid? Probably, but that doesn't mean they're not after you.

Here's my beef. Yes, I've got a horse in the race, but I'm no mere music maker – I'm a music lover. I'm a disciple. Hell, I'm a music fundamentalist. And I believe that music – in fact all art – is an essential expression of the human condition as we ride our one-way ticket on this spinning rock. Not just essential to enjoy but essential to make. Art is the crowning jewel in our species' accomplishments; it is the very essence of what makes us human, and it's a limitless manifestation of our deepest truths. Art is the mirror that reflects our common beauty, evil, struggles and love. It is the language that unites us all and is a portal to our personal gods or demons. Art ignites the flame in our heart, nourishes our soul and floods us with wonder. Art kills fascists. Art is what makes life worth living. I like art.

But art is a human sport – by humans, for humans. It requires a human heart, human flaws, human fears and human love. No machine will ever be able to create art that truly resonates on the primordial, godlike level that transcends dimensions and electrifies bones. I mean, it'll give you a damn good approximation, but nothing more. By its very nature (no pun intended) AI can only ever produce an algorithmic repurposing of stuff that already exists but which won't be infused with any relatable human pain, adventure or ecstasy. And why the hell would we want it to anyway? It's not like we're in short supply of the holy water, is it? I mean, we're fucking drowning in music out here, man! We've already got more music than we will ever be able to listen to in a hundred lifetimes. So it's not a supply issue. And it's certainly not an access issue – musicians are literally giving the stuff away for free now. Why, then, would we willingly watch our most treasured gift being tossed on the scrapheap of history to be replaced by a cheap, artificial, disposable substitute?

On our part – mine and yours – it's a laziness issue. A convenience issue. As always. It's why we'd rather have tinny digital music streamed directly into our earholes than get off our arses and put a record on through a good set of speakers – or better still, go to a live show. I'm not saying I'm any better; I'm just saying we're trading the real deal for lazy convenience. And on the industry side, it's a making-truck-loads-of-money-without-ever-having-to-pay-anyone issue. As always. Having the Terminator rattling out songs 24/7 will be a gold rush for the music industry villains the likes of which they have never known. And it's coming.

Does it matter? Well, if you care for innovation, human expression, creative genius and having the hairs on the back of your neck stand up, then yes, it matters a lot. It also matters if you have a passing interest in truth. We're already living in a post-truth nightmare where politicians lie, corporations lie, the media lies – I don't want my fucking music to lie to me as well. Music is the antidote to everything that sucks about life, and I want to know that when I listen to my heroes, I'm listening to my heroes – not a clinical AI doing a digital impression of them and singing things they never sang and saying things they never said. I want to marvel in awe at the uber-human ability of some people to eclipse their mortal boundaries and blow our minds with their impossible magic and talent. To be inspired by their example. The type of shit that's easy for a computer to knock out is not so easy for us – and that's part of the appeal. Leave me my magic.

Which brings me to my next point: effort. Like I said, art is not only essential to enjoy, but essential to make. Nothing so good ever came easy. Not only is there an immense amount of value and reward in creating something from nothing by yourself, but the pursuit of doing so will bring purpose, vision, meaning, self-discovery, adventure, discipline and growth into your life – and that's all good stuff. Any monkey can push the 'generate' button, but where's the fun in that? Where's the sense of achievement, of pride? Where's the skill, the devotion, the self-expression? So paint your own damn painting. Write your own damn book. And play your own damn music. I mean, what else are we gonna do? The devil makes work for idle hands – remember that. Art is a noble and necessary endeavour – be an artist. And what of the reward for the listener, too? Where's their human connection? Where's their emotional investment?

Music made by AI will only ever be a cheap cover version of something already made previously by the 'real guys'. Even if you can't tell the difference, that's not the point. Do we want to make an entire industry redundant? I always thought that the purpose of technology was to take the shit jobs off our hands so we can sit around philosophising, creating art and smoking weed. But it seems I had it all backwards. For soon, the technology will be creating art all day and 'expanding its consciousness, man', while we scrape our way through some desperate, dusty existence like a grubby subspecies and people sit at home in their VR headsets thinking they're watching an actual Kurt Cobain. He's dead, people – get over it!

So who wants this? I'll tell you who wants it – Enemy Number One and Enemy Number Two. And the first ones on the fire will be the library music guys. You know that harmless instrumental background music you hear in adverts and TV shows? AI can already churn that stuff out like mincemeat, so those guys will be KO'd in one, swift blow. Next up, the electronic music producers. Music made entirely with electronic sounds is much easier for a machine to pull off convincingly, and most people won't be able to tell the difference. So bye bye, Zed. Then will go the songwriters. Why would a label give up a slice of its feast to some needy songwriters when it can get RoboCop to do it for free? And then it'll be the performers. No more will you need an actual singer or guitarist, for AI will provide you with a plethora of the best mouths and fingers in the known universe. Unconstrained by vocal range, speed or physical possibility. And if you want 'actual Ed Sheeran' or 'actual Taylor Swift' on your song, you can have them – for the last-ditch attempt to stay relevant for the upper 1 per cent of artists will be to license the sound of their voice to the labels and let AI do the rest.

Of course, all this stuff is commonplace already – we know that – but we're still in the 'gawping-at-the-gimmick' stage right now. Like, 'Dude, that fake Drake song sounds just like Drake, sick!' The wholesale erosion of the music industry from bottom to top has yet to pick up cancerous speed, but the tentacles are taking position as we speak. And by the time you read this, I will already be light years behind the times. Soon, music made and performed by humans will be viewed like handmade trinkets at a market stall – a cute throwback to an ancient time when people did stuff by hand. Something for the mantlepiece, perhaps, but ultimately a bit pointless.

The music industry has a real opportunity right now *not* to make the same disastrous, ignorant mistakes it made with the arrival of digital music not so long ago. To have some foresight, brave leadership and vision – but our track record in those areas is not good. If you think about it, the music industry has already been the crash-test dummy for several major technological shifts that went on to dominate all other areas of our lives – so we're well placed to heed the warnings this time around and insist on playing an active part in the direction this is going before it's too late. But I'm not confident. Serious issues are going to flare up around copyright, plagiarism, royalties and redundancy of skill sets – and we should be getting our shit together right now to nail down tight boundaries around what exactly the role of AI will and *should* be in the music industry.

There are endless useful applications for AI to help actual artists do their art. Editing, social media, content organisation, planning, scheduling, massaging our ego or answering our never-ending bloody emails. But creating and performing the music? Fuck that. Like I told you, I'm a music fundamentalist. I'm not naive, though, and I know that regardless of whether I or anyone else likes it or not, the times they are a-changin' – a-changin' forever. Sure, there have always been old fucks fearing the future and lamenting the loss of some mystical past – but there have also always been vultures ready to trash the planet, art, people and nature in order to make a quick buck. So are we to expect artist-friendly regulation to come from the same cartel who stand to make a killing off of the coming gold mine? What do you think?

Sadly, there has always been an acquiescent third party willing to allow the vultures to let rip, which brings me to Enemy Number Three – us. We are on the cusp of a new dawn in the human story – one that is significantly less human than ever before, and there will be no going back. If ever there was a time to sharpen up and get wise to the coming tsunami, it's now. It doesn't seem as if any help is likely to come from above – so this one's on us. All of us. It's time to take a side. Do we stand with artists, and art? Or do we choose the mindless consumption of a blizzard of content rattled out by unfeeling machines? It's our choice. Let's not forget who was there for us when we needed them. Who provided the soundtrack to our lives, our good times, our bad. And who were even cool about it when their trade became profitless, but still carried on dishing out the good stuff despite being unable to eat. So when the time comes, they can count on us to have their backs, right? We are human. We are real. Our ancestry goes back millions of years and it lives on within all of us. No machine could ever stir up our most primal, animalistic desires – only a fellow human can do that. And musicians have been doing exactly that for us since the birth of sound – don't let them be thrown to the flames. When the choice comes, choose the human, choose the real.

Is this new, corporate-approved music-by-algorithm going to scream at us to rise up against injustice and fight the power? Or will it be daft, banal background noise designed to aid mass consumption and obedience to our masters. Do you really trust our government-affiliated big-tech overlords to have our best interests at heart? Recent fuckery in social media (shadow-banning, data mining, censorship, disinformation and the rest) should tell us all we need to know about *that* evil alliance. And what of innovation? New sounds and new movements? I would argue (and I will) that all new musical movements are sparked by struggle and the insatiable need for us to express ourselves despite those struggles – in fact, because of them. The blues, hip hop, punk rock – none would exist were it not for the social climate that forged them. And a robot knows no struggle; it knows no pain; it knows only its master – and its master ain't us.

In case you couldn't tell, I think machines have no place in the arts. Machines should do machine stuff. For too long, humans have been doing machine stuff (labouring, transporting, mining – stuff that's dangerous and detrimental to human health) – let the machines handle that shit and leave the art to us. Let's say it one more time for the people at the back: the arts are a miraculous expression of the human condition, the human journey and human emotion – they should be created and performed by humans. Disagree at your own peril. Although I fear the takeover will be inevitable eventually. It will begin like it always does – seemingly innocent at first, just a bit of fun – and before you know it, there'll be no going back. It is in this honeymoon period where we have our last chance to lay down some rules. Perhaps AI creators should have to be registered as a corporate entity, and the users of their content should have to pay a royalty like they would with any other. This could ensure that human artists aren't priced out of the market, and the money earned by these AI artists could be funnelled into support programmes for human musicians and artists. And AI productions must be clearly labelled as such so that people know what they're getting. We're starting to see this happening on more and more platforms already – and so we should. We do this with food already (organic, vegan, no GMOs etc.) and as far as I'm concerned, music is food. Who knows? But regulation there must be, or we're all toast.

More than likely there will be winners and losers like there have been with every major model change in music – and who might the winners be this time? Correct. The new boss will be the same as the old boss. The gargantuan, global record-industry monopolies who own all the mega-catalogues will be just fine, and the even bigger and more powerful tech companies, who own the platforms and the tech, will be even better. The rest of us? I shudder to think. Embrace the new, they'll say. And, as always, we'll try. Get with the times, Grandad, they'll say – and, of course, we'll have to. But the times of which they speak will be times in which art in any true, human sense will be dead and buried. Music will be a throwaway, forgettable soundtrack to further consumption and compliance, coming at us so fast we'll have no time to think, to feel or to question. Checkmate. Just where they want us. Music finally overthrown as a conduit to human progress and co-opted as a tool of the system. Thankfully, due to my questionable relationship with self-care, I will have tapped out of this mortal coil long before it all gets too ridiculous.

Art is our species' proudest moment. An unparalleled achievement that tells our extraordinary story and enriches our one-way journey. Treasure it, for the battle has already begun. Don't say I didn't warn you. Fellow humans, we need you. And you need us. Look at history. See the pattern. Think of what's at stake. Make the right choice. For, as always, it's on us. Which side are *you* on?

17.

THE NOISE

Less is more. I hate that saying. It's a tired, dilapidated cliché usually smugly uttered by the pompous faux-cool who don't know what it means but say it because they think it sounds clever. The phrase has been popularised by Jazzers (urgh) espousing the idea that it's 'the space between the notes that matters as much as the notes themselves, bro'. Or some shit. Rubbish. More is more and I want more of it. Turn it up, speed it up, load it up and double it. Fuzz it up, punk it up and pour a little trouble in it. Give it to me both barrels. Pin me to the wall. Grab me by the throat and *make* me fucking listen. Less is more? Piss off.

But get this... even I'M starting to think that, these days, a little less might not be the worst idea in the world. Allow me to explain. Right now, at this very moment, you've got over 100 million songs in your phone ready at the swipe of a finger. There are nearly twenty billion videos on TikTok and around 100 million pictures are posted on Instagram every single day. By the time you read this, those numbers will be the quaint throwback to simpler, sepia times. We are living in a world that has far overtaken our ability to process it. We are punch-drunk from a non-stop bombardment of images, sounds, videos, adverts, arguments and propaganda that is causing a mental health epidemic and trashing our brains and nervous systems. We are being made sick from having too much. Our attention spans have dwindled to the shameful, our bodies, reward system is partied out, we're distracted, addicted, confused, insecure, anxious and, despite having more information than all of human history in our pockets, more clueless than ever before. Why? Because we've got too much stuff. We just can't keep up with it, and the more we try, the more it burns us out.

I'm ancient enough to remember life before it was thrown into technicolour warp speed, and having played out one half of my life at a slower pace and the other half in the Brave New Weird, I reckon my generation's got an interesting vantage point from which to understand the current crisis of more, more, more. Now, surely I don't need to caveat this with some grovelling preamble about how much I love technology and the new powers it has given us all? Please tell me I don't need to first prove how thoroughly 'down with the kids' I am and that this isn't going to be the ramblings of an old, out-of-touch dickhead. And I'm sure we all want me to skip the part where I try to remind you that I am – and have been for a long time – an outspoken evangelist for the new digital music model and a salty, bitchy critic of the old one. So then let's proceed.

Because us Gen Xers and millennials grew up right across the transition line between the old world and the new – and, as such, I believe we have a unique insight on the world of today. Some of us do anyway. I can vividly remember a time when there was no Internet. No mobile phones. No social media, no music streaming, no selfies, no influencers and no doomscrolling. I'm *not* saying it was better. I'm just saying. There was a lot that was woefully shit about it. Like shelling out twenty quid for a huge chunk of plastic so we could listen to the few measly songs that we liked. That sucked. Learning guitar meant hunting down some old blues dude in town and forking out even more of our hard-earned cash, *or* trying to find something remotely cool to play in our dad's dusty old guitar books – instead of just firing up YouTube and getting lessons direct from our heroes. Discovering new music meant whatever the guy at the local music store thought was cool that week. The music press was a handful of magazines who were all in the pocket of the major labels. There was no file sharing, no MP3s, no up- or downloading. Everything was either on a big, chunky piece of plastic… or it didn't exist.

And then came along the digital age and bestowed us with wonders that teenage me would have traded a leg for. Man, I would have *killed* to have had YouTube when I was a kid. But with the benefit of being prehistoric, I can also see what it has taken away from us. Like time. Time to think. To process. To digest. To create and to dream. And time to truly *listen*. When you've only got twenty albums, you have to deep-dive the hell out of them. Because they're all you've got. So you savour each aspect of every song, discovering new layers of wonder with every spin. It's a beautiful thing. I mean, there wasn't much else to do back then – no phone to check, selfies to take or web to surf. So listening to music meant lying back and listening to the whole glorious album as you dreamed impossible dreams, undisturbed and un-bombarded.

There's immense value in that, and I mourn the days when my mind could roam freely, thinking and dreaming for hours at a time. There's no time for that any more. I've got newsfeeds to scroll, messages to reply to, links to check out, arses to look at, strangers to argue with and an online persona requiring constant maintenance with new pictures, videos and updates on my every move and fleeting thought for God knows who to consume. As artists, we now spend less and less time making music and more time editing photos, making videos, managing social media profiles and jumping through hoops for algorithms.

Along with time, this new wonderland has robbed us of our headspace. How can we think straight, let alone process information, create art, form our own opinions, learn something properly or truly innovate anything, when our head is being bashed in every second of the day with chatter, gossip, adverts, arguments, chat groups, bad news and media content? We can't. It's content overload over here, and our brains are just simply unable to make sense of it all. Which is why it's now being fed to us in ever-shorter servings. Get this... what's considered to be a high attention retention rate on TikTok is a few seconds. Read that again – a few fucking seconds! I'm just gonna throw this out there – no great work of art will ever be created or enjoyed in a world where people can't wait more than a few fucking seconds. As with politics, as with art – we get what we'll take. If we're cool with high-speed, throwaway junk food for our ears and our soul, then guess what we're gonna get more of? And who, ultimately, will be to blame for that? I'm not even gonna let that hang; I'm just gonna say it – we fucking will. We get the culture and the politicians we deserve – and we, my friends, we deserve better.

But what has any of this got to do with music? Well, everything! If you're a struggling musician drowning in the static of a billion other bands, if you're an old fart lamenting the end of the classic band, or if you're a music lover desperately yearning for a deeper connection but not feeling it in a cheesy three-second video reel, then this is the reason why. We've all got way too much stuff and no time to wade through it all. We've been sucked into the irresistible pull of the sugary vortex, and now it's spinning so fast we can't even imagine a life outside of it. Technology has given us many incredible riches, but it's also making us increasingly untethered from our innate need for connection and community – two things that us old bastards used to have in warm, cuddly busloads while huddled around a spinning piece of plastic with good friends and time to kill. No phones pinging, no one documenting anything – just the liberating luxury to listen and lose yourself for hours and hours in the healing waves of music's therapeutic witchcraft. I know it exists because I've been there – and those who haven't are really are missing out.

THE NOISE

I call it the noise. The incessant migraine of content tugging at our attention every second of the day. Of messages, opinions, trolls, bots, adverts and jingles. Too much time in the noise and it erodes your ability to think, to feel, to dream and enjoy. Too much time in the noise and the anxiety takes hold, the feelings of worthlessness and overwhelm. Too much time in the noise and you might start believing that Roger Waters is an actual Nazi because he played one in a fucking play. The noise is bad. Bad for you, bad for society, bad for the body and bad for the mind. And it's bad for art, especially music. Music was the noise's first victim. It was the noise that convinced us all that music has no inherent value. That a musician's true destiny is to spend their time making crappy little videos for dorky tech companies to make billions from. The noise is the reason your amazing songs can't find an audience. The noise is the reason that more and more twentysomethings are gravitating towards music that was made before they were even born. The noise is a problem.

The sick joke in all this, of course, is that inside the noise, it is *us* that's the product. Our data, our shopping habits, our voting habits, our musical tastes and our twisted sexual interests. Scooping all that shit up and selling it to shadowy corporations and government agencies to further exploit *us* is what the game is really all about. So they keep hitting us with another hit, another dose, another fast fix – until we're too addicted to the noise and too bamboozled to know what's even going on any more.

Old-timers like me remember life before the noise very well, and we know that a world of less has got a lot going for it. As I said, the reason more people don't truly LOVE bands the way they used to is that there's just too many of them now. We're drowning in songs here, so who cares? When you've only got those twenty albums I mentioned, you really have to commit to them. You study the inlay card, learn the words, wear the T-shirt with pride and that band becomes your gang, your cult, your tribe, your identity. Sure, this is all still alive and well – Swifties and The Black Hearts Club, we salute you – but for too many of us, there's just no time. Listen to a whole song? That's ten lifetimes in TikTok years, you mad man! And hey, I'm not dissing anyone here; things change, and I get that, but I fear we're straying far from the land of developing deep and meaningful connections to music or anything else. And we need that. We really do. The good news is that we can still have it, but we're gonna need to slow the fuck down.

What's all this stuff *for* anyway? What's the need to be constantly entertained and distracted at such breakneck speed? What's behind that? What does it say about us? Are we happy? Is this a modern-day opiate of the people keeping us numb and dumb under the perpetual hypnosis of our flickering screens? I'll put money on it that if you want to be more creative, produce better work, enjoy music like never before and deepen the bond between artist and listener – whichever side of that divide you're on – you've gotta unplug from the noise now and again. You need the headspace. Listen to Grandpa here. I *know* more people are yearning for that connection; I meet them every day. It's like we've been force-fed a diet of fast food for so long that our soul is just begging for some nourishment. And that nourishment is out there – but first we've got to wean ourselves off the noise.

We don't have to be willing prey to the toxic tech dystopia; we can snuggle our way back into a 1995 state of mind any time we like – because the remedy to all of this is dead simple. Let me walk you through it. Ready? You just turn that shit off. Just turn it off. Rip the fucking plug out. Then pick just ONE album to listen to. Sit back, close your eyes and dreeeeeeeeam! You're allowed, my friend – do it. You don't have to be plugged into the noise all of the damn time. Say, 'Fuck it, I'm off to the nineties for the rest of the night. See you all later.' Put that album on, lie back and *do* absolutely nothing. Let each song run right to the end and relish the whole album in the order it was intended. Take a trip to another dimension. It's heavenly, it's transformative and there's nothing else like it.

If you do this, I guarantee two things will happen. Firstly, your mind will start to think again. It'll begin to wander and wonder. To dream and explore. No longer simply a sponge to be battered with incoming content, the furnace of imagination will fire up again and excitement will rush through your veins as you start to feel, for the first time in so long... connection. Connection to something higher, deeper and more potent than a few likes on a fucking selfie. Ideas will appear. Inspiration will strike. Songs will get written. Solutions will surface. You'll realise you never realised just how good that band's frigging bass player is! And you'll want to put another record on. The second thing that will happen is that all the anxiety, that subtle tension that's been wired into us by too much exposure to the noise, will start to melt away. You will lose yourself, literally, in the music. This is music's true power. To heal, to take us to a higher plane and return us to the eternal. Free time for our mind to play is a human and artistic necessity – and we can reclaim it any time we want to.

So this is a call to down tools. To simplify. To downsize. To slow down. To enjoy less stuff – but enjoy it more. If done en masse, I believe it could be a strong shot in the arm for the entire music industry. Because by spending more time with less music and *really* getting to love it, we can enrich the connection we feel to that music. Artists would be able to build stronger fanbases, labels would be able to better service those fans, and by everyone focusing more on fewer things, we'd all benefit. Physical products could stage a comeback, smaller bands could tour more and grass-roots music scenes could flourish once again. There was a lot to hate about the music industry of old, but there's also a hell of a lot we can learn about life outside of the noise by revisiting those not-so-distant years – a lot that could just save our asses.

All of us, artists and fans alike, need to spend far less time mindlessly consuming garbage content – we deserve better. And ignore what dickweed music influencers will tell you; it is NOT our job as an artist to 'get with the times', 'make short-form content' and 'feed the platforms' and neither should it be. That's a self-perpetuating cycle of pointlessness that erodes the soul of everyone involved. When we all say, 'Fuck it, I'm getting off the ride,' the circus is over. I'm not saying the Internet isn't one of the best things to ever happen – I could never have done my thing as an independent artist without it – but there's a reason that so much of our culture right now, especially in music, is looking backwards to a time that existed before it. We're burnt out. We can't keep up. We're confused and we're anxious. The antidote? Kill the noise, turn up the music. Make albums great again. Bring back boredom. Reconnect to the real. In a world that's hurtling ever forward towards God knows what next, slowing down is a revolutionary act. And I suspect we're not missing much, either.

Less is more. I think I get it now. So that's it – my phone is off, the drink is poured and the record is spinning. Ah, ignorance really is bliss.

18.

THE FUTURE

When predicting scenarios for the future of humanity, experts generally settle on two likelihoods:

1) *Star Trek* or 2) *Terminator.*

That's because whichever way it goes down, one thing is certain – our future will be determined and dominated by technology. And that will either lead us to an egalitarian, enlightened utopia or a bleak, brutal hell. Seeing what I've seen about the tendencies of powerful interests and human nature, I'm putting my money on *Terminator* – or more likely, *The Matrix. Terminatrix*, if you will. We're racing in that direction already, with all of us unknowing cogs, in one way or another, locked into the machinery of global tech giants making us unwitting pawns for the powerful interests woven into them. Some say that most of us could soon be made entirely redundant as technology does more and more of the work historically done by humans – especially the arts.

But not everyone is a nihilistic, cynical arsehole like me. Some propose that it'll all be all right in the end because the power of human compassion will triumph over evil and we'll all live in a blissed-out, ultra-modern, equal society where robots do all the dirty work while we laze about writing poetry and pondering philosophy all day. I'm not sure these people have been paying attention to history, but maybe I'm wrong. I really hope I am. Either way, the future is coming and it's coming fast, so we'd better stop doomscrolling and start paying attention.

So what's happening? What are the definites? Well, we know for sure that AI is gonna be the biggie. It won't be long before most of the music we hear on adverts and movies will be made by machines. It won't be long after that before more and more commercially released music is written, produced and performed by machines – that's happening already. Practically everything that us human artists can do, machines will soon be doing faster and for free. The fat-cat label execs will be rubbing their grubby little nubbins together with a wide, demonic smile. There is going to be seismic turbulence in the music industry over the coming years, and many, many artists are going to either fall by the wayside, give up or die trying. If you thought music streaming was bad for us lot, you ain't seen fucking nothing yet. There is a content tsunami a-coming, and copyright and the concept of intellectual property will soon cease to be relevant in a world where most artists will just be glad that someone, somewhere actually heard their creation.

And then there's the metaverse. That's right, a virtual world where we all disappear into a fully immersive but entirely fake version of life that we'd rather pretend we live in. In the metaverse, we'll all have six-pack abs, a jet-setting lifestyle and be forever twenty-five years old. And who wouldn't prefer that to the barren Hunger Games that will exist outside in the 'old world'? There, avatars and robot celebrities will reign supreme, with a cornucopia of sensory experiences impossible for humans to ever match. Who'll be providing this new escape from the reality they helped destroy? Why it's our good friends over at big tech, and we all know how much respect they've shown so far for our data, our content, control of public discourse and the propagation of propaganda. Yeah, I'm sure it'll all be fine.

So where's the *Star Trek* in all of this? Well, there are some glimmers of hope, some counter-blows brewing in the underground resistance movement that could, if we got involved, potentially save our asses. And no, it's not NFTs. People, NFTs are the MiniDisc of the new world. What's a MiniDisc? I rest my case. NFTs were a fleeting fashionable gimmick for those with too much money and not enough sense. For artists, they promised a new way to make a decent buck but only if you already had a platinum album giving commercial value to your content. Absolutely useless, therefore, for the rest of us – especially if you're an underground punk band from south Wales. By the time you read this, NFTs will already be dead in the water. Beware the next big thing, for there will be many – and they will die a quick death.

No, there is something *way* better coming that we should all be paying attention to – it's called decentralisation. Our Internet is evolving, and while one branch is sprinting in the direction of strengthening big tech behemoths and the centralised control of everything on Planet Earth, another is cooking up something with the potential to be much more equal, democratic, artist-friendly and collectively owned. For many years, the buzz around the so-called Web 3.0 has been growing steadily. A new internet experience built upon collectively operated networks and blockchains where there is no central power that determines who succeeds, who fails, who gets heard and who gets censored. It's not here yet, but it's coming and it could change everything. No longer would artists have to dance like monkeys for private tech firms to make billions in profit while the content creators go hungry. No longer would artists have to dilute their art to this week's algorithmic whims or have their material completely erased from existence by a platform because they didn't like the words in it – yes, I'm *still* pissed about *Make Anger Great Again*. Soon we could have a new reality, whereby online content is not hosted by one mega-company who can remove it at will but is instead hosted collectively by all of us, with no central authority wielding influence over the artists, the fans or the platforms at any point. After years of us all having to constantly jump through hoops in order to appease a private company who may or may not allow people to hear our songs, read our posts or watch our videos, that sounds like a big breath of fresh air to me.

You see, the pattern so far has been one of ownership – first by the kings who commissioned the classics, then by the record labels and now by big tech. You make it; they own it. That's been the music industry since day one, and that's the way the billionaire overlords want to keep it – but soon, we stand a very real chance of being able to say 'fuck you' to all of them and, for the first time *ever*, actually own and control our own work. For the only people who *should* own an artist's work are the artists themselves and the people who love it. This is not about a new app or a trendy new platform rented to us from on high – this is a *system*, a whole new way of doing things, a process that we're all a part of. We've been banging our drums about the great democratisation of the music industry for a long time, but decentralisation could offer the first real genuine shot at it. The problem with democracy, though, is that it only works if we take part in it, and the problem with humans is that we like shiny things. It remains to be seen whether more people would engage in a communally owned network where art, ideas and dissent can flourish, or whether they'll plough their heads deep into the metaverse and gawp at the arses of celebrity avatars. And that's the stinger – collectively owned, decentralised systems of universal empowerment are only as powerful as the numbers of people engaged in them. But if you're an optimist, you'd be right in thinking that, at least in theory, decentralisation could soon disrupt the whole establishment from finance to politics and art – and that's pretty fucking punk rock.

Don't go getting too comfy though, for the battle is never won and the vultures will always be attacking en masse to find new ways to co-opt, steal and own our shit. The kings of this world aren't gonna go out without a fight, and the battle lines are getting drawn. So whose side will you be on when they start throwing multisensory, multidimensional AI extravaganzas at us? A feast for the feels unlike anything ever known. Will you be entranced into their saccharine world of make-believe while they rinse you of your voice, your talent, your money, your potential and your power? Or will you be part of the resistance, hunkered down in the trenches with the artists, the rebels and the dreamers? Ultimately, it's gonna be on you.

But what *exactly* is this new decentralised dreamland of which I speak? Where is it and how do we sign up? While platforms already exist for blockchain-based music distribution, I don't feel that we're 'there yet'. The current incarnations of this model are either frustratingly basic and lacking in features or unfathomably complex and riddled in nerd-speak. I've seen nothing yet that could rival the usability and appeal of the mainstream giants. And, of course, they don't have the numbers yet. Artists want to put their music where the people are – and right now, the people are on the Devil's jukebox. The people want to hear the bangers, the classics and the hot new releases – and these are mostly all owned by the major labels who will have nothing to do with a decentralised distribution network, so it's unlikely we'll see the Beatles, Drake, Ed Sheeran or Coldplay in such a place any time soon. Although I take that as another win.

Things are moving so fast, though, that by the time you read this, I'll be ten dog years behind, so let's not get too caught up in the detail of the who, the where, the when and the how, but instead wrap our heads around the fact that what we're talking about here... is *systemic change*. We're talking about a mindset change so that, when the time comes, you're ready to jump aboard the decentralised pirate ship as soon as it sets sail. It can only be as strong as the number of people using it, and together we can finally give a colossal, collective middle finger to the labels, big tech and all their murky middlemen, forever. Or not.

And let's keep it real. Is a decentralised web going to magically make us all rich and famous rock stars living a life of abundance? No. Will we still have all of the same problems of being a tiny drop in an ocean of content? For sure. Will there still be spammers, freeloaders and dickheads? Most definitely. But at least we'll have a role in shaping how 'our' platforms develop because they'll exist for our benefit, not private profit. Almost all barriers to us doing our thing will be removed, and no one – *no one* – will own or control us (except our fans, but that's the way it should be). And we're not talking about idealisms here either; we're talking about the future of the Internet and where it's headed whether we like it or not. Luckily for us, there are two very different roads forking out ahead of us – one that sucks badly and one that could finally put the power in our hands. There will be screw-ups, there will be obstacles and there will be harsh resistance from you-know-who, but whatever happens, we'll all be far better off doing our thing on a decentralised, ownerless network that's run by all of us collectively than what the other team are stirring up. So keep a look out for that pirate ship on the horizon, and when it comes, defect immediately.

Now, you may notice that none of this has anything to do with *making* music and everything to do with *surviving* in music. Well, unfortunately, those are our options. But there's also a third option that I mentioned earlier in the book. We could just turn off the noise altogether. We could just pull the fucking plug on all of it and get back to playing music to rooms of fellow humans and reminding ourselves that the real world isn't behind a screen – it's 'out there', where the air and the beer is. So what if we're no longer relevant on some Mickey Mouse social media platform? Ninety-nine per cent of us were never *really* relevant on them anyway. It's a self-perpetuating circus; it exists only because we all buy into it – but it ends the second we decide to go and do something more meaningful with our time... like make some music. We don't have to join the crazy train; we can cut the cord and go play some guitar.

Disappear back to that 1995 headspace and let the world fritter and waste its hours on gimmicks, blue lights and robots while we kick back and spin those black circles.

And speaking of circles, it's inevitable that we'll all end up doing a 180 at some point anyway. It's what we do. We go around in revolutions. After too long in the metaverse, there'll be a push-back and we'll all yearn for something different, something simpler, more artisanal and real. Artists will get bored of merely issuing commands to a machine and letting it do all the fun stuff, and instead begin to long for something more enriching, more stimulating and more challenging. We'll want to be involved in the process again, and people will start to 'go retro' – retro in this case meaning not having a cable plugged into your head. Just as we always do, people will look back to a simpler past and they'll long to hold an instrument again or be awed by the spectacle of an actual human doing something impressive. It would only be a matter of time before we'd see a resurgence in human-made music, since things do as they always do – go full circle. So long as we don't lose too much along the way, that is.

So what is the future of the music industry? No one knows for certain, and beware of anyone who claims to, but I'm certain about one thing: the age-old battle between the artist and the industry will continue – we'll just have different toys to argue over. Because here's the thing: there's only ever really been one story. The story of them and us. Whether it's the kings, the government, the record labels, big tech or massive tech, the story is the same. There are those with the talent who create the work, and those who seek to steal it, control it, sell it and take all the money. For the first time in our history, a decentralised web *could* be the start of a different story – but I put 'could' in italics for a reason. And I may also be colossally wrong. Another certainty is that interesting times are coming, potentially very dark times for our precious art form. So as we stumble forward blindly, I urge you to remember our story and what it's always been. Beware the smiling salesman who 'really loves your music', and beware the hot new platform that promises to be 'all about protecting artists' but is covertly owned and controlled by the same old foes in high places. Go forth with vigilance and duty to protect the realm. Don't let the bastards win the next round, and let's take back what was ours all along. Together we can build the first truly powerful decentralised artist collective where all of us can thrive and support one another, free from exploitation. It's time.

So what's it gonna be? *Star Trek*, *Terminatrix* or unplug completely?

I know what I'll be doing. I'll see you on the pirate ship.

19.

SAYONARA

As I bid you farewell on another journey, I'm easing into that blissful timelessness that only music can deliver. The vinyl spinning, the coffee smelling, the world looking like a brighter place. It's usually at this point in a book where one is expected to give thanks – to their agent, their researcher, their ghostwriter, their publisher for 'their endless patience and support', their god and the 'real muse' who inspires their work, their lover. I'm not going to be doing that. Other than thanking you for reading this thing, everyone else can piss off. No, instead, I'm going to give my thanks to the real star of the show here – music.

Thanks for the memories, the adventures, the lessons and the growth. Thanks for the struggles that have bettered me, the friends for life, the travels and the insights. Thanks for saving me – from myself, from conformity, from boredom and the dreaded office cubicle. Thanks for the ecstasy, the tears and the goosebumps. Thanks for giving me a reason, a purpose and a gang. Thanks for always being there when I needed you. For being my friend. Thank you for the magic. Thank you for the music.

And to that end, I must thank you. The fellow lifers out there, the creators, the dreamers, the rebels and pioneers. Thanks to all those who preserve and progress this most beautiful of art forms. And to those who support this cause – the fans and music lovers who play an equally vital part in keeping this music thing breathing – thank you from the bottom of my heart. To the soldiers on the frontlines and the heroes behind the curtains, thank you. I thank you all for your part in the bustling ecosystem that has been the story and the soundtrack to my life. To all of you – artists, dreamers, creators, game-changers, misfits, rebels and underdogs – I urge you to continue the good fight no matter what the future may hold. I know that you will. Good luck and go give 'em hell.

Now, back to the vinyl.

Support artists. Support venues. Buy physical. Kill the machines.

ACKNOWLEDGEMENTS

All right, all right, I suppose I should share some love with the people who helped make this damn thing happen, shouldn't I? First, a standing ovation for the awesome Amy Feldman, who championed the book when it was merely a seed of an idea, fought its corner, and found it a loving home with the Calon Books brigade. Take a bow, Amy. A million thanks for your unwavering belief and backing – this is totally your fault.

Next, a riotous applause for the talent, dedication, contribution (and patience!) of my brilliant editors, Abbie Headon, Dave Holwill and Rob Harries for their evil genius in sculpting this prickly slab of hyperbole into the glistening diamond you hold in your hand. For calling me out on my BS, adding their secret sauce and fixing my lousy grammar – please raise the roof for them. They've made this a better book, and I thank them dearly.

Thirdly, a relentless 'scream for more' for all the super-cool dudes and dudettes at Calon Books for their passion, creativity, energy and belief in my *Loud Medicine*. It has been an absolute pleasure serving with you all, and I do hope you're proud of the good trouble we've made here!

And of course, the final heckle goes to you for reading this thing. I do hope you enjoyed it, but if not, don't worry – there'll be a deluxe hardly-any-different-to-the-last-version-but-hey-it's-got-a-different-colour-cover edition out soon, which you'll totally love. I promise!

Thank you, and ciao for now, comrades. See you on the next one.